The Premier Football Betting Handbook 2010/11

The key stats and strategies to give you an edge betting on the Premier League

by Matt Finnigan and Pete Nordsted

HARRIMAN HOUSE LTD

3A Penns Road
Petersfield
Hampshire
GU32 2EW
GREAT BRITAIN

Tel: +44 (0)1730 233870
Fax: +44 (0)1730 233880
Email: enquiries@harriman-house.com
Website: www.harriman-house.com

First edition published in Great Britain in 2010 by Harriman House.

978-1-906659-82-0

British Library Cataloguing in Publication Data
A CIP catalogue record for this book can be obtained from the British Library.

Printed in the UK by CPI William Clowes, Beccles NR34 7TL

Risk Warning

Gambling is addictive and can lead to serious losses. Please remember that this book cannot and does not guarantee success – and that no one can. Always gamble responsibly:

- only gamble with money set aside for the purpose, and which you can afford to lose
- do it just for fun or for the challenge, rather than to gain money that you need
- know that you are often very unlikely to win in the long term
- do not chase after losses
- *never* borrow money to gamble.

If you recognise or fear that you or anyone else may have a problem with gambling, please check out the guidance at www.gambleaware.co.uk.

Contents

Introduction

Since bookmakers started to accept single bets on football, their turnover and profits have shot through the roof. Betting on football is by far the biggest sport in terms of turnover through the online bookmakers; the latest generation of punters are not interested in horse racing, and with a live televised game broadcast almost every day during the season who can blame them!

If, like most people, you lead a busy life, you simply do not have the time to analyse the key stats before placing a bet on the weekend's Premier League football. Often you'll end up betting on hunches rather than the really important facts and the best possible analysis. And you'll receive bog-standard odds, rather than knowing how to detect the best value ones out there. If that is the case, then this is the book for you. Our aim is to give you all the necessary ammunition needed to take on the bookies and beat them at their own game!

Who we are

The Premier Football Betting Handbook 2010/11 has been written by Matt Finnigan and Pete Nordsted.

Matt Finnigan is a professional punter/sports trader who specialises in making money on horse racing and live soccer. Matt also runs a successful Betfair education program at: www.the-xclub.com and since 2007 has mentored no less than five traders to full-time status. He also has a strong bookmaking pedigree, having worked for a leading bookmaker as one of their company spokespersons before making his living as a professional punter.

Read Matt's blog and follow him on Twitter at:

www.mattfinnigan.com

www.twitter.com/mattfinnigan

Pete Nordsted is also a full-time sports trader. He specialises in analysing the sporting markets to pinpoint various trading opportunities and it was this knowledge that led him to write *Mastering Betfair* (Harriman House, 2009). Pete is launching a brand new live football trading service for the 2010/11 season at www.tradeonfootball.com and you can trade alongside him on all the big Premier and Champions League matches. He has been working with Matt for over a year, researching fixed-odds betting on football. It is this ongoing work that inspired the writing of this book and *The Essential World Cup Betting Guide 2010*.

Read Pete's blog and follow him on Twitter at:

www.petenordsted.com

www.twitter.com/petenordsted

Who the book is aimed at

The Premier Football Betting Handbook 2010/11 is firmly aimed at the casual punter who enjoys a weekly bet on the Premier League football markets*. We feel this is the perfect opportunity to bridge the gap between small staking punters, who enter the markets to enhance their enjoyment of the match, and the short-term higher staking investor whose sole purpose is to obtain a return on investment. This book's goal is to help the former enjoy some of the success of the latter, without them having to go through too much of the fun-sapping hard work on their own.

*Whilst the extensive 'form book' and analysis of Part II is dedicated to the 20 teams of the 2010/11 Premier League, and we use Premier League examples throughout, the principles and strategies shared in Part I will also be of great use to those who bet on foreign or lower leagues. The number of bets available at bookmakers and punters engaged on the exchanges may, of course, differ.

We are not going to promise that the content in this book will grab you untold fortunes; as a punter the odds are, so to speak, against you. The bookmakers ensure that happens! But we want to put you in a position where you have a better understanding of your options, the quality of the odds and what to look out for in placing your bets. This should help you become a better punter and hopefully turn that loss into a profit.

There is nothing *wrong*, per se, with how you bet now and we're not going to claim that we have all the answers. However, as professional punters/traders we have a code of practice that maximises our opportunities for securing long-term profits. We want to pass this on – along with all the stats and strategies that we, as professionals, rely on – so that the next time you have the urge to place a bet you have more options at your disposal than betting on a whim, guess or gut feeling. Spontaneous betting can and does make watching a match more enjoyable; but winning those bets more often than losing them makes it even better.

In truth, bookmakers make their money because of the ignorance of punters. If you show any amount of ability, the chances are your account will either be restricted or even closed down. If that happens as a result of reading this book, then take that as a huge compliment and switch to the exchanges; there you can pretty much stake what you like and they offer almost the same number of markets.

It's through a combination of ignorance, laziness and greed that 99% of all football punters lose long-term. And when you add into the mix the complete lack of understanding as to how odds are compiled, you have a sure-fire recipe for losing money. We want to address all these factors with an easy-to-follow guide. So this book is all about ensuring that you are correctly prepared to take on the bookmakers or exchange bettors and hopefully claim back some of that edge they have held over you for years!

What you should expect from the book

As well as highlighting a variety of Premier League football markets you can bet on, we offer you structured analysis of the main markets – such as match odds, Asian handicaps, corners, bookings, first and last goal scorer – by pinpointing the best angles to secure a steady stream of profits throughout the season.

We also provide a breakdown of each Premier League side's statistical performance over the previous season, backed up by unique and comprehensive reports. We have also graded each team and analysed how these sides have performed against each other and this unique analysis will instantly highlight if the bet you are considering is value or not. Armed with this information, you will have that all important edge necessary to take on the bookies.

If there is money to be made betting on the Premier League, then *The Premier Football Betting Handbook* will show you how.

www.premier-betting.com

This handbook is dedicated to laying the foundations for a successful season of Premier League betting, and to build on this match by match we have launched a dedicated website to accompany this book at www.premier-betting.com. Forgive us for getting this plug in early, but the interactive nature of football betting, and the twists and turns of a full Premiership campaign, inevitably requires something up-to-the-minute to deal with the unexpected as well as to go further in depth.

Don't worry – this book isn't a brochure for the website! We've tried really hard to make it a must-have reference work for every step of the 2010/11 campaign, and the website will only augment that; you'll still get all the value out of this handbook even if you don't sign up. But if you find this book helpful, the website should be of interest too.

During the 2010/11 season we will be individually analysing all 380 matches played in the Premier League as they come up, taking into account the kinds of short-term form, news and other considerations that a book cannot. You can have direct access to our innermost thoughts on every single Premiership fixture, starting at just £8 a month. You will also gain access to Premier Betting's 'True Odds' database, which will enable you in a split second to identify any potential value in the markets being offered by the bookmakers for any given game. We have done this work, so you don't have to!

Our aim is to make Premier Betting the hub for punters who want to bet on the Premier League, by providing them with all the odds and analysis in one place so they can have the latest and most important betting information at the click of a mouse.

Plug over – let's get stuck into the book.

Part I

The Premier Football Betting Toolbox: Odds, Markets and Strategies

1

Betting Development

Casual Punter vs Short-term Investor

Before we get down to highlighting the numerous kinds of Premier League bets available and how you can best profit from them, it is important to begin by knowing where you are at the moment. Hopefully by reading this book you will eliminate all of the bad habits you have picked up over the years and start taking your punting seriously. At the very least, after reading this book you should only be placing your hard-earned money on bets that offer value.

Below is a definition of both a Casual Punter and Short-term Investor: their habits, hopes and ambitions. What do you recognise of yourself in either – or both?

It is our goal that by following the ideas presented in this book you will make the full transition to the second, the short-term investor, wherever you are in the process now. This means ultimately making your money go further, and getting more out of one of the most compelling past-times in the world: following football. It's a journey we've both made, as you'll see from our stories at the end of this chapter; and it's one anyone else can also accomplish.

Casual Punters

Definition

The largest section of football punters are casual ones who generally have a bet on live TV games to enhance their enjoyment, especially if they are watching two neutral teams play. They also like to play the fixed-odds coupons (a weekly bookmakers' football coupon that displays the odds for each match taking place at the weekend) accepting whatever odds are on offer, and on many occasions look at placing bets on long odds accumulators (accumulators are bets placed where two or more selections need to win in order for your bet to win). They will generally be small-staking punters who are looking for big returns.

Profile

The casual football punter will eat, drink and sleep football and will probably class themselves as very knowledgeable about the game. They will usually have a set amount they can bet each week and are unlikely to keep a record of their bets for future reference.

They are also unlikely to shop around for the best prices because their stakes are small and they will take the view that it is not worth the hassle for a few extra pounds; indeed they may have no concept at all of obtaining the best value with their bets.

Their mindset is that of a losing punter – even though they hope to win each time they bet, they don't actually believe they will beat the bookmaker.

Objectives

- To potentially win a decent amount from a small stake.
- To enhance their enjoyment of watching the game.

Resources

Will place bets via all available options – high street, telephone, online and TV – but will probably stick to the same bookmaker they have an account with.

May follow tipsters for bets, but will certainly be led by pundits or peers who have strong opinions on the outcome of a match.

Short-term Investor

Definition

Generally betting through the internet, this is probably the fastest growing section of those who make bets on Premier League football (although still quite niche). They see matches as a short-term opportunity to make money.

Profile

Like the casual punter they will be very knowledgeable about football, but will delve deeper into the stats and will have an analytical approach to betting.

They will almost certainly have a structured plan and be working with a dedicated betting bank. They will understand the concept of, and need for, always obtaining the best value.

They will have multiple bookmaker accounts and will shop around for the best prices, keeping a record of all the bets they place. A grading system of bets may be adopted by this type of punter and they will stake accordingly to the strength of the grade.

As they work to a structured staking plan they're more likely to be a higher staking punter than the casual punter (although not necessarily true in all cases).

Strike rates are also important to them and they will take a long-term view that to beat the bookmaker over a period of time, they will have to make consistently good short-term decisions.

Objectives

- To take a calculated risk based on statistical and analytical assessments.
- Will only place bets that offer value and a decent risk v reward ratio.

Resources

Will always use odds-checking websites to obtain the best value and they will also take advantage of various bookmaker offers.

They may also use software programs to aid with their research and will not be averse to using betting systems.

Our Stories

Pete

When I first started betting on football I had no concept at all of the meaning of value and would take whatever price the bookmaker would offer me. If Manchester United were playing a team like Aston Villa I would bet on Manchester United regardless of the price on offer. My thoughts were: 'Well, a winner is a winner'. This is a classic, subtle and – in the long term – devastating error. Basically I was betting on 1.50 (66%) chances, when in reality the chances of winning were much more like 1.75 (57%) (see our explanation of the 'over round' in Chapter 2, for part of the reason for this). So instead of averaging 66 winners every 100 bets (which were the odds I was betting at), I was averaging around 57 out of 100. Consequently I was a losing punter.

With the dawn of the internet and various football stats sites, I became a lot more knowledgeable about the game. I started to take into account previously ignored factors, and greater statistical detail, such as how differing standards of teams actually (and not presumably) performed against each other, and I also took the time to learn how to compile my own odds. This threw up a number of surprises, which you'll get to see and use for yourself later in the book.

This then culminated in devising and using the kinds of ratings we'll share with you later. These ensure that every time I place a bet I am doing so at value and when the odds are in my favour: so that, if I win, I win well; and if I lose, which should be less regularly than before, it doesn't badly affect me. Now I don't want to give the impression that this was an easy task – I have put in many hours of hard work to get to this stage. But it has been well worth it, because, as well as being a fascinating process for a football fan, I am now a profitable punter.

Matt

Back in the '90s I was like the vast majority of football punters. I would make my weekend pilgrimage to the bookmakers to place an accumulator on the fixed-odds coupon. I was a big fan of the one from each section bet, which is basically a bet where the bookmaker groups together a number of matches and you have to pick one team from each section. All selections then have to win for your bet to win. I had no sense of value: typically I would place my bet based on little research; sometimes the first time that I had really looked at the matches was when I picked up the coupon that morning.

I didn't expect to win and considered my bet as a weekly expense on the way to play or watch football that afternoon. I probably got greater satisfaction in the bar after the match saying this or that team let me down, than I would have done had my bet won.

My whole outlook to this game was changed overnight when I joined Ladbrokes as one of their company spokesmen. When I say it changed, I actually gave up betting on football altogether for a while – the amount of time the odds compilers put into their work, not to mention their knowledge, left me feeling quite deflated and indeed embarrassed about my approach to betting.

During my time at Ladbrokes I learned many aspects of the business, from basic bookmaking through to odds compiling and managing liabilities. I also learnt a great deal about the ever-increasing variety of markets that were being offered on football.

To this day, it's very rare that I bet on football in the traditional fashion – I am a sports trader who manages risk before and during the game, mostly betting on the exchanges, so I view each match as a short-term investment opportunity but don't especially care about the outcome of the match. It's not important when trading. What is important is how the game can provide you with trading signals. Then you can look to the markets to see if they're ready to serve you. And if both are right, that's your opportunity to open a position.

I do not bet for a living; I make a living as a sports trader. When I do place a bet I bring my sports trading and statistical knowledge of the game to the fore, and treat a weekend of Premier League football no differently to a stock market trader engaging in the FTSE. (Except of course it's a lot more fun!) This is where mostly betting on the exchanges comes in: they allow me to do the kinds of things, in the kind of timescales, that share traders get up to every day.

Nevertheless, readers of our previous book may be aware that we took the bold step of posting all our straightforward bookie bets for the World Cup on the morning of every game at premier-betting.com. The 2010 tournament was a tough ride for punters, with endless shocks in the group stages, so to come out in front was some achievement. I was pleasantly surprised with my success. I'm not sure we'll see quite so peculiar a tournament – at least in the first round, anyway – again!

2

Getting the Best Odds

Decimal Pricing

All prices quoted throughout this book are decimal odds. Decimal odds differ from the odds traditionally quoted in the UK in that they include your stake as part of your total return. (If you're *au fait* with decimal odds, feel free to skip this explanation – we'll see you again at 'How Does a Bookmaker Make Money?')

If you place a bet of £10 at decimal odds of 4.0 and win, then your total return (including stake) is £40.

In the UK this would traditionally be quoted as 3/1, returning to you winnings of £30 plus your original stake of £10.

Decimal odds are simpler to use than traditional odds, and are the most common form of odds quoted in countries outside the UK.

In addition, for the mathematically minded, decimal odds relate more closely to probability. For example, in a cup final with two equally matched teams, the probability of each team winning and lifting the cup is 50%. Each team will have traditional odds of 1/1 or decimal odds of 2.0. Hence, the probability of an outcome equals 1 divided by its decimal odds (1/2.0 = 50%).

Decimal odds also offer many more incremental prices – bookmakers can then offer every price between 1.01 and 2.0 to two decimal places.

Converting decimal odds to traditional odds

Decimal odds minus 1.0 = traditional odds (x to 1)

For example, 4.0 = 3/1, 1.80 = 4/5 (0.8 to 1)

Converting traditional odds to decimal odds

Traditional odds (x to 1) plus 1.0 = decimal odds

For example, 7/1 = 8.0, 1/2 = 1.50

Decimal odds conversion chart

Fractional	Decimal	Fractional	Decimal
10/1	11.00	Evs	2.00
9/1	10.00	10/11	1.91
8/1	9.00	5/6	1.83
7/1	8.00	4/5	1.80
13/2	7.50	8/11	1.73
6/1	7.00	4/6	1.67
11/2	6.50	8/13	1.62
5/1	6.00	4/7	1.57
9/2	5.50	8/15	1.53
4/1	5.00	1/2	1.50
7/2	4.50	4/9	1.44
10/3	4.33	2/5	1.40
3/1	4.00	4/11	1.36
5/2	3.50	1/3	1.33
2/1	3.00	2/7	1.29
15/8	2.88	1/4	1.25
13/8	2.62	2/9	1.22
6/4	2.50	1/5	1.20
5/4	2.25	1/6	1.17
6/5	2.20	1/7	1.14
11/10	2.10	1/8	1.13

How Does a Bookmaker Make Money?

It is essential that you know how a bookmaker makes a profit and the importance of identifying a bookmaker's 'over round'.

A bookmaker takes money from the bets placed by customers, pays out the winners and keeps the money of losers. It's quite a simple concept. However, this doesn't explain how a bookmaker can make money in the long run.

The over round

When a bookmaker sets the odds, he builds what is known as an 'over round' into the odds. This over round is sometimes also known as 'juice'.

For example, in a Premiership football match between Fulham and Tottenham, there are three possible outcomes: a Fulham win, a Tottenham win and the draw.

Fair odds on this match would probably be:

```
Fulham 2.94, Tottenham 2.63 and the Draw 3.57
```

This equates to the following percentages:

TEAM	ODDS	PERCENTAGE
FULHAM	2.94	34.01
TOTTENHAM	2.63	38.02
DRAW	3.57	28.01
TOTAL %		100.04

As you can see, this then equates to over a 100% book.

So in this case if you were to place £34 on Fulham, £38 on Tottenham and £28 on the draw you would get your money back

(£34 + £38 + £28 = £100); the available odds reflect the true 100% (£100) chance of that event happening.

However, as we can see, a traditional bookmaker would not offer odds that equate to 100% over all three events.

In this example, Ladbrokes are offering the following:

Match betting			
Selection	Home	Draw	Away
Fulham vs Tottenham	2.60	3.20	2.37

As you can see from the following table, this equates to a near 112% book:

TEAM	ODDS	PERCENTAGE
FULHAM	2.60	38.46
TOTTENHAM	2.37	42.19
DRAW	3.20	31.25
TOTAL %		111.90

So the bookmaker in this example has stated that:

- Fulham have a 38.46% chance of winning,
- Tottenham have a 42.19% chance of winning, and
- there is a 31.25% chance of the game ending in a draw.

If we add all of the percentage chances together we come up with 112%; so the book value is 112% in this example. And this 12% over 100 is known as the bookmaker's *over round*.

You can then see that if the bookmaker took our original amount of money from the 100% book on Fulham, Tottenham and the draw, they would win regardless of the outcome.

TEAM	ODDS	BET
FULHAM	2.60	34.00
TOTTENHAM	2.37	38.00
DRAW	3.20	28.00
£ TOTAL		100.00

For example, if they took £34 on Fulham, £38 on Tottenham and £28 on the draw, they would then take £100 and pay out £90.06 maximum on the winner. This means that, in this case, the bookmakers are making a profit of at least £9.94 for every £100 bet *regardless of the final result.*

TEAM	ODDS	BET	PAYOUT
FULHAM	2.60	34.00	88.40
BOOKMAKER'S PROFIT			11.60

TEAM	ODDS	BET	PAYOUT
TOTTENHAM	2.37	38.00	90.06
BOOKMAKER'S PROFIT			9.94

TEAM	ODDS	BET	PAYOUT
DRAW	3.20	28.00	89.60
BOOKMAKER'S PROFIT			10.40

So we can see from this example that beating the bookmaker is going to be an uphill struggle: the odds are stacked in the bookmaker's favour from the beginning. **However, we can begin to combat this by calculating our own odds and seeing if the bookmakers have made a mistake in pricing up the matches.**

How to Calculate Your Own Odds

When betting on an event like football you have to accept that you are going to have a run of losing bets. You are going to have to come to terms with the fact that you are not going to win every weekend, and you should simply be setting yourself the goal of attaining a steady *long-term* profit.

Knowing that you are going to have your fair share of losers, the only way you are going to achieve this profit is by backing selections whose odds are larger than the actual chance of the team you are betting on winning. That way, your wins, when they come, are substantial enough to offset your losses. In other words, *before you even consider having a bet your selection must offer value.*

To achieve this it helps greatly if you can compile and calculate your own odds.

In this section we will be explaining a method that you can use to price up a match yourself. However, it should be remembered that pricing up an event can be all down to individual preference and judgement – the calculations you make depend upon what data or range of data you consider relevant. Some people, for example, put more emphasis on the form of, say, the last six games than they do on the records of a previous 38-game season, and will ignore results outside such a window.

So pricing up a football match takes a little time to learn. With each match-up you need to decide how far you're going to go back, which games (or kinds of games) you think might deserve extra or less emphasis, and so on. However, with continued practice you will find that putting in a couple of hours' work a week can pay off handsomely.

Whichever way you decide to price up a match, we believe it is important to stick to the following overriding rule.

When compiling your own odds, ensure that you do not look at any bookmakers' prices beforehand. You will find that you become influenced by these prices. Or they will cause doubts to set in and unnecessarily undermine confidence in your own compilation process. Remember, you're trying to detect loosely priced bookmaker odds – not ape them. The only time you need to be concerned is when your method repeatedly shows **every** possible bet to be wildly mispriced and ridiculously good value – bookies, whatever they are, are not stupid!

Compiling your own odds

In the following example we are going to look at a match between Arsenal and Aston Villa, which took place on 27 December 2009.

One way of determining what the odds should be is by looking at the two team's previous 16-game home and away form matches. As this was played at the Emirates, in this example we will be looking at Arsenal's previous 16 home games and Aston Villa's previous 16 away games. (Remember, choosing what stats you take into account is where the real thought comes into it.)

In their last 16 home matches, Arsenal's form was:

```
Won 11 Drawn 3 Lost 2
```

In their last 16 away matches, Aston Villa's form read:

```
Won 5 Drawn 5 Lost 6
```

We would then suggest the following equations. (Don't worry, there's no voodoo involved; all we're doing is adding together relevant stats – e.g. Arsenal's strength, in their wins, and Villa's weaknesses, in their losses; and vice versa. Then, as you'll see, we work out the mean of this total against all of the outcomes.)

To start to get Arsenal's home price:

We would take Arsenal's 11 home wins and add them to Aston Villa's 6 away losses = 17

To get the draw price:

We would take Arsenal's 3 home draws and add them to Aston Villa's 5 away draws = 8

To get Aston Villa's away price:

We would take Arsenal's 2 home losses and add them to Aston Villa's 5 away wins = 7

So then we are left with the following:

Arsenal 17

Draw 8

Aston Villa 7

To get the percentage chance we divide each team's individual score by the combined total of all three outcomes, which in this case is 32 (17 + 8 + 7).

So, to get Arsenal's percentage you divide 17 by 32 = 53.12%.

To get the Draw percentage you divide 8 by 32 = 25.00%.

To get Aston Villa's percentage you divide 7 by 32 = 21.88%.

Then to get the odds you simply divide 100 by the percentage figure.

So in this case we have:

```
Arsenal 100/53.12 = 1.88

Draw 100/25.00 = 4.00

Aston Villa 100/21.88 = 4.57
```

So now we have priced up our match. And we have:

- Arsenal at 1.88
- Draw at 4.00
- Aston Villa at 4.57

If we then take a look at an odds checker we find the following:

Figure 2.1 – Bookmakers' Odds for Arsenal v Aston Villa

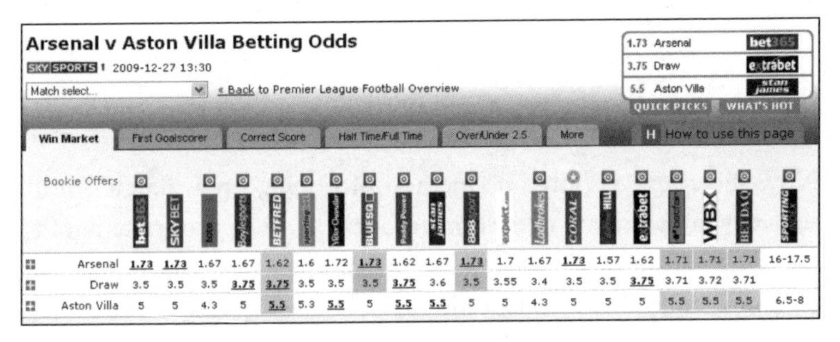

Arsenal v Aston Villa Betting Odds

SKY SPORTS 1 2009-12-27 13:30

Match select... « Back to Premier League Football Overview

1.73 Arsenal bet365 | 3.75 Draw extrabet | 5.5 Aston Villa stan james

QUICK PICKS | WHAT'S HOT

Win Market | First Goalscorer | Correct Score | Half Time/Full Time | Over/Under 2.5 | More | How to use this page

Bookie Offers	bet365	SKYBET	tote	Boylesports	BETFRED	sporting	Victor Chandler	BLUESQ	Paddy Power	stan james	888sport	expekt	Ladbrokes	CORAL	HILL	extrabet	betfair	WBX	BETDAQ	SPORTING
Arsenal	1.73	1.73	1.67	1.67	1.62	1.6	1.72	1.73	1.62	1.67	1.73	1.7	1.67	1.73	1.57	1.62	1.71	1.71	1.71	16-17.5
Draw	3.5	3.5	3.5	3.75	3.75	3.5	3.5	3.5	3.75	3.6	3.5	3.55	3.4	3.5	3.5	3.75	3.71	3.72	3.71	
Aston Villa	5	5	4.3	5	5.5	5.3	5.5	5	5.5	5.5	5	5	4.3	5	5	5	5.5	5.5	5.5	6.5-8

As we can see (Fig 2.1), the best odds available for Arsenal are 1.73 (57.80%) and we believe they should be 1.88 (53.12%). So we would not bet on them – the bookmakers believe Arsenal have more chance of beating Aston Villa than we do, with a 4.61% difference between us.

Aston Villa are best priced at 5.50 (18.18%) and we have them at 4.57 (21.88%) chance. So there is 3.70% value in backing Aston Villa, as we believe they stand a 21.88% chance of winning the game and the bookmakers have them at 18.18%.

The draw is best priced at 3.75 (26.66%) and we believe it only offers a 4.00 (25%) chance. So we would not bet on the draw, as the bookmakers believe there is a 26.66% of the draw happening whereas we only believe there is a 25% chance of this happening.

In the event, Arsenal won 3-0 – this despite the fact that, as the *Guardian* reportage noted, "Villa [we]re unbeaten in three visits to Arsenal (won one, drawn two) and ha[d] won their last five league games". Our method identified a genuine good price, for a reasonably probable outcome; and then the unpredictability of an injured Fàbregas turning in two remarkable second-half goals (followed by a Diaby strike on 90) let us down. A useful reminder that this is not going to be infallible – but, as you can see, it did everything possible to get us in a position to profit handsomely from an outcome that was very much a possibility.

And by always placing such good-value bets, where you stand to win bigger because of the quality of the odds, over the long term you will neutralise the inevitable losses you'll experience.

Other methods to consider

Now the above is only one method of pricing up a match – it all depends on what you determine to be the most appropriate data to take into account. You could, for example, base your book on some of the following suggestions:

- The last 20 home and away matches for each team (AKA seasons never lie).
- The last 10 home matches (for home side) and the last 10 away matches (for away side) (AKA form is king).
- How a team has played against similar opposition. This could be broken down as 'big four' sides, top-half non-'big four' sides, bottom-half teams, bottom six sides (AKA it's all about the opponent).

- Check the prices available from the corresponding fixture last season. You can then assess if either of the teams have improved or deteriorated since the last time they met, and price up the match from there.
- Some or all of these in combination.

The main thing is to find a method that suits you and which you have complete confidence in. Our carefully organised stats in Part II should offer food for thought, as well as all the data you need no matter how inventive or subtle you want to be.

Beginning with the draw

One quite clever method that some people prefer is to begin with the draw. It needs a little explanation – though all it is, in effect, is taking advantage of the fact that the draw is usually given too much chance by bookies; even when reliable stats are used as the basis of the odds, the fact is that, *match by match*, a draw is only really about a 27% to 31% probability in the Premier League. So, for example, if after your calculations for the 32 matches highlighted previously the stats had the home team on 10 wins, the draw at 16 and the away team on 6 wins, this would suggest that the home team be priced at 3.20 (31%) the draw be priced at 2.00 (50%) and the away team be priced at 5.26 (19%).

But in reality there is about a 28% chance of the draw happening (we always price the draw as a 28% chance, based on our experience). So, in this case, you would adjust the draw down from 50% to 28% and then divide the remaining 72% of probability between the two sides pro rata, redrawing their odds based on this 28% and the stats which provided your original estimate of odds. In this case you have the home side on 10 wins and the away side on 6 wins, so you do the following calculation.

Take the 72% and divide by the total number of home and away wins. Which in this case is 16 (10 home wins + 6 away wins).

```
72/16 = 4.5
```

Then you simply multiply this figure by the number of home wins (10 x 4.5 = 45) and away wins (6 x 4.5 = 27).

You then convert the figures into percentages. So, in this example, you have:

- home team 45%
- the draw 28%
- away win 27%

Which equates to the following odds: Home 2.22, Draw 3.57, Away 3.70. Now you can start to look for value in the odds on offer.

One of the software options available on the Premier Betting site allows you to price up a match within seconds using a tried and tested statistical model. You can set the parameters between 8 and 38 matches and experiment with different time frames. Pricing up the weekend fixtures takes only a few minutes, so this can be an excellent tool to have in your armoury. Taking a more manual approach isn't the end of the world, though, and certainly allows the pundit in you to come to the fore, which can be part of the fun now and then.

How much value do you require?

This is a very difficult question to answer, but obviously the more value you gain the better.

Personally we do not place a bet on a particular team unless we find at least 5% value on top of the price that we have calculated them at; and at least 1% value when it comes to the draw. So, regarding the Arsenal v Aston Villa match, we would not have made a bet.

This is a major advantage that the punter has over the bookmaker. You only need to bet when you decide to bet – the bookmakers are obligated to offer prices on every match.

If it seems too good to be true, it probably is

Finally just a quick word of warning – if you price up a match and you find that you are receiving excellent value and it seems too good to be true, then you need to check the prices and the team news. It can mean that the manager is either resting players or that key players have been injured. Or you could have made a simple mistake in your calculations. **So always double-check your figures, facts and team news before placing what you consider to be a value bet.** More on this subject will be covered later in the book.

Odds Comparison

So, now you've priced up your matches and are looking to place your bet. To get a good overall view of the market you need to go to an odds comparison site. The best one in our opinion is oddschecker.com, and it's probably also the most popular. It has many useful features, which we will look at over the next few pages. However, its main purpose is to highlight all of the odds available on a specified event across the major bookmakers.

Here we will take you through the process of logging on to Oddschecker and placing a bet through the site on the Birmingham v Chelsea match which took place on 26 December 2009.

On loading up the screen you will be presented with the front page (Fig 2.2). And on the left-hand side of the screen you will see all of the sports listed in a column.

As you can see, football appears just below horse racing.

Just click on 'Football', and then click on the English tab that pops up underneath it.

Figure 2.2 – Oddschecker front page

This will give a list of the upcoming Premier League matches. As you can see, we have highlighted the Birmingham v Chelsea match. To see the odds available on this match, simply click the 'all odds' tab (Fig 2.3).

Figure 2.3 – List of Premier League matches

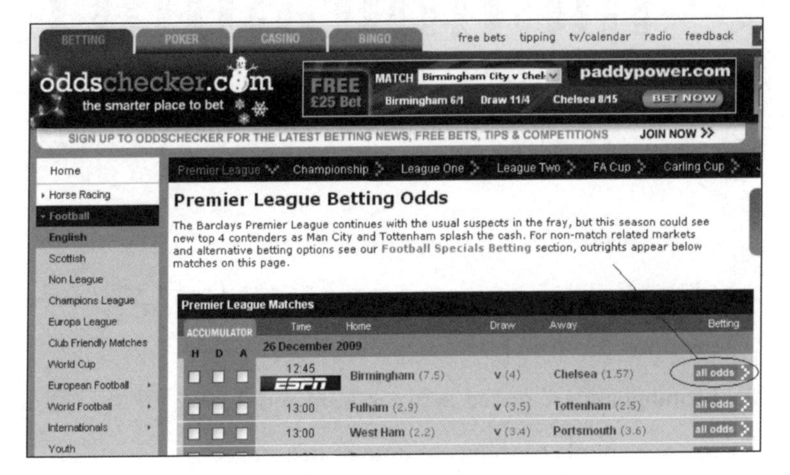

This then presents you with a list of markets available on the Birmingham v Chelsea match (Fig 2.4).

Figure 2.4 – List of available markets for Birmingham v Chelsea

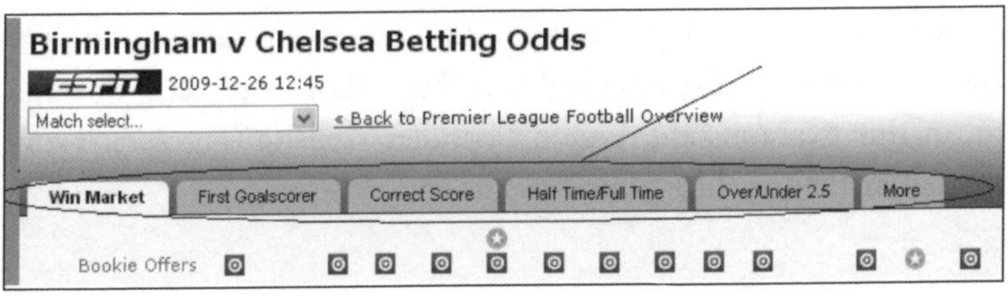

If we then click on the win market* (Fig 2.5) we will see a list of all the match odds and the various bookmakers offering these odds.

*('win market' tab has recently been replaced with 'winner').

Figure 2.5 – Match odds for Chelsea v Birmingham

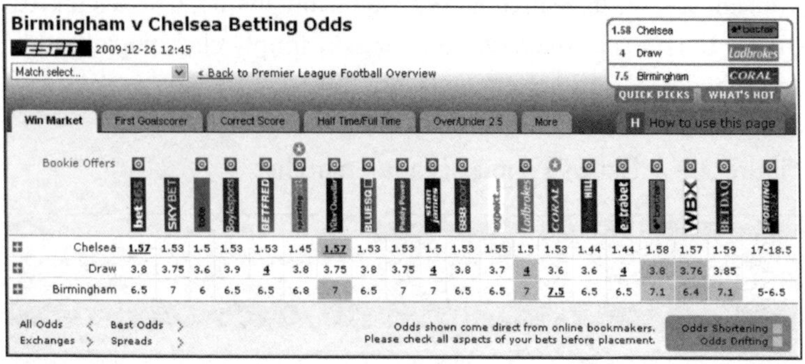

Birmingham v Chelsea Betting Odds

ESPN 2009-12-26 12:45

Match select... « Back to Premier League Football Overview

1.58 Chelsea betfair
4 Draw Ladbrokes
7.5 Birmingham CORAL

QUICK PICKS | WHAT'S HOT

Win Market | First Goalscorer | Correct Score | Half Time/Full Time | Over/Under 2.5 | More

H How to use this page

Bookie Offers	bet365	SKY BET	tote	Boylesports	BETFRED	sportingbet	Victor Chandler	BLUESQ	Paddy Power	stan james	888sport	expekt	Ladbrokes	CORAL	HILL	extrabet	betfair	WBX	BETDAQ	SPORTING INDEX
Chelsea	1.57	1.53	1.5	1.53	1.53	1.45	1.57	1.53	1.53	1.5	1.53	1.55	1.5	1.53	1.44	1.44	1.58	1.57	1.59	17-18.5
Draw	3.8	3.75	3.6	3.9	4	3.8	3.75	3.8	3.75	4	3.8	3.7	4	3.6	3.6	4	3.8	3.76	3.85	
Birmingham	6.5	7	6	6.5	6.5	6.8	7	6.5	7	7	6.5	6.5	7	7.5	6.5	6.5	7.1	6.4	7.1	5-6.5

All Odds < Best Odds >
Exchanges > Spreads >

Odds shown come direct from online bookmakers.
Please check all aspects of your bets before placement.

Odds Shortening
Odds Drifting

As you can see:

- Chelsea's odds for this match range from 1.44 to 1.57
- the draw is priced between 3.60 and 4.00
- Birmingham are priced between 6.00 and 7.50.

There are a couple of things to note at this stage.

The best odds available are always highlighted in bold. Also, you will see that if a team's odds are drifting this will be highlighted by the box being shaded pink. If, on the other hand, the team's odds are shortening, the box is highlighted in pale blue.

As we can see, the best odds being offered on Chelsea are 1.57.

Let's say we decide these are the odds we wish to take; we simply click on the 1.57 (Fig 2.6) and this then takes us directly through to, in this example, the Victor Chandler website (Fig 2.7). From there you simply place your bet.

Figure 2.6 – Chelsea odds offered by Victor Chandler

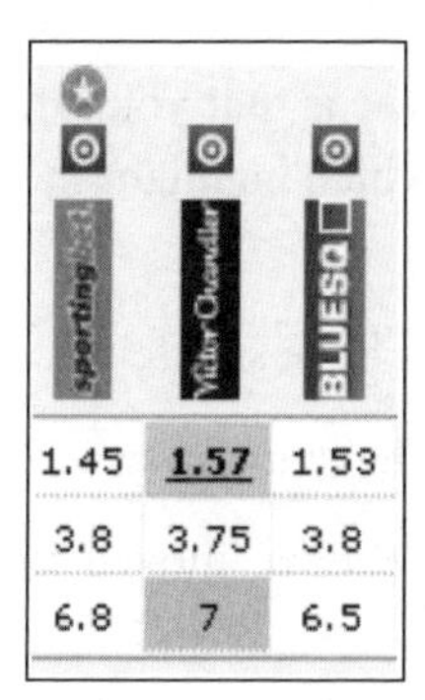

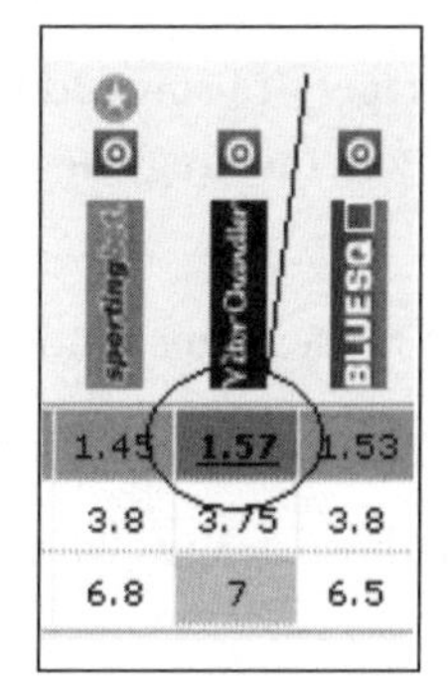

Figure 2.7 – Victor Chandler betting slip for Chelsea to beat Birmingham

Email updates

One of the major advantages of using Oddschecker is that you can have email alerts sent to you on a regular basis, which highlight the following:

- Steamers: highlights those teams whose odds have shortened.
- Drifters: highlights those teams whose odds have increased.
- Movers: highlights those teams whose odds have moved in either direction.

You can choose to have these emails sent to you every day, Monday to Friday or Saturday to Sunday. You can also have the odds displayed in decimal or traditional formats, and sent hourly between 0900 and 1800.

To access this service you simply sign up on the right-hand side of the screen (Fig 2.8).

Figure 2.8 – Sign up form to receive email alerts

On logging in you are then presented with a series of options, including the market reports as shown in Figure 2.9.

You simply highlight the reports you require and the frequency with which you require them – and they are then sent directly to your email account.

Figure 2.9 – Market report options

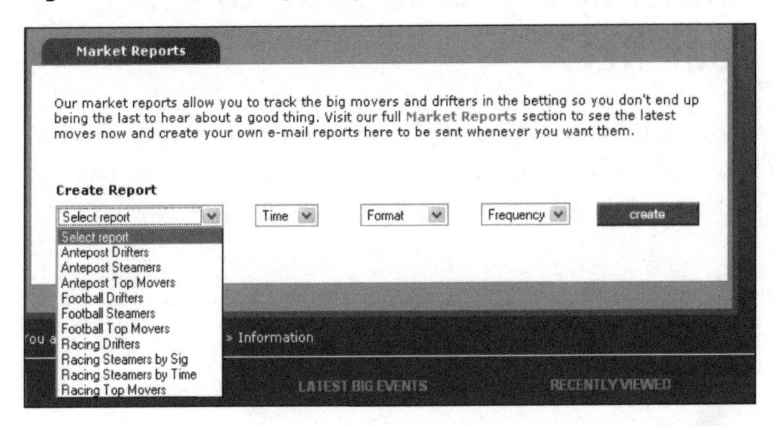

One of the major advantages of signing up to this service is that you can see and highlight any early market movement. This can then help you in ensuring that you place your bet at the optimum time, ensuring you receive the best odds available.

This now brings us nicely onto our next subject: knowing the best time to place your bet.

Knowing the Best Time to Place Your Bet

Knowing the correct time to place your bet is very important. It is a keystone of our one rule that should never be broken (and we make no apology for repeating it throughout our book):

Always ensure that you are placing your bet when you perceive that there is value to be had. This way you maximise your profits without increasing your risk.

It can be extremely frustrating when you place a bet on a team a couple of days before the match only to find you have put your bet on too early and the odds started drifting. However, the opposite can happen and you may find that the best odds available were only on offer the moment the market opened.

You are never going to get this right every time. However, with regular practice you will soon become accomplished at placing your bet at the best time.

It makes sense to assume that if you have already priced up your match you will know the price you are prepared to take in order to receive value. So often the best time to place your bet is early, when the betting markets are in their infancy and are just forming. At this stage the bookmakers are putting the feelers out to see where the sentiment lies. If they are attracting no money for the favourite, they then know they have priced this team incorrectly and will have to lengthen the odds. If they take money for the favourite very quickly then they know that they will have to shorten the price of this selection. The odds tend to get shrewder the closer to kick-off, and mispricing shrinks.

Ensure you are organised

This is where you need to be organised: you need to ensure that you are engaged as soon as the markets are formed by the bookmakers – the times that markets are formed can vary, but generally you find prices a week before a game is due to kick off. Good prices do not hang around for long, as other value punters are also around snapping up the early prices as soon as they become available.

Football betting markets will fluctuate in the early stages due to value takers. The time to bet early in any market is when your fancy is priced at value odds; a good proportion of your bets will be struck at this early stage.

Another factor that needs to be taken into account (and again you are going to have to be organised) is a team's fixture list. As an example, Wolverhampton Wanderers experienced their first away victory against Spurs on 12 December 2009. Their next fixture was away at Manchester United on the 15th, before facing a home fixture against Burnley on Sunday 20 December. It soon became apparent that Wolves manager Mick McCarthy did not fancy his team's chances at Old Trafford; he changed all 10 outfield players from the team that beat Spurs the previous Saturday.

This then alerted value punters to the Burnley match after this – it was obvious that McCarthy had identified the Burnley game as a must-win match and was saving his first team for Sunday's encounter. At this stage Wolves were priced at 2.40 to beat Burnley. This was when the value punters got in; and Wolves eventually started the game at 2.10. Wolves won 2-0.

Always consider competitions outside the Premier League

As with the above example it also pays to keep an eye out on team news and selections outside of the Premiership matches. These days managers have many differing priorities to consider and this can lead to weakened sides being selected in, and because of, the following competitions:

- The Champions League (group stages tend to have less priority, where feasible, than Premier League games; knockout stages have higher priority)
- The FA Cup (rarely prioritised by big teams till semi-final stage; Chelsea have been a notable exception of late)
- The Carling Cup (rarely prioritised by big teams, in most years, even to the final)
- The Europa League (rarely prioritised in most years; peculiar seasons – see Liverpool and Fulham in 2009/10 – can change this)

It therefore pays to keep an eye on how teams approach the above competitions, as bookmakers sometimes quote prices early without giving thorough consideration to the upcoming fixture list. They can also throw up additional opportunities.

Once the team news leaks through that the manager has decided to field a weakened side it is almost guaranteed that the odds on his side will drift and the price of the opposing side will contract. This means, when bearing in mind the upcoming fixtures list and impact of squad changes, sometimes getting in early and sometimes getting in late.

Let's look at three examples.

In the first example we will see what happened to the odds when Sir Alex Ferguson prioritised the Premiership after already qualifying for the knockout stages of the Champions League, and in the second we will see how the odds were affected when he initially rested his top striker Wayne Rooney for the Carling Cup final. In the third we'll see what happened when Arsène Wenger prioritised the Champions League in the midst of injury doubts over his best player.

Premiership priorities

The first example shows both kinds of complications that arise with games affected by these multiple priorities. You need to be flexible – sometimes getting in early, sometimes waiting, always mindful of the price you're looking for. In the Man United v Besiktas game on 25 November 2009, having qualified for the knockout rounds, Sir Alex Ferguson then decided to field a youthful and experimental line up. As soon as it was announced – an hour before kick off – with both Rooney and Berbatov missing, the price on Manchester United immediately went out from 1.41 to 1.48, and the Under 2.5 goal market went down from 2.00 to 1.74 within an hour.

Figure 2.10 – Man United v Besiktas, pre-match Man United price

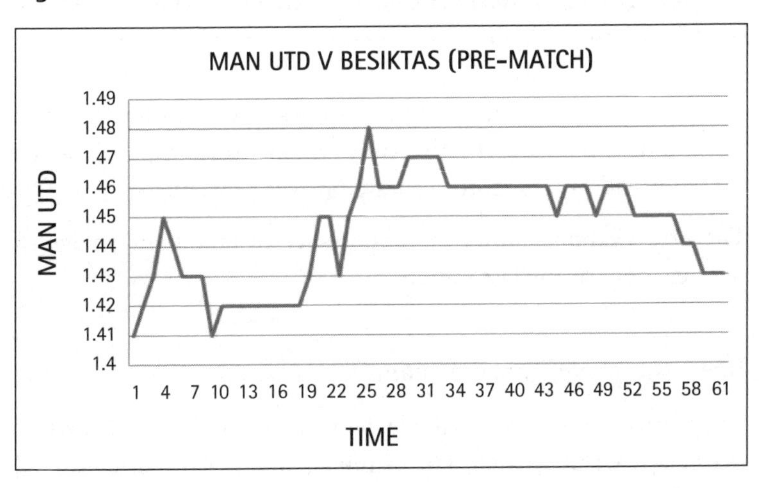

Figure 2.11 – Man United v Besiktas, pre-match Under 2.5 price

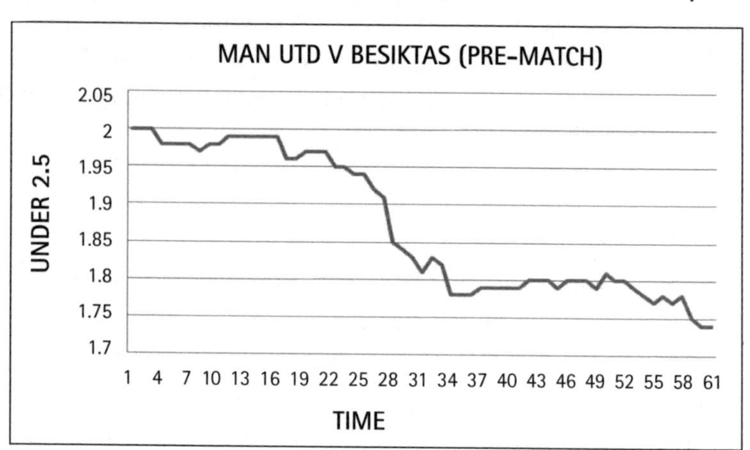

- In the match odds, if you still fancied Manchester United to win, and had quietly expected this kind of team change, *waiting till this reaction moment with the team sheet news* would have assured you the best possible odds – the price started to move out rapidly.
- Conversely, again quietly expecting this kind of team change and having identified the Under 2.5 goal market as a good one to get into (without Rooney and Berbatov, where are the goals going to come from?), *you would have done best by getting in as early as possible*, when the price was 2.00 – as further news could almost certainly only make this tighter, when information was more accurate (as was proved).

The next example shows the importance of taking advantage of overreactions at the last minute.

Does one player make a team?

The answer: yes – at least when it comes to how the betting markets react pre-match. For example, when Manchester United played Aston Villa in the Carling Cup final at Wembley on Sunday 28 February 2010, it was thought that Manchester United would field a full-strength side. When the teams were announced, including the surprise news that Wayne Rooney was on the subs bench (being spared for the Premiership campaign) and was being replaced in the starting line-up by Michael Owen, this had a dramatic effect on Manchester United's odds – their price drifted sharply from 1.91 to 2.02 within five minutes of the team news being released. This is classic overreaction – because, of course, on the pitch against a relatively weaker side, one player sitting on the bench (able to come on and play at any moment) cannot be said to have seriously impeded their chances of success. Man United won; Rooney scored the winner; and with canny alertness you'd have snapped up some good value on the back of nothing, just at the last minute.

Figure 2.12 – Man United v Aston Villa, pre-match Man United price

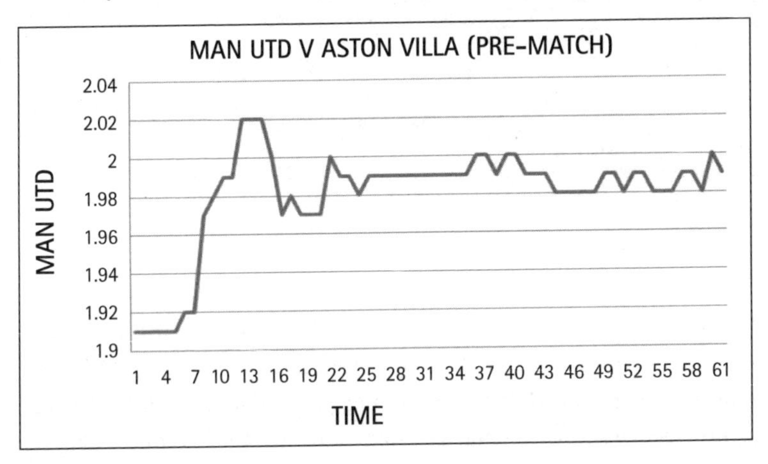

Prioritising the Champions League

For our next example we will see the importance of reading market sentiment and getting in early if prudent.

In the days before Arsenal's Champions League tie on Tuesday 26 August 2009 there had been plenty of 'will he/won't he?' rumours surrounding whether Fàbregas would (or indeed could) play. Figure 2.13 represents Arsenal's odds movement during this period leading up to the European tie with Celtic. We have also pointed out the key story developments that contributed to the movement of Arsenal's match odds.

Figure 2.13 – Arsenal's price movement

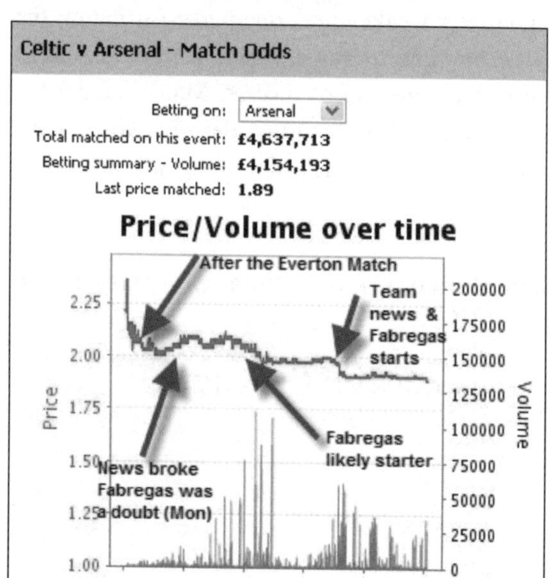

Before the Everton game on Saturday 23 August 2009, Arsenal were available at prices ranging between 2.20 and 2.30; but the market started to attract real money around the 2.12/2.14 price point. Because of Arsenal's flying start to the Premier League season they started to attract plenty of backers, which forced the price down to around 2.00/2.02 Monday lunchtime.

News then broke on Sky Sports that Fàbregas was doubtful for the game. As you can see on the chart, the price then drifted all the way back to 2.10 before settling at 2.06/2.08, which it held most of Tuesday before coming into 2.00 around 6pm.

Although there was no concrete news as to the fitness of Fàbregas, it is pretty safe to assume that as the market price had not drifted any further than this, those in the market clearly thought that it was safe to take for granted that he was indeed going to play. How this information gets out to enough of those taking up (or offering) positions is not always obvious, but the fact is that word does leak. It usually isn't very hard for someone to have found out from someone, or somewhere, the truth at a club. Indeed various fan websites, blogs and Twitter posts are some of the best ways to find out if an injured player is playing or not; although some of these postings are rumours, many have inside sources that prove to be accurate.

When the team news filtered through at around 6.45pm, the Spaniard was included in the team and there was a further price movement from 2.00 down to 1.90. So you would have been well advised, seeing the indications of the stabilising price, to get in as early as you could – knowing that confirmation could only worsen the available odds. You would have got in at an ultimately enviable price.

⚽ ⚽ ⚽

The above examples highlight the need for quick thinking, adaptability and patience. You should only bet when the odds are in your favour. Sometimes this may not be early in the market. Sometimes it will be. The key, each time, is to know in advance the kind of odds you're happy to accept – and then take into account the squad and cup priorities that are likely to affect this. A bit of canny thinking and timing goes an awfully long way to maximising your profits without increasing your risk.

Betting Exchanges

Although this book primarily highlights the markets available with the traditional bookmakers, we have included this small section on Betfair (and other betting exchanges), covering how to place a simple bet and why you should never assume that Betfair et al. always offer the best odds.

Should you require a more detailed publication dealing with how you can best exploit some of the opportunities provided by betting exchanges, we would of course suggest you check out Peter Nordsted's own *Mastering Betfair*, if you haven't already. Naturally, though, much of the thinking and stats in this book will be relevant to those who use Betfair: getting the best price and understanding market movements is equally important there. If you've used Betfair before, skip to 'Betfair vs bookmakers'.

A simple trade

When you log onto the Betfair site and start looking at a market, you will be presented with a table highlighting the current available odds. In the example below we are going to look at a football match between Tottenham and Newcastle (Fig 2.14).

In a football match we are presented with six possible options. We can back or lay the home win, the away win or the draw.

- If you back a team or individual you are stating that you are expecting that this event will occur.
- If you lay a team or individual you are saying this event will not occur.

In this particular case:

- If you were to back Tottenham you are expecting Tottenham to win.

- If you lay Tottenham you are saying that Newcastle will win the match or it will end up being a draw.

The best available prices are always displayed in the middle of the table. In the example below, the best odds available for Tottenham to win the match are currently 1.73.

However, there is also money available at odds of 1.72 and 1.71. This money is from the punters who are laying the Tottenham win but do not want to accept the current price of 1.73.

Should someone back Tottenham at 1.73 with £866, the odds at 1.73 would disappear and be replaced by the next price in the queue (i.e. those people who have laid at the odds of 1.72).

Figure 2.14 – Odds available Tottenham v Newcastle

Tottenham v Newcastle
Going in-play Live Scores Matched: GBP 121,771 Refresh
Back & Lay Market Depth More options

Selections: (3)	100.4%		Back	Lay		99.5%
Tottenham	1.71 £748	1.72 £505	1.73 £866	1.74 £193	1.75 £2071	1.76 £233
Newcastle	5.7 £542	5.8 £162	5.9 £211	6 £340	6.2 £226	6.4 £675
The Draw	3.8 £1644	3.85 £422	3.9 £961	3.95 £253	4 £457	4.1 £951

On the lay side you will see that £193 is available to lay at 1.74 and the odds of 1.75 and 1.76 come from those who have backed Tottenham hoping to gain a better price than is currently available.

Backing

As you can see from the preceding table there is £866 available to back Tottenham at the odds of 1.73.

If you were to back at the lower price of 1.72, your bet would automatically get filled at the higher price of 1.73 – providing that the total monetary value of your bet is available.

One thing to remember is that Betfair always automatically matches your bet at the best available odds whether you are backing or laying.

In this example, if you back Tottenham you are saying: I bet £100 that Tottenham will win this match and want to receive 1.73 times my stake. In this case, should Tottenham win, your return would be £173. The 1.73 represents 1 + .73, the 1 being your stake of £100 and .73 being the £73 risk that the layer is putting up for you.

Just to clarify, should you want to back and ask for better odds than are currently available your bet will appear on the *lay* side of the market.

Laying

If you lay Tottenham, you are saying that Tottenham will not win the match. In other words, you are saying the game will result in either a:

- Newcastle win
- or a draw.

If you were to lay Tottenham for £100 and they did not win, you would win £100. However, should Tottenham win, then the odds of 1.74 represent your stake, 1 (here £100), plus your risk of .74, which in this case would be £74. So a Tottenham win would represent a loss of £74.

Betfair commission

Betfair charge a commission on your net winnings, so you only pay commission if you have a winning trade. If you have a net loss on a market you do not pay commission. Commission is calculated by multiplying your net winnings by the Market Base Rate; a win of £100 on a market with a Market Base Rate of 5% would result in you paying £5 in commission. To find the Market Base Rate you go to the Rules tab of the market you are trading (Figure 2.15).

Commission is generally charged at 5%.

Figure 2.15 – Market Base Rate commission

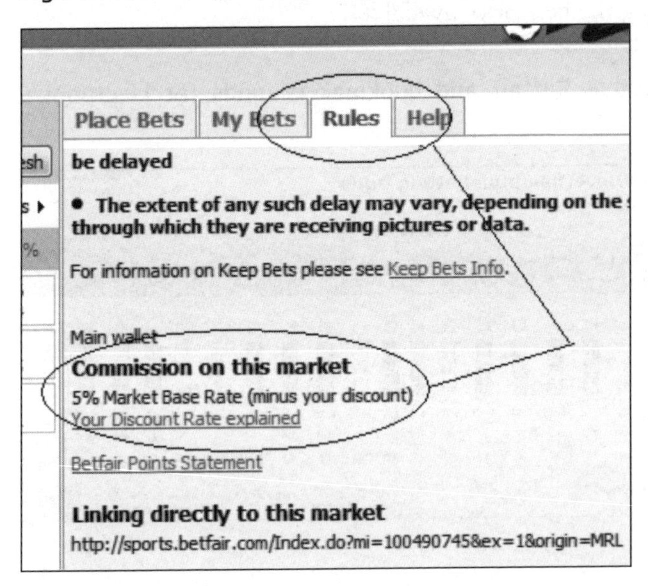

Betfair vs bookmakers

One thing that should be noted is that it is completely false to assume that Betfair always offer the best odds.

As we can see from the example (Fig 2.16), in the Liverpool v Wolves game it would appear that Betfair are offering the best price on the match odds at 1.30, along with Victor Chandler and Coral.

However, what these prices do not take into account are the 5% deductions on winnings that apply to all bets placed on Betfair. If you were to place £100 on Liverpool to beat Wolves with Corals you would gain a £30 profit. If you were to place £100 on Liverpool to beat Wolves with Betfair you would gain a £28.50 profit.

Again, this represents a 5% difference on the profit gained.

When deciding to place a bet with Betfair, always take into account the 5% deduction; you will see that on many occasions Betfair are not offering the best price available.

Figure 2.16 – Betfair and bookmakers' odds for Liverpool v Wolves

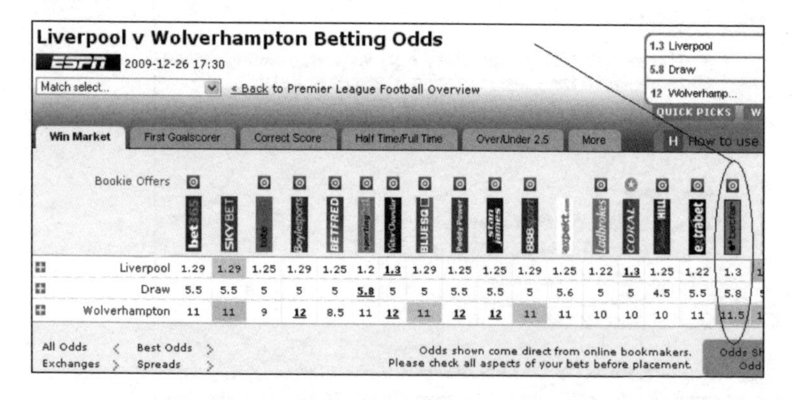

Liverpool v Wolverhampton Betting Odds

ESPN 2009-12-26 17:30

Match select... « Back to Premier League Football Overview

1.3 Liverpool / 5.8 Draw / 12 Wolverhamp...

QUICK PICKS

Win Market | First Goalscorer | Correct Score | Half Time/Full Time | Over/Under 2.5 | More | How to use

Bookie Offers

	bet365	SKY BET	tote	Boylesports	BETFRED	sportingbet	VictorChandler	BLUESQ	Paddy Power	Stan James	888sport	expekt	Ladbrokes	CORAL	William Hill	extrabet	betfair
Liverpool	1.29	1.29	1.25	1.29	1.25	1.2	1.3	1.29	1.25	1.25	1.29	1.25	1.22	1.3	1.25	1.22	1.3
Draw	5.5	5.5	5	5	5	5.8	5	5	5.5	5.5	5	5.6	5	5	4.5	5.5	5.8
Wolverhampton	11	11	9	12	8.5	11	12	11	12	12	11	11	10	10	10	11	11.5

All Odds ‹ Best Odds ›
Exchanges › Spreads ›

Odds shown come direct from online bookmakers. Please check all aspects of your bets before placement.

3

Match Bets

The Win Markets

Good value for the victory

When looking to place any bet on football it is essential that you give yourself the best chance of succeeding, as said, by *always ensuring that you obtain the best price available.* And you'd be surprised how true (and easy) this is even for a straightforward traditional 'win' bet (i.e. backing a particular team to win a given match) – so that you can often find some value without doing any calculations at all.

For example, if we take a look at the Boxing Day 2009 clash between Fulham and Tottenham and we fancy Tottenham to win we can see from the odds comparison site Oddschecker that there is a large disparity in the odds the different firms are offering.

In the screenshot (Fig 3.1), Tottenham's price ranges from the 2.63 being offered by Victor Chandler through to the 2.25 which is being offered by both William Hill and Sky Bet.

The punter placing £20 on Tottenham to win at Victor Chandler would expect to show a profit of £32.60 should Tottenham go on to win. However, if he had placed his £20 with William Hill he could expect to profit by only £25 in comparison.

This represents an incredible 30.4% difference in return. By just taking a few minutes to search for the best value, you have gained £7.60 should Tottenham go on to win the game.

Figure 3.1 – Bookmakers' odds for Fulham v Tottenham

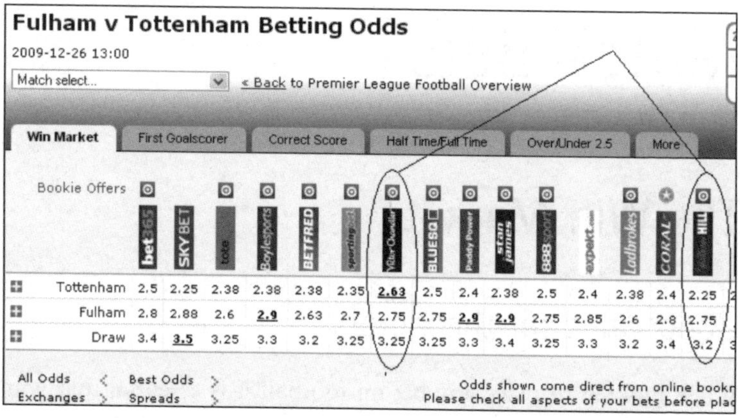

Fulham v Tottenham Betting Odds

2009-12-26 13:00

Match select... « Back to Premier League Football Overview

Win Market | First Goalscorer | Correct Score | Half Time/Full Time | Over/Under 2.5 | More

Bookie Offers

	bet365	SKY BET	tote	Boylesports	BETFRED	sporting	Victor Chandler	BLUESQ	Paddy Power	stan james	888sport	expekt	Ladbrokes	CORAL	HILL
Tottenham	2.5	2.25	2.38	2.38	2.38	2.35	**2.63**	2.5	2.4	2.38	2.5	2.4	2.38	2.4	2.25
Fulham	2.8	2.88	2.6	**2.9**	2.63	2.7	2.75	2.75	**2.9**	**2.9**	2.75	2.85	2.6	2.8	2.75
Draw	3.4	**3.5**	3.25	3.3	3.2	3.25	3.25	3.25	3.3	3.4	3.25	3.3	3.2	3.4	3.2

All Odds < Best Odds >
Exchanges > Spreads >

Odds shown come direct from online bookm
Please check all aspects of your bets before plac

Open numerous accounts

Bookmaking is one business where it does not pay to be a loyal customer; opening one account and blindly taking whatever odds are available is, to be honest, pointless. If you are to take your Premier League betting seriously it is essential that you open numerous accounts, giving yourself the best advantage possible.

Obviously initially this will take some hard work and you are best keeping a notebook handy so you can record all of your login, password and contact details for each different bookmaker. But once this is done you can then always, and promptly, take advantage of situations like the one highlighted above.

However, this does come with a very serious word of warning: if you are placing bets with your ordinary debit card through numerous bookmakers, your bank statement does not make for good reading – especially if you have up to 10 different entries every week. It simply does not look great if you are applying for any type of finance such as a loan or mortgage. We combated this by opening separate bank accounts to be used solely for our betting.

Odds on the draw

As we have previously stated, the only way you are going to profit in the long term is by finding selections that offer decent value.

Backing the draw

It is now that we would like to bring your attention to the draw and the value that can be had by backing it.

Most punters prefer to back one team or another. These single team selections are many punter's weekend bets; if they do not think a team will win they simply do not bet on that match. So this is where you can find value and often make a nice profit; you are more likely to find value on these bets because these are the type of bets the bookmakers have problem taking money on.

For example, all of the major clubs now have a resident bookmaker installed on the premises. In Arsenal's case it is Ladbrokes. Now how many punters do you think will be opposing the home side? Not many, we would suggest – the travelling fans and who else? And who, out of all the expectant ticket holders, will back a draw? So the bookmakers are more than willing to take your money, even if it is at a price which suggests you're getting good value. They do this purely and simply because there is so much money being backed on one side or the other or both (in the case of the draw).

Before placing a bet on the draw we personally like to see if we can find around 2%-3% value.

Before we discovered how profitable backing the draw could be we were also just two of those punters who would never even consider looking at the draw. But now we regularly wager on a match finishing a draw and it has paid dividends.

Half time/full time

The half-time/full-time bet is generally favoured by punters when a strong favourite is playing at home or away against weaker opposition. However, our advice is: beware. It can look like a sure fire way of getting value. It isn't.

For example, in a recent Premiership match Manchester United were playing Blackburn at home and were priced at 1.17 to win. They were also priced at 1.40 to be leading at both half time and full time. Obviously not many punters were tempted at backing Manchester United at 1.17 but many may have been tempted by the 1.40 on offer for Manchester United to be leading at both half time and full time. As it turned out, Manchester United beat Blackburn 2-0 – but were drawing 0-0 at half time.

The following tables highlight the records of the top seven clubs, and, as you can see, winning at both half time and full time is rarely as easy or common as it would seem. The average odds for a top-seven home side achieving this are 1.93. Looking at the away stats, even the 2009/10 champions, Chelsea, only achieved the half-time/full-time win result in eight of 19 matches, which equates to odds of 2.38.

Average punters almost always overestimate a team's chance of achieving this bet and bookmakers know this by offering them very poor odds.

So our advice is – always tread with care; ensure that you are receiving good value if you go for this bet. And as for backing the big teams away from home with this bet, leave well alone.

Team	Home matches	Half time/full time	Percentage	ODDS
CHELSEA	19	12	63.15	1.58
MAN UNITED	19	9	47.37	2.11
ARSENAL	19	11	57.89	1.73
SPURS	19	13	68.42	1.46
MAN CITY	19	10	52.63	1.90
ASTON VILLA	19	4	21.05	4.75
LIVERPOOL	19	10	52.63	1.90
TOTAL	133	69	51.87	1.93

Team	Away matches	Half time/full time	Percentage	ODDS
CHELSEA	19	8	42.11	2.37
MAN UNITED	19	5	26.32	3.80
ARSENAL	19	4	21.05	4.75
SPURS	19	4	21.05	4.75
MAN CITY	19	5	26.32	3.80
ASTON VILLA	19	6	31.58	3.17
LIVERPOOL	19	1	05.26	19.01
TOTAL	133	33	24.81	4.03

Draw no bet

'Draw no bet' can be a very useful wager, especially when looking to bet on those games where you believe your selection will definitely not lose but may draw. As the name implies, if the match you are betting on ends in a stalemate then you receive your full stake back, and if your selection wins you receive the odds you placed the bet at. Should the opposing side win then you lose your stake. Once again, when looking to place this bet you should always look for value. Here's an example of how to do so with this particular kind of wager.

Let's look at a match from last season between Everton and Birmingham. The best available prices at the bookmakers were as follows:

Bookmaker's odds		Percentage
Everton	1.89	53
Draw	3.60	28
Birmingham	5.00	20

We had done our calculation and came up with the following odds:

Our book		Percentage
Everton	2.13	47
Draw	3.45	29
Birmingham	4.17	24

Birmingham had been on a good run and we identified that there was 5% value in backing them. However, although we did not think they would lose, we were not fully confident in them winning – we believed Everton could possibly hold them to a draw.

We then decided to see what odds where available at the bookmakers.

Best draw no bet odds		Percentage
Everton	1.30	76.92
Birmingham	4.00	25.00

I then saw that Birmingham were best priced at 4.00 draw no bet to win this match. We then did the following calculation to ensure that we were still receiving at least 5% value.

We took our original book figures and took out the draw figure of 3.45 (29%).

Our book		Percentage
Everton	2.13	47
Birmingham	4.17	24

This then left Everton with 47% and Birmingham with 24%. To calculate Birmingham's chances without the draw we simply added Everton's 47% to Birmingham's 24%, which left us with 71. We then divided Birmingham's 24 by 71 and multiplied this figure by 100.

This left us with 33.80.

This 33.80 represents the percentage chance of Birmingham beating Everton when taking away the draw. When converting to odds this equates to 2.96. So according to our book, Birmingham should be priced at 2.96 and had a 33.8% chance of beating Everton without the draw. The bookmakers were offering 4.00 – a 25% chance. According to our figures, there was therefore 8.8% value in backing Birmingham draw no bet.

This is the bet we took; the game ended 1-1; and we had not lost any money.

When looking to place this bet, never overlook the draw – especially if you believe the draw price offers some value also.

Double chance

As we saw earlier in the book, the beauty of Betfair is that you can lay a side not to win a match. Now, many punters believe this cannot be done at a traditional bookmaker – but indeed it can, with the double chance bet.

When you are laying a side on Betfair you are effectively backing the other two outcomes. For example, in the following example (Fig 3.2) we can see that we have laid Arsenal for £25 not to beat Aston Villa.

Figure 3.2 – Betfair odds for Arsenal v Aston Villa

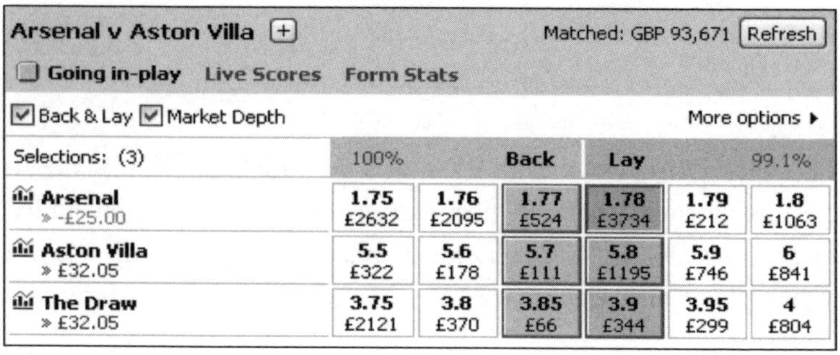

Arsenal v Aston Villa (+) Matched: GBP 93,671 Refresh

Going in-play Live Scores Form Stats

Back & Lay Market Depth More options ▸

Selections: (3)	100%		Back	Lay		99.1%
Arsenal » -£25.00	1.75 £2632	1.76 £2095	1.77 £524	1.78 £3734	1.79 £212	1.8 £1063
Aston Villa » £32.05	5.5 £322	5.6 £178	5.7 £111	5.8 £1195	5.9 £746	6 £841
The Draw » £32.05	3.75 £2121	3.8 £370	3.85 £66	3.9 £344	3.95 £299	4 £804

So if the game ends up with Aston Villa winning, or the game is a draw, we will win £32.05. When we deduct the 5%, this then amounts to £30.44.

To calculate the odds of this – the two outcomes other than the Arsenal win – we take our potential winnings, in this case £30.44, and divide them by our potential loss of £25 (our stake). This comes to 1.21. We then add 1 (our original stake) and this gives us odds of 2.21 on the game ending in either an Aston Villa win or a draw.

So now we know that the equivalent of laying Arsenal is backing Aston Villa and the draw at true odds on Betfair of, in fact, 2.21.

We then need to see if better odds are available at the bookmakers.

On opening up Oddschecker we see that, in the double chance market (Fig 3.3), William Hill are offering 2.25, which is better than the 2.21 being offered on Betfair.

Figure 3.3 – Bookmakers' double chance odds, Arsenal v Aston Villa

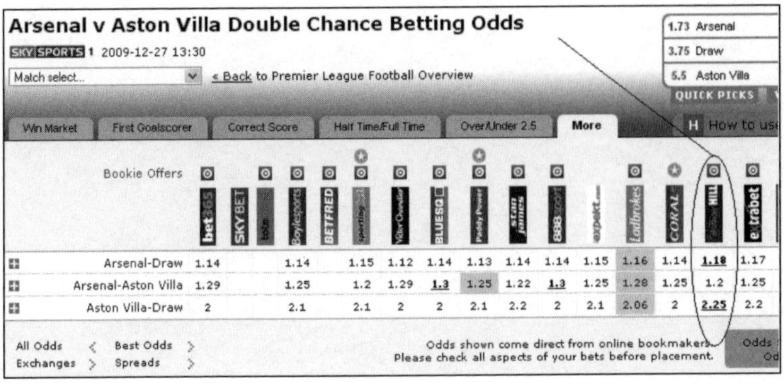

Arsenal v Aston Villa Double Chance Betting Odds

SKY SPORTS 1 2009-12-27 13:30

Match select... « Back to Premier League Football Overview

1.73 Arsenal
3.75 Draw
5.5 Aston Villa
QUICK PICKS

Win Market | First Goalscorer | Correct Score | Half Time/Full Time | Over/Under 2.5 | More

How to use

Bookie Offers	bet365	SKY BET	tote	Boylesports	BETFRED	sportingbet	Victor Chandler	BLUESQ	Paddy Power	stan james	888sport	expekt	Ladbrokes	CORAL	HILL	extrabet
Arsenal-Draw	1.14			1.14		1.15	1.12	1.14	1.13	1.14	1.14	1.15	1.16	1.14	**1.18**	1.17
Arsenal-Aston Villa	1.29			1.25		1.2	1.29	**1.3**	1.25	1.22	**1.3**	1.25	1.28	1.25	1.2	1.25
Aston Villa-Draw	2			2.1		2.1	2	2	2.1	2.2	2	2.1	2.06	2	**2.25**	2.2

All Odds < Best Odds >
Exchanges > Spreads >

Odds shown come direct from online bookmakers. Please check all aspects of your bets before placement.

Once again, never assume that the best prices are always available on Betfair. The commission and bookmakers' promotions, combined with increased competition, mean that on many occasions better odds can be found. Typically it is just a case of taking the time to find these opportunities.

4

Score Betting

This chapter deals with the bookmakers' markets that relate to either the number of goals scored in a match (the unders/overs markets, i.e. less than or more than a certain number of goals) or what the final score of a match will be.

Over/Under 2.5 Goals

When it comes to Premier League bets relating to the number of goals scored, over/under 2.5 goals is probably the most popular market.

In the following example we are going to look at the match between Manchester United and Liverpool that took place on 21 March 2010 at Old Trafford.

As with the previous match odds example in Chapter 2 we will be compiling our own odds by again looking at the two teams' previous 16-game home and away form. In this example we will be looking at Manchester United's previous 16 home games and Liverpool's previous 16 away games.

In their last 16 home matches, Manchester United had:

- four games that contained under 2.5 goals
- 12 games that contained over 2.5 goals.

In their last 16 away matches, Liverpool had:

- 12 games that contained under 2.5 goals
- four games that contained over 2.5 goals.

We then do the following equations.

To get the under 2.5 goal price

To begin working out the under 2.5 goal price, we would take Manchester United's four home games that contained under 2.5 goals and add these to Liverpool's 12 away games that also featured under 2.5 goals. This gives us a total of 16.

To begin working out the over 2.5 goal price, we would take Manchester United's 12 home games that contained over 2.5 goals and add these to Liverpool's four away games that also featured over 2.5 goals. This also gives us a total of 16.

So then we are left with the following:

```
Under 2.5 goals = 16 Matches

Over 2.5 goals = 16 Matches
```

To get the percentage chance of each, we divide the under and over totals by the combined total of the two outcomes, which in this case is 32.

```
So to get the under 2.5 goal percentage you
divide 16 by 32 = 50

To get the over 2.5 goal percentage you divide
16 by 32 = 50
```

Then to get the odds you simply divide 100 by the percentage figure:

```
Under 2.5 goals 100/50 = 2.00
Over 2.5 goals 100/50 = 2.00
```

So now we have priced up our under/over 2.5 goal market. And we have:

- Under 2.5 goals 2.00
- Over 2.5 goals 2.00

Oddschecker shows us the following:

Figure 4.1 – Bookmakers' over/under 2.5 odds, Manchester United v Liverpool

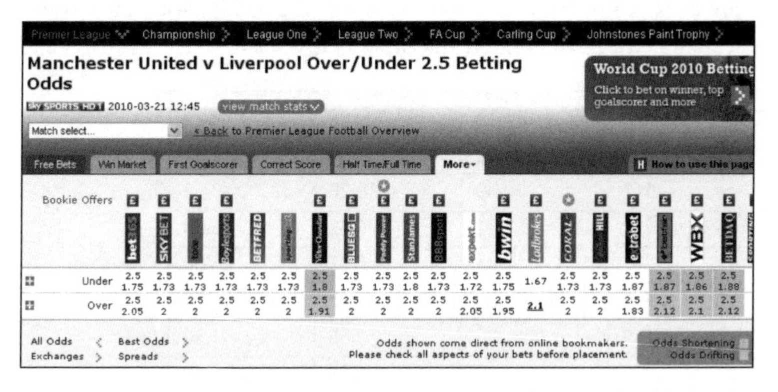

As we can see (Fig 4.1), the best odds available for under 2.5 goals are 1.8 (55.55%) and we believe they should be 2.00 (50.00%); so we would not bet on under 2.5 goals here. The bookmakers believe there is more chance of this game finishing with under 2.5 goals than we do – with a 5.55% difference.

Over 2.5 goals is best priced at 2.10 (47.61%) and we have this priced up as a 2.00 (50.00%) chance. So we believe there is 2.39% value in backing over 2.5 goals in this game. If you were happy with the value offered by this, it is the bet you would take.

The game ended 2-1, and with a stake of – say – £50, we would have won a handsome £55 on top of getting our stake back again. That's £5 more than what we calculated as reasonable – and it's precisely that sort of regular extra, from only taking good value bets, that stands you in good stead against inevitable losses.

Correct Score

When it comes to pricing up a correct score market, the mathematics of the equations involved are far too complicated to be included in a book like this.

However, to give you some idea of the odds you should be receiving, we have created the table below.

Score	No of games	Percentage	Real odds
0-0	32	8.42	12.00
1-1	39	10.26	9.50
2-2	21	5.52	18.00
3-3	4	1.05	95.00
1-0	33	8.68	11.50
2-0	33	8.68	11.50
3-0	23	6.05	16.50
2-1	42	11.05	9.00
3-2	8	2.10	47.50
0-1	25	6.66	15.00
0-2	14	3.70	27.00
0-3	3	0.78	125.00
1-2	19	5.00	20.00
1-3	8	2.12	47.00
2-3	5	1.33	75.00
OTHER	55	14.49	6.90

We've got a more in-depth and up-to-the-minute look at the odds you should be getting on the correct score markets at www.premier-betting.com.

Never back 0-0

There is one thing that you should always remember with correct score betting. Never back 0-0. If you do fancy a 0-0 score line, you should consider backing the 'no goal scorer' in the first goal-scorer market instead.

The reason for this is that, if the game finishes 1-0 and the winning goal was scored by an own goal, according to bookmakers' rules this goes down as a 'no goal-scorer'. So you get extra protection: your 0-0 bet cannot be disrupted by some particularly hopeless defensive blunder. A game can end 1-0 and your 'bet' on 0-0 will pay out.

5

Player Betting

First/Last Goal Scorer

The first/last goal scorer market is an extremely popular market and is a very straightforward bet to make. All you are doing is backing a player to either score the first goal or the last goal. You must always remember in this market that **own goals do not count**.

Once again, all you have to ask yourself is – are you receiving the best odds? And once again, it's an informed statistical approach that will help you here. In this case we've put together a very helpful form sheet for all your 2010/11 first/last goal scorer bets. Here's how.

In the following table we have brought together last season's top 10 goal scorers, and how many times they scored either the first or last goal of the game. From this we then reverse engineered the odds of their being the first/last goal scorer throughout the 2009/10 term, based on the number of times each player would have produced a winning bet. This gives you a really useful reference for the 2010/11 season – just check any odds on offer for these players being first/last scorer against this table. There's no reason for there to be any wild divergence – though temporary form or niggling injuries, should such things arise, will obviously have to be taken into account. (We've only done this for the top scorers of 2009/10 – if you fancy evaluating anyone else, just use the process outlined below; we've put together relevant stats for the top 31 scorers of last season on p.68.)

To produce the odds we started by dividing the number of goals by the games scored in. So, for example, Wayne Rooney scored the first goal 10 times in 32 matches.

```
10/32 = 0.31

Multiply the 0.31 by 100 = 31

Then simply divide 100 by 31 = 3.22
```

So, the real odds of Wayne Rooney scoring the first goal are 3.22.

Player	Goals scored	Matches started	No of times scored first goal	Real Odds	No of times scored last goal	Real odds
Drogba	29	31	8	3.85	9	3.45
Rooney	26	32	10	3.22	6	5.26
Rooney Last goal scored in 1-0 Victory once						
Bent	24	38	13	2.92	7	5.43
Bent Last goal scored in 1-0 Victory four times						
Tevez	23	32	6	5.33	7	4.57
Lampard	22	36	3	12.00	8	4.50
Defoe	18	31	7	4.43	2	15.50
Torres	18	20	8	2.50	4	5.00
Fàbregas	15	26	4	6.50	3	8.67
Adebayor	14	25	6	4.17	5	5.00
Adebayor Last goal scored in 1-0 Victory twice						
Agbonlahor	13	35	7	5.00	5	7.00
Agbonlahor Last goal scored in 1-0 Victory twice						
Saha	13	26	3	8.67	5	5.20

Anytime Goal Scorer

We have gone through the same procedure to find the real odds of a player scoring a goal anytime during the match. (Once again, we've only done this for the top scorers – if you fancy evaluating anyone else, just use the process outlined above; we've put together relevant stats for the top 31 scorers of last season on p.68.)

Player	Goals scored	Matches started	No of times scored goal anytime during game	Real odds
Drogba	29	31	20	1.55
Rooney	26	32	18	1.78
Bent	24	38	17	2.23
Tevez	23	32	14	2.28
Lampard	22	36	14	2.58
Defoe	18	31	12	2.58
Torres	18	20	12	1.67
Fàbregas	15	26	9	2.88
Adebayor	14	25	12	2.08
Agbonlahor	13	35	12	2.92
Saha	13	26	9	2.89

First Goal Scorer Each Way

As well as being able to bet on the first and last goal scorer in a football match, many bookmakers are now offering each-way terms on the first three goals. This means you could end up profiting even if the player you select does not score the first goal; if he scores the second or third goal then you will still get a return on your money. This then allows you to be a little more adventurous with your selections.

To understand this bet further we need to take a look at a full explanation of the rules that underpin it.

Essentially you are having two bets:

1. The first is that the player you are betting on will score the first goal; this is settled at the full odds.
2. The second is that the player you are betting on will score either the first, second or third goals; this is settled at 1/3 of the odds.

Let us look at an example of placing this kind of bet before looking at the rest of the rules. In this example we shall look at the Birmingham v Chelsea match on Boxing Day 2009.

Here we have looked at the relevant odds and we fancy that Birmingham striker Cameron Jerome may score the first goal. We go onto Oddschecker and see that Jerome is best priced for first goalscorer at 10.00 with Bet365 (Fig 5.1).

Figure 5.1 – Bet365 first goal scorer odds, Birmingham v Chelsea

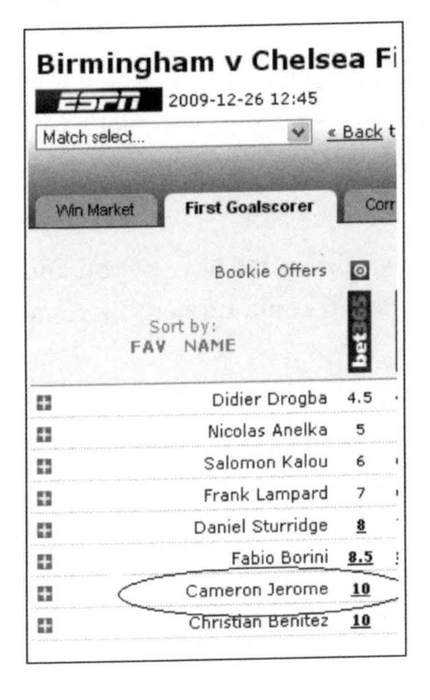

We then click on this best price; the Bet365 betting slip opens up (Fig 5.2).

Figure 5.2 – Bet365 first goal scorer betting slip

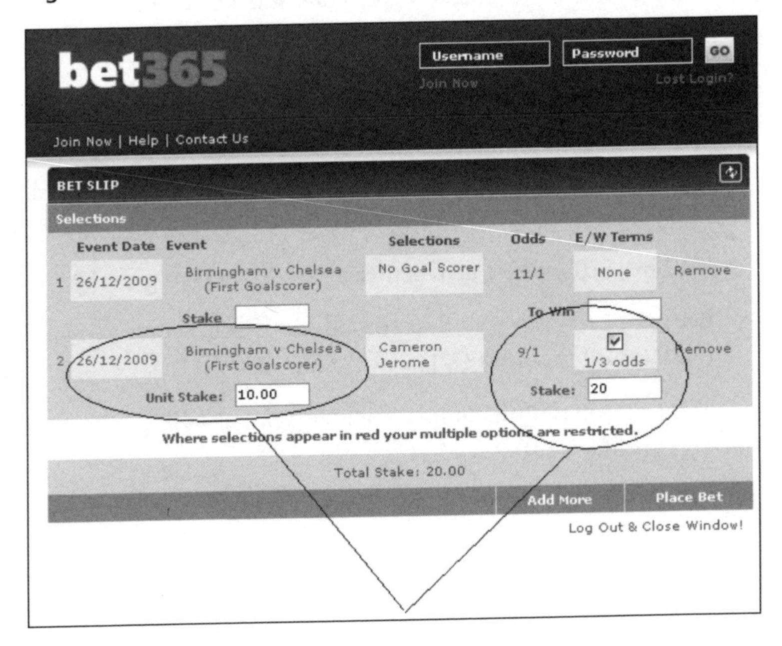

To place an each-way bet you simply tick the box which highlights 1/3 of the odds.

You then put in the amount of your unit stake. At this stage you must remember that you are having two bets. So if you place £10 in the unit stake your total stake will be £20. If you only wish to risk £10 in total then the unit stake would be £5.

We will now take a look at the details of what we have bet on and what we will receive depending on when, if at all, Cameron Jerome scores one of the first three goals.

First goal scorer

Should Cameron Jerome score the first goal you will have two winning bets:

- Bet one: £10 on first goal scorer at 10.00 (9/1) = win £90.
- Bet two: £10 each way first, second, third goal scorer at 10.00 (9/1) 1/3 odds = 4.00 (3/1) = win £30.
- Total return: £120 (including original stake of £20).
  Total profit = £100.

Second and third goal scorer

Should Cameron Jerome score the second or third goals you will have one winning and one losing bet:

- Bet one: £10 on first goal scorer at 10.00 (9/1) = lose £10.
- Bet two: £10 each way first second, third goal scorer at 10.00 (9/1) 1/3 odds = 4.00 (3/1) = win £30.
- Total return: £30 (including original stake of £20).
  Total profit = £10.

So, as you can see from the previous example, providing Cameron Jerome scores one of the first three goals in the match against Chelsea, we will end up in profit.

Further rules to take into account

Other rules that need to be noted before placing this bet are as follows:

- Players who do not score until after three goals have been scored will be treated as losers.
- If less than three goals are scored, then settlement will be based on the actual goals scored. Where no goals are scored, all each-way bets will be treated as losers.
- If a player scores the first goal, both the win and place parts of the bet will be winners. If the same player scores the second and/or third, fourth or fifth goal, **no additional winnings will be paid.**
- If a player scores the second, third, fourth or fifth goal, the place part of the bet will be successful. If the same player scores more than once, **no additional winnings will be paid.**
- If the selection does not take part or comes on after the first valid goal is scored (i.e. not an own goal), **both the win and place parts of the bet will be void.**
- Players that are substituted/sent off before the first goal is scored will be settled as losing bets for both the win and place parts of the bet.
- Own goals do not count.

Advantages of this bet

One of the major advantages of the each-way first goal scorer markets is that you can afford to be more adventurous with your selection. For example, the following players on many occasions are priced at 20 or above to score the first goal – but many times they are on the score sheet at some stage of the match:

> John Terry (Chelsea), Michael Carrick (Man United), Darren Fletcher (Man United), Glen Johnson (Liverpool), Michael Dawson (Tottenham), Thomas Vermaelen (Arsenal), William Gallas (Arsenal).

Also, when staking on these games we would suggest that you choose a team who are superior to their opposition. Should the opposition not score, your chances of winning on this bet improve dramatically.

Season's Top Scorer (Golden Boot)

Last season there was an 11.78% increase in the number of goals scored in the Premier League compared to 2008/09, and a 5.19% increase on the 2007/08 season. This increase in the number of goals resulted in five players scoring over 20 league goals apiece – something you have to go back to 1994/95 and 1993/94 for, at a time when the league contained 22 rather than 20 teams.

We've included this table of the top 30 or so scorers from last term so that you can evaluate the odds available on them to be top scorer this time round. We've also included enough detail to help you evaluate odds for them in the first, last, each way and anytime goal markets.

2009/10 Premier League top goal scorers

The following table represents in order of goals scored the top 30 goal scorers in the Premier League for the 2009/10 season. So, if we look at Didier Drogba, we see he started 31 matches and scored 29 goals. He was the first goal scorer eight times ('First' column) and he scored the last goal of a match on nine occasions ('Last' column). In the 'Each way' column, we see there were 17 times he scored either the first, second or third goal of a match, and in the 'Anytime' column we see there were 20 occasions he scored at anytime during a match.

Player	Team	Started	Goals	First	Last	Each way	Anytime
Didier Drogba	Chelsea	31	29	8	9	17	20
Wayne Rooney	Man United	32	26	10	6*	16	18
Darren Bent	Sunderland	38	24	13	7*	16	17
Carlos Tévez	Man City	32	23	6	7	14	14
Frank Lampard	Chelsea	36	22	3	8	12	14
Fernando Torres	Liverpool	20	18	8	4	11	12
Jermain Defoe	Tottenham	31	18	7	2	12	12
Cesc Fàbregas	Arsenal	26	15	4	3	9	13
Emmanuel Adebayor	Man City	25	14	6	5*	10	12
Gabriel Agbonlahor	Aston Villa	35	13	7	5*	11	12
Louis Saha	Everton	26	13	3	5	7	9
Dimitar Berbatov	Man United	25	12	4	2	8	11
Florent Malouda	Chelsea	26	12	3	3	7	9
Nicolas Anelka	Chelsea	31	11	7	2*	9	9
Andrei Arshavin	Arsenal	25	10	3	4	5	10
John Carew	Aston Villa	22	10	2	3*	9	9
Cameron Jerome	Birmingham	32	10	4	1*	8	8
Craig Bellamy	Man City	26	10	0	2	4	8
Carlton Cole	West Ham	26	10	2	1	9	10
Hugo Rodallega	Wigan	38	10	5	5*	8	9
Robin van Persie	Arsenal	14	9	5	2*	7	8
David Dunn	Blackburn	20	9	4	3*	8	8
Steven Gerrard	Liverpool	32	9	4	2	5	8
Dirk Kuyt	Liverpool	35	9	4	2	8	8
Kenwyne Jones	Sunderland	24	9	2	2	6	7
Kevin Doyle	Wolverhampton W	33	9	5	2	7	8
Ivan Klasnic	Bolton W	12	8	4	1	6	7
Matt Taylor	Bolton W	29	8	1	4	7	7
Tim Cahil	Everton	33	8	4	2	4	6
Bobby Zamora	Fulham	27	8	5	2	8	8
Peter Crouch	Tottenham	21	8	6	3*	7	7

*Explained later in the book under the individual teams.

Tips for the Top Scorers

Let's take a closer look at the key players to watch out for in the 2010/11 season when betting in the scoring/goals markets. The guide odds next to them are for their chances in the Golden Boot market. They are in order of our Premier Betting guide odds, from the favourite down.

Fernando Torres (Liverpool) – Premier Betting guide odds 7/2 (4.50)

	Started	Goals	First	Last	Each way	Anytime
2009/10	20	18	8	4	11	12
2008/09	20	14	4	3	7	8
2007/08	29	24	7	8	16	18
Total	69	56	19	15	34	38
%			27.54	21.74		55.07
Break-even odds			3.63	4.60		1.82

During the past couple of seasons the Spaniard has been plagued with injury problems, but it didn't stop him almost averaging a goal a game last season. In the 69 matches he started for Liverpool over the past three seasons he has scored anytime in 38 matches (55.07%), meaning backing at any odds over 1.82 during this period would have yielded a level stake profit.

It should be noted that 40 (71.42%) of Torres' goals have been scored at Anfield and any consideration of getting involved with a bet on the player should probably be when Liverpool are playing at home.

Premier Betting 2010/11 value tip – back Torres anytime scorer when playing at Anfield.

Wayne Rooney (Man United) – Premier Betting guide odds 5/1 (6.0)

	Started	Goals	First	Last	Each way	Anytime
2009/10	32	26	10	6	16	18
2008/09	25	12	5	4	10	11
2007/08	25	12	3	3	7	9
Total	82	50	18	13	33	38
%			21.95	15.85		46.34
Break-even odds			4.56	6.31		2.16

Wayne Rooney took up the goal-scoring mantle when Cristiano Ronaldo left for Real Madrid after the 2008/09 season. In his previous two seasons Rooney was often played out wide for the benefit of the team. That's why we we feel it wise to pay more consideration to this last season's stats than the previous two seasons' – and fully expect him to carry a similar threat in 2010/11. In the 32 matches he started in 2009/10 he scored anytime in 18 matches (56.25%), a percentage on par with Torres.

Premier Betting 2010/11 value tip – back Rooney to be first scorer any price over 3.50.

Didier Drogba (Chelsea) – Premier Betting guide odds 5/1 (6.0)

	Started	Goals	First	Last	Each way	Anytime
2009/10	31	29	8	9	17	20
2008/09	15	5	2	2	3	4
2007/08	17	8	4	1	6	6
Total	63	42	14	12	26	30
%			22.22	19.05		47.62
Break-even odds			4.50	5.25		2.10

Following a couple of indifferent seasons, the Ivory Coast striker has thrived under Carlo Ancelotti, winning the Premier League Golden Boot for the first time since 2007, and scoring a staggering 29 goals from 31 starts, netting in 20 matches (64.52%) – which equates to him being a 1.55 shot to score anytime.

We don't see this changing in the 2010/11 season if he stays injury free. Given the dramatic improvements in his form since the new managerial arrangements came in at Chelsea, as with Rooney at Man United we should probably lay an emphasis on last season's stats – and expect to be maintained next season.

The generally impressive way Chelsea play away from Stamford Bridge makes him a huge consideration for first scorer or anytime scorer when they're on the road.

Premier Betting 2010/11 value tip – back Drogba to be first scorer any price over 3.50 when playing away.

Robin Van Persie (Arsenal) – Premier Betting guide odds 12/1 (13.0)

	Started	Goals	First	Last	Each way	Anytime
2009/10	14	9	5	2	7	8
2008/09	24	11	3	3	7	8
2007/08	13	7	3	2	5	6
Total	51	27	11	7	19	22
%			21.57	13.73		43.14
Break-even odds			4.64	7.29		2.32

The 2009/10 Premier League season was an injury-plagued one, but we feel the Dutchman will play a major part in the success of Arsenal in the 2010/11 season. We had a glimpse of things to come in his cameo appearances at the backend of 2009/10, and any double figure quotes for him to win the Golden Boot should be considered seriously.

Carlos Tévez (Man City) – Premier Betting guide odds 14/1 (15.0)

	Started	Goals	First	Last	Each way	Anytime
2009/10	32	23	6	7	14	14
2008/09	18	8	3	3	5	5
2007/08	31	14	3	6	10	11
Total	81	45	12	16	29	30
%			14.81	19.75		37.04
Break-even odds			6.75	5.06		2.70

A fantastic first season at Eastlands following his switch from Old Trafford, and there are two ways you could look at the 2010/11 season (bearing in mind that this book was written before any summer signings had been made by Man City).

Having missed out on Champions League football, it would be a total shock if Mancini doesn't strengthen his forward line. This will either complement Tévez or could result in him reverting to a similar role as played in his final season at Man United.

To us, as he has form as a match-winning striker that battles until the end, he is more likely to score the last goal of the game than the first, and provided you can back him at odds over 5.0 he should enter into your betting. We do recommend a watching brief whilst the expected revamped City team bed in, though.

Darren Bent (Sunderland) – Premier Betting guide odds 20/1 (21.0)

	Started	Goals	First	Last	Each way	Anytime
2009/10	38	24	13	7	16	17
2008/09	21	12	2	5	9	10
2007/08	11	6	3	3	3	6
Total	70	42	18	15	28	33
%			25.71	21.43		47.14
Break-even odds			3.89	4.67		2.12

Darren Bent won the Paddy Power Top Scorer (Handicap Market) for the 2009/10 season. He also had a habit of popping in the first goal of the game. Considering that he was playing for a team not competing at the business end of the table, to be first scorer 13 times is a staggering achievement. Blindly backing him in any match last season would have yielded a level stake (staking the same amount of money on each bet) profit, but is he a one-season wonder?

After all, in his previous two seasons he was a bit-part player, often coming off the bench for Spurs (hence scoring more last goals as a proportion of his record), but his overall scoring history is pretty healthy.

Premier Betting 2010/11 value tip – back Bent to be first scorer any price over 5.0.

Jermain Defoe (Tottenham) – Premier Betting guide odds 20/1 (21.0)

	Started	Goals	First	Last	Each way	Anytime
2009/10	31	18	7	2	12	12
2008/09	23	10	3	5	9	9
2007/08	15	12	4	5	9	10
Total	69	40	14	12	30	31
%			20.29	17.39		44.93
Break-even odds			4.93	5.75		2.23

This England striker's form tailed off towards the backend of last season, Defoe scoring just four league goals in 2010, having been in electric form just before Christmas.

If we look at his overall record over the past three seasons you would need to be getting over 5.0 to obtain any value backing him for first scorer, a price you will certainly find difficult against lesser sides.

That said, he does offer a threat and would certainly enter the equation for an anytime scorer against top sides at odds bigger than 2.75 if starting the game.

Premier Betting 2010/11 value tip – look to back Defoe anytime scorer against top sides if starting and odds are 2.75 and above.

Emmanuel Adebayor (Man City) – Premier Betting guide odds 25/1 (26.0)

	Started	Goals	First	Last	Each way	Anytime
2009/10	25	14	6	5	10	12
2008/09	21	10	4	4	6	7
2007/08	32	24	9	7	15	17
Total	78	48	19	16	31	36
%			24.36	20.51		46.15
Break-even odds			4.11	4.88		2.17

Adebayor is a striker that should enter your thoughts when considering first scorer – 39.58% of his goals scored over the past three seasons have been the first goal of the game. We should note the 46.15% figure on anytime scorer over the last three seasons, with a 48% strike rate last season.

It's a similar story to Tévez for 2010/11, though. It's very hard to predict what is going to happen at Eastlands – he could even make way for another striker at the club. But if he remains there, and in the first-team, all season, he should be considered for anytime scorer if you can get odds near 2.50.

Premier Betting 2010/11 value tip – look to back Adebayor anytime scorer if odds are 2.50 and above.

Nicolas Anelka (Chelsea) – Premier Betting guide odds 25/1 (26.0)

	Started	Goals	First	Last	Each way	Anytime
2009/10	31	11	7	2	9	9
2008/09	33	19	5	9	14	15
2007/08	28	11	4	3	8	9
Total	92	41	16	14	31	33
%			17.39	15.22		35.87
Break-even odds			5.75	6.57		2.79

Anelka won the Premier League Golden Boot in the 2008/09 season, but Drogba's gain has been Anelka's loss with the advent of Ancelotti seeing him playing a different role in the 2009/10 season to the previous one.

One thing we can note is the number of times he has scored at anytime (just 35.87%), the lowest of all the strikers covered so far. This makes us feel that he offers very little value in any of the scoring markets; his odds are likely to be very short most weeks.

Dimitar Berbatov (Man United) – Premier Betting guide odds 25/1 (26.0)

	Started	Goals	First	Last	Each way	Anytime
2009/10	25	12	4	2	8	11
2008/09	29	9	3	5	9	9
2007/08	33	15	7	3	10	11
Total	87	36	14	10	27	31
%			16.09	11.49		35.63
Break-even odds			6.21	8.70		2.81

Berbatov has not set the world alight since arriving at Old Trafford from Spurs, and he tends to go missing for long periods of the game, especially in the big matches, where he failed to score against any of the top six sides last season. He enters the equation when United play mid to low-ranking sides, when the number of team chances are increased and more goals are scored. You could possibly take a punt on him scoring at anytime if he starts the match against those sides.

Premier Betting 2010/11 value tip – look to back Berbatov anytime scorer against mid and low-ranking sides if starting and odds are 2.50 and above.

Frank Lampard (Chelsea) – Premier Betting guide odds 33/1 (34.0)

	Started	Goals	First	Last	Each way	Anytime
2009/10	36	22	3	8	12	14
2008/09	37	12	3	3	10	12
2007/08	23	10	4	4	7	7
Total	96	44	10	15	29	33
%			10.42	15.63		34.38
Break-even odds			9.60	6.40		2.91

Lampard had a fantastic 2009/10 season, scoring the same number of goals as the previous two seasons combined. Despite this increase in the number of goals, as you can see first scorer isn't really on his radar and offers very little value based on the last three seasons.

The England midfielder comes into most punters' minds because he is the penalty taker and it should be noted that Chelsea were awarded a higher number of penalties last season compared with previous seasons. Statistically it is highly unlikely that Chelsea will be awarded so many penalties this coming season and it is for that reason that we would avoid backing Lampard in the 2010/11 season – we think he will offer little or no value in the vast majority of games, as the bookmakers will price him up purely on the number of goals he scored last season, hoping that the average punter will not realise that this was due to Chelsea's extraordinarily high penalty count. (Which won't be repeated.)

Steven Gerrard (Liverpool) – Premier Betting guide odds 33/1 (34.0)

	Started	Goals	First	Last	Each way	Anytime
2009/10	32	9	4	2	5	8
2008/09	32	16	5	6	11	11
2007/08	32	11	3	6	11	11
Total	96	36	12	14	27	30
%			12.50	14.58		31.25
Break-even odds			8.00	6.86		3.20

Despite starting the same number of games in the 2009/10 season as the previous two seasons, it seemed a stop-start term for Gerrard and he never really hit top gear.

In compiling this data we were surprised by how few matches he has actually scored in over the past three seasons. He certainly offers no value in either first or last scorer markets, based on this form, and if you can obtain below the break-even odds on the betting exchanges for any of the scorer markets then taking him on should be a strong consideration.

6

Stats Betting

There are numerous statistical markets and they seem to grow year after year.

These markets include:

- Team goals
- Total corners
- Total cards
- Penalty in match
- Team that will kick off first
- Home clean sheet
- Away clean sheet
- Total goal minutes (e.g. If a goal is scored in the thirtieth and fortieth minutes, then the total goal minutes are 70)
- Total shirt numbers (e.g. If a goal is scored by the player wearing shirt number 10, and a goal is then scored by a player wearing shirt number 16, the total shirt numbers are 26)

So, as you can see, you will never be stuck for variety. Without doubt, two of the most popular markets in this section are the markets relating to bookings and corners. In the section below we will look at an example of the corners market, giving you an angle into how you may be able to profit in it. We'll also take a close look at the bookings market. (Detailed coverage of all of the data-heavy stats markets cannot be crammed into a book without making it the *War and Peace* of football, though, so for more do check out www.premier-betting.com.)

Corners Market

With stats betting there are numerous approaches you can take to profit in the markets – sadly far too many to do justice to here. But the key thing is to take a statistical approach. By highlighting in this section a simple strategy for profiting from the corners market, we hope you'll not only know how to do that in future, but also have an idea of how to best approach all stats markets. Our comprehensive stats for every team in Part II will be your friend here! Many bookmakers price up their corners markets with the punter having to state whether the total corner count in a match (total number of corners forced by both sides) is above or below a certain number. The industry standard is generally over or under 10.5 corners.

Alternative corners markets that punters can bet on include above or below 8.5, 9.5 or 11.5 corners. Betfair also has three markets that punters can bet on:

- 9 or less corners
- 10-12 corners
- 13 or more corners

In the table below, we highlight the corner records over the last two seasons of the 24 games played between the traditional top four clubs. The table includes the relevant stats for:

- the home team
- the away team
- the total number of corners in the match
- the Betfair market to which the corner count relates to (9 or less, 10-12, 13 or more)
- the number of corners by which the home or away team were superior to their opposition.

When looking at the corners market involving matches between two of the big four, a pattern of note is that there will be generally less than 13 corners. You would expect this pattern to recur in these types of games, as they are usually close matches where chances are few and defences are tight. And indeed if we look at the tables for the last two seasons, nine or less corners featured in 14 of the 24 games. That equates to 58% of matches or odds of 1.72. *So if you see in any of these big four matches in future that the price is above 2.00 (50%) for 9 or less corners then you are receiving good value.*

Alternatively, if betting with the traditional bookmakers you would be able to bet on the under/over 9.5 corner markets, and if betting on under 9.5 corners in these matches you will generally receive odds of 2.5. A £20 bet on under 9.5 over the past two seasons in all of these big four matches would have resulted in a £220 profit. Again, by doing your homework and working out the probabilities – a reasonably simple, quick process – some good value bets can be struck. On the premier-betting.com website we highlight team corner counts against sides of similar ability, so if you can't be bothered to do the hard work for yourself, you don't need to!

Total corners for matches involving traditional big four clubs (2008/09 Premier League season)

Home team	Away team	Total corners	Make-up	Supremacy
Manchester Utd	Chelsea	9	9 or less	Home +3
Manchester Utd	Liverpool	13	13 or more	Home +7
Manchester Utd	Arsenal	8	9 or less	Away +4
Chelsea	Manchester Utd	11	10-12	Home +3
Chelsea	Liverpool	6	9 or less	Home +2
Chelsea	Arsenal	5	9 or less	Home +1
Liverpool	Manchester Utd	9	9 or less	Home +1
Liverpool	Chelsea	13	13 or more	Home +11
Liverpool	Arsenal	12	10-12	Home +12
Arsenal	Manchester Utd	11	10-12	Away +1
Arsenal	Chelsea	8	9 or less	Home +4
Arsenal	Liverpool	3	9 or less	Home +1

Total corners for matches involving traditional big four clubs (2009/10 Premier League season)

Home team	Away team	Total corners	Make-up	Supremacy
Manchester Utd	Chelsea	6	9 or less	Draw
Manchester Utd	Liverpool	3	9 or less	Away +1
Manchester Utd	Arsenal	11	10-12	Home +1
Chelsea	Manchester Utd	7	9 or less	Away +7
Chelsea	Liverpool	13	13 or more	Away +3
Chelsea	Arsenal	12	10-12	Away +4
Liverpool	Manchester Utd	6	9 or less	Home +4
Liverpool	Chelsea	14	13 or more	Home +4
Liverpool	Arsenal	7	9 or less	Away +1
Arsenal	Manchester Utd	13	13 or more	Home +3
Arsenal	Chelsea	7	9 or less	Home +1
Arsenal	Liverpool	9	9 or less	Away +3

Bookings Market

The referee's influence

It seems as though it is almost a weekly occurrence that a Premier League referee takes centre stage in the media for the decisions they made during the 90 minutes of play. We first started researching the referees at the beginning of the 2008/09 season and we have been astounded by the patterns that emerge with certain officials.

In this section we hope to pinpoint possible betting opportunities that can be exploited in the 2010/11 season. We have ignored individual clubs in this report, and obviously if you combine the discipline records of certain clubs and referees together it will provide you with a better strike rate than our bare ratings here. However, these are the key stats and patterns you need for however you wish to approach a varied but compelling betting market.

The bookings markets and how they operate vary an awful lot from bookmaker to bookmaker, and for the details of how each one operates it's best to check out the bookies' websites to be doubly sure. All of the stats and analysis brought together in this chapter should prove directly relevant, or easily adaptable, no matter who you bet with. But, for a couple of reasons, we're looking at the bookings market (and analysing our stats) from the perspective of how it operates on Betfair. This is because of this market's increased liquidity on Betfair of late – in simple terms, the sheer number of punters involved in it means there are some excellent betting opportunities available there.

The Betfair bookings market explained

Betfair splits the bookings market into three outcomes by allocating points for bookings and red cards:

- 2 points for a booking
- 5 points for a red card
- It should be noted that, if two yellow cards are shown to a player, thus producing a red card, it is scored as 7 (2 points for the first yellow card and 5 points for the subsequent red card).

The market is split into the following outcomes on which you can bet:

- A total of 5 points and under
- 6 to 8 points
- 9 or more points.

In the following two tables we give a full breakdown on each referee over the past two seasons.

Referee booking table Premier League 2008/09

First name	Games	Yellows	Reds	Yellows average	Reds average	5 point matches	6–8 point matches	9+ point matches
Mike Dean	30	116	6	3.9	0.2	7	12	11
Mike Riley	23	89	4	3.9	0.2	6	7	10
Steve Bennett	22	78	0	3.5	0.0	4	14	4
André Marriner	21	74	4	3.5	0.2	7	8	6
Howard Webb	34	119	6	3.5	0.2	14	8	12
Stuart Attwell	5	17	2	3.4	0.4	2	2	1
Chris Foy	24	82	3	3.4	0.1	6	11	7
Lee Mason	16	54	3	3.4	0.2	4	6	6
Steve Tanner	11	37	3	3.4	0.3	4	4	3
Martin Atkinson	26	85	6	3.3	0.2	10	6	10
Michael Jones	12	40	3	3.3	0.2	3	6	3
Phil Dowd	30	97	6	3.2	0.2	10	10	10
Robert Styles	26	78	5	3.0	0.2	10	7	9
Alan Wiley	28	81	2	2.9	0.1	8	9	11
Lee Probert	11	26	0	2.4	0.0	6	4	1
Keith Stroud	5	12	0	2.4	0.0	4	1	0
Peter Walton	27	66	3	2.4	0.1	13	8	6
Mark Halsey	28	39	1	1.4	0.0	23	4	1
Mark Clattenburg	1	0	0	0.0	0.0	1	0	0

Referee booking table Premier League 2009/10

First name	Games	Yellows	Reds	Yellows average	Reds average	5 point matches	6-8 point matches	9+ point matches
Martin Atkinson	32	126	5	3.94	0.16	4	13	15
Stuart Attwell	15	58	2	3.9	0.1	4	5	6
Mike Dean	30	114	6	3.8	0.2	7	10	13
Steve Bennett	29	108	5	3.7	0.2	6	11	12
Howard Webb	28	101	3	3.6	0.1	9	7	12
André Marriner	28	97	9	3.5	0.3	9	6	13
Lee Probert	22	74	6	3.4	0.3	8	5	9
Michael Jones	20	64	1	3.2	0.1	7	10	3
Kevin Friend	12	40	4	3.33	0.33	3	6	3
Alan Wiley	26	81	5	3.1	0.2	7	10	9
Phil Dowd	29	87	5	3	0.2	14	8	7
Lee Mason	22	62	6	2.8	0.2	11	5	6
Chris Foy	26	69	2	2.7	0.1	12	7	7
Mark Clattenburg	31	84	5	2.7	0.2	12	11	8
Peter Walton	27	66	4	2.4	0.1	12	9	6
Anthony Taylor	2	5	0	2.5	0.0	1	1	0
Mark Halsey	1	0	0	0.0	0.0	1	0	0

Looking at the points system, you would automatically assume there would be a bias towards the 6-8, or 9+, brackets – with only three to five bookings required to cover those points.

However, if you look at the next table you can see how even the spread is between the brackets over the course of a season. The 2009/10 season suggests that there is a trend towards more bookings being given out, if you compare it with 2008/09, but we think this trend is all down to one referee missing from the ranks of the Premier League list nearly all of last season due to illness, and who is unlikely to return to the role.

2008/09 Season	5 point matches	6-8 point matches	9+ point matches
Number of matches	142	127	111
Percentage	37.36%	33.42%	29.21%

2009/10 Season	5 point matches	6-8 point matches	9+ point matches
Number of matches	127	124	129
Percentage	33.43%	32.63%	33.94%

In the 2008/09 season, the very restrained Mark Halsey officiated at a total of 28 Premier League matches, giving out an exceptionally modest total of 39 yellow cards and 1 red card in the process. Out of the 28 matches, in a staggering 23 (82%) you would have won by backing 5 points and under.

In the table below we have taken the Mark Halsey matches out of the equation, giving the overall percentages for the remaining 352 matches of that season.

2008/09 Season	5 point matches	6-8 point matches	9+ point matches
Number of matches	119	123	110
Percentage	33.80%	34.94%	31.21%

Now the trend to more bookings isn't as severe when we look at the basic stats. It would suggest that the overall percentages are fairly consistent over the past couple of seasons. The Mark Halsey stat equates to over 16% of all matches (Premier League and other) containing two or less bookings during the 2008/09 season.

Following on from this stat we have compiled the following tables to show the strike rate of each referee at each end of the market. A quick check of these is vital before placing a bet. We haven't shown the strike rate for the middle market, because looking at the two extremes is the best way to profit from the market when dutching two of the three markets. We'll show you how, and explain dutching for those who haven't really heard of it before, in a moment!

In the first table, the referees are ranked according to their likelihood, based on past form, for producing a match that ends in under 9 booking points. You'd check this if you were interested in betting on the 9+ market, as it shows you the stats and probabilities arrayed against or in favour of your bet. The higher the percentage in the final column, the worse the likelihood of a 9+ back bearing any fruit.

Referee percentages under 9+ (2009/10 season)

Referee	Games	5 point matches	6–8 point matches	9+ point matches	S/R (The percentage of times the game finished with under 9 booking points)
Anthony Taylor	2	1	1	0	100.00%
Mark Halsey	1	1	0	0	100.00%
Michael Jones	20	7	10	3	85.00%
Peter Walton	27	12	9	6	77.78%
Phil Dowd	29	14	8	7	75.86%
Kevin Friend	12	3	6	3	75.00%
Mark Clattenburg	31	12	11	8	74.19%
Chris Foy	26	12	7	7	73.07%
Lee Mason	22	11	5	6	72.73%
Alan Wiley	26	7	10	9	65.38%
Stuart Attwell	15	4	5	6	60.00%
Lee Probert	22	8	5	9	59.09%
Steve Bennett	29	6	11	12	58.62%
Howard Webb	28	9	7	12	57.14%
Mike Dean	30	7	10	13	56.67%
André Marriner	28	9	6	13	53.57%
Martin Atkinson	32	4	13	15	53.13%

Next is the table for checking the stats and probabilities when considering a bet on the 5 and under market. The higher the percentage, the worse the prospects for backing the 5 point bet.

Referee percentages over 5 points (2009/10 season)

Referee	Games	5 point matches	6-8 point matches	9+ point matches	S/R (The percentage of times the game finished with over 5 booking points)
Martin Atkinson	32	4	13	15	87.50%
Steve Bennett	29	6	11	12	79.31%
Mike Dean	30	7	10	13	76.67%
Kevin Friend	12	3	6	3	75.00%
Stuart Attwell	15	4	5	6	73.33%
Alan Wiley	26	7	10	9	73.07%
Howard Webb	28	9	7	12	67.86%
Andre Marriner	28	9	6	13	67.86%
Michael Jones	20	7	10	3	65.00%
Lee Probert	22	8	5	9	63.64%
Mark Clattenburg	31	12	11	8	61.29%
Peter Walton	27	12	9	6	55.55%
Chris Foy	26	12	7	7	53.84%
Phil Dowd	29	14	8	7	51.72%
Anthony Taylor	2	1	1	0	50.00%
Lee Mason	22	11	5	6	50.00%
Mark Halsey	1	1	0	0	0.00%

Probably the most interesting table, from a tips point of view, is that detailing the percentages of games ending in above 5 points: the top three referees in this table had 6 bookings points or above in over 80% of the 91 matches they officiated at last season. This means that, as long as your combined odds when dutching 6-8 and 9+ points was bigger than 1.25, you would have showed a level stake profit on Betfair.

Dutching the bookings market

For those relatively new to betting, *dutching* is the term given to betting on two or more selections in an event in order to improve your chances of backing a winner.

So, for example, you could have:

- the 5 points and under market priced at 3.20
- the 6 to 8 points market priced at 2.50 and
- the 9 and over points market priced at 3.50.

And we are looking to 'dutch' the 6 to 8 points market and the 9 points plus markets. In other words, we do not think it will be 5 points or under and are looking to bet on the 6 to 8 points and the 9 points plus markets at the same time.

To work out the odds of dutching 6 to 8 points and the 9 points plus, we first convert the odds to their percentage chance by dividing into 100.

```
6 to 8 points = 40.00% (100 divided by 2.50)
9 and over points = 28.57% (100 divided by 3.50)
```

The next stage is to add the percentages together:

```
40.00 + 28.57 = 68.57%
```

Now you need to work out how much to place on each bet.

To get this figure you divide each individual bet percentage by the overall percentage figure. Finally, you multiply this figure by the amount you wish to stake (which in this case is £50). So we now have the following:

6 to 8 points

`40.00 divided by total percentage of 68.57 = 0.583`

`0.583 multiplied by your £50 stake = £29.17`

Total staked on 6 to 8 points = £29.17

9 points plus

`28.57 divided by total percentage of 68.57 = 0.416`

`0.416 multiplied by your £50 stake = £20.83`

Total staked on 9 points plus = £20.83

So as you can now see, we have placed two bets:

- Bet 1: £29.17 on 6 to 8 points at odds of 2.50
- If the bet wins, returns = £72.92 - £50 = £22.92

- Bet 2: £20.83 on 9 points plus at odds of 3.50
- If the bet wins, returns = £72.91 - £50 = £22.91

So in this scenario, should the bookings points be 6 to 8 or 9 points plus, then you will be profiting by at least £22.91 after staking a total of £50.

This then equates to having a bet at odds of 1.46 (72.91/50.00).

For ease of reference, when betting on the bookings market for any match and referee in the 2010/11 season, check out 'The Referees' chapter in Part II. There we've got the form book for each of them stretching back over the years, detailing the yellows and reds awarded each season, their averages for those cards, and the number of games in a season where they've produced five, six to eight, or nine-plus point matches. We've also provided our betting tips for each for the 2010/11 season.

7

Asian Handicaps

What Are Asian Handicaps?

Asian Handicaps are a relatively new type of bet, which eliminate the draw and create more equal odds for the two remaining outcomes by awarding a theoretical advantage to the weaker side/disadvantage to the stronger side.

For example, if Chelsea are playing Southend United in an FA Cup tie you would expect Chelsea to be very strong favourites and their odds to be priced up at around 1.10 to win the match. Obviously, having to stake £100 to win only £10 does not hold much appeal to the average punter. Nor would any bet on Southend United's chances. So, to make these bets more appealing, the Asian handicap is applied by bookies – for the sake of the bet on Southend to win, Southend could be 'given' a +2.5 goal head start; which is the same, for the sake of the bet, on Chelsea to win, as Chelsea being 'given' a -2.5 goal deficit. In other words, the handicap is 2.5 – applied either positively to Southend or negatively to Chelsea, depending on which you back. In either case, this produces a starting score line of Chelsea 0 - 2.5 Southend. In this case, with the much weaker Southend receiving a

2.5 goal head start, you could now expect both teams' odds to be around 1.90, as each side now has a roughly equal chance of winning. (And, you might notice, no chance of drawing – since it's impossible for Chelsea to score half a goal.)

Now all of sudden you have got some decent odds to bet at, if you can formulate a view on the outcome of the game.

Advantages of betting on Asian handicaps

These Asian handicap bets are increasing in popularity and tend to be offered on most football matches. The bookies offer them because the close-to-50/50 odds they provide encourage a balanced amount of wagering on either side of the match, and therefore help to defray their inevitable losses.

They're also attractive from the punter's perspective:

- You bet on only two outcomes, the home or away team victory – the draw is eliminated. Because of this, you have a 50% better chance of winning than when betting on the match odds. You will get more frequent returns from your stakes.
- You can win your bet even if the team you have bet on draws or loses the match.

Perhaps one of the biggest advantages of betting on the Asian handicaps, though, is that the bookmakers tend to make very low percentage profits on these bets. Unlike 90-minute match bets that include the draw, the bookmakers' over round tends to be a lot smaller because there are only two possible outcomes instead of the traditional three (home, draw, away), so there is less room to build in value for themselves. This is one of the major reasons why Asian handicap bets can represent very good value bets for the punter.

How All the Varieties Work

Instead of just betting on a team to win, you are betting on them to overcome or take advantage of a handicap.

In the above example you would back Chelsea if you thought they could win by at least three clear goals. Alternatively, you might think that Southend can keep a tight defence and concede less than three goals; in which case you would back Southend.

It's important to note that teams can be given a full goal handicap, half a goal handicap, and a quarter goal handicap (also called ball handicaps). This is where it gets confusing, so we will illustrate with examples. The key thing when appraising a bet is to remember that the handicap produces the same starting score line, whichever side you're backing. What you're interested in is whether to pick the side that has to defend it or overcome it. The way to work out if you've won is to add the pre-match goal scoreline to the final score. Simple. In the first Chelsea v Southend match in 2009, the result was 1-1. The handicap starting score line was Chelsea 0 - 2.5 Southend. So the result for the Asian handicap was: Chelsea 1 - 3.5 Southend. A victory for Southend and a loss for Chelsea.

Full-goal handicap (when a whole number is used in the handicap)

1 goal handicap: Arsenal (-1), Blackburn (+1)

In this example, Arsenal are at home to Blackburn and have been given a -1 goal handicap, i.e. a one-goal handicap is being applied to the game – negatively to Arsenal, positively to Blackburn. The way this works out, whichever side you're backing, is with a starting score line of: `Arsenal 0-1 Blackburn`

We then decide to back Arsenal -1 goal.

- If Arsenal score two goals and the final real-world score is 2-0 to Arsenal, then the handicap score would be Arsenal 2 - 1 Blackburn. In this case we win the bet.
- If Arsenal score one goal and the final real-world score is 1-0 to Arsenal, then the handicap score would be Arsenal 1 - 1 Blackburn. This is a draw and our stake is returned.
- If Arsenal score no goals and the final real-world score is a 0-0 draw, then the handicap score would be Arsenal 0 - 1 Blackburn. In this case we lose the bet.
- Obviously if Blackburn win by any margin, we lose too.

You can see the advantage of betting with a full-goal handicap, as there is the possibility of getting our stake back in full should things not quite pan out exactly how we envisioned (a narrow failure can produce a draw, impossible with half and quarter goals), and the odds are so much better than if you backed on the half-goal handicap.

Half-goal handicap (when 0.5 is used in the handicap)

0.5 goals handicap: Arsenal (-0.5), Blackburn (+0.5)

For simplicity's sake, we will use the same teams as before. In this example it's the FA Cup and the Arsenal manager Arsène Wenger has decided that he will field a side comprised mainly of reserves.

Arsenal have a -0.5 goal handicap (which is the same as saying that Blackburn have a +0.5 goal handicap), so the goal line before the game, regardless of who you back, is:

```
Arsenal 0 - 0.5 Blackburn
```

We then decide to back Arsenal -0.5 goals.

- If Arsenal score one goal and the final real-world score is 1-0 to Arsenal, then the handicap score would be Arsenal 1 - 0.5 Blackburn. In this case we win the bet.
- If Arsenal score no goals and the final score is a 0-0 draw, then the handicap score would be Arsenal 0 - 0.5 Blackburn. In this case we would lose the bet.

What you should notice with a half-goal handicap is that the possibility of a draw has been eliminated. There's no way a team can score half a goal. The main advantage of this bet is, if you fancy the outsider to win, that you have the draw on your side – as the outsider generally receives the 0.5 goal advantage.

Quarter-goal handicap (when 0.25 is used in the handicap)

0.25 goals handicap: Manchester United (-0.25), Liverpool (+0.25)

Using the quarter-goal handicap is probably the most confusing of them all but hopefully all will become much clearer after the following example.

You tend to only see the 0.25 handicap occasionally; it is used mainly in closely contested matches such as Manchester United v Liverpool. When it is a quarter-goal handicap your stake is automatically split in half.

1. Half of your stake will go on a 0-goal handicap (i.e. 0-0 starting score line; this portion of your bet is then on the out-and-out victor, with this half of your stake to be returned in the event of a draw)
2. Half of your stake will go on a 0.5-goal handicap (i.e. Man United 0 - 0.5 Liverpool starting score line, either to win depending on who you back).

So effectively it is two bets. Let's now work through what happens in this example.

Man United have a -0.25 goal handicap (which is to say, Liverpool have a +0.25 goal handicap – same difference). So the goal line before the game, whoever you back, is:

```
1. Man United 0 - 0 Liverpool (half of our stake
   backing a victor out of this at the end)
2. Man United 0 - 0.5 Liverpool (half of our
   stake backing a victor out of this at the end)
```

In this case if we back Manchester United and they win by any goal line then we win both parts of the bet. Let's say Man United win

1-0; you just add that goal to the score lines we had before the game, and in this case they read:

```
1. Man United 1 - 0 Liverpool (Win)
2. Man United 1 - 0.5 Liverpool (Win)
```

In both cases we have won.

What happens if the game is a draw?

Let's say the game is goalless and finishes a 0-0 draw. Again, we must refer back to the pre-match handicaps and we would have the following:

```
1. Man United 0 - 0 Liverpool (Draw)
2. Man United 0 - 0.5 Liverpool (Loss)
```

As half of our money was on 0-0 or the draw we are returned that stake (e.g. we are returned 50% of the total stake).

We would have lost on the other half, as Liverpool had a +0.5 goal head start. We lose the other 50% of our stake.

In-running Asian handicaps

As well as offering odds on the 90-minute result, many bookmakers also offer the Asian handicap in-running market.

However (and this needs to be remembered), bets on the Asian handicap market in running are settled according to the score line for the remainder of the game **after** the bet has been struck.

Any goals prior to the bet being placed are ignored for settlement purposes.

We would recommend that you read and ensure you understand the rules fully before you enter this market.

Below is a table that displays the various basic outcomes possible when placing an Asian handicap bet.

Handicap	Team Result	Bet Result	Handicap	Team Result	Bet Result
0	Win	Win	0	Win	Win
	Draw	Stake refund		Draw	Stake refund
	Lose	Lose		Lose	Lose
-0.25	Win	Win	+0.25	Win	Win
	Draw	Lose half		Draw	Half win
	Lose	Lose		Lose	Lose
-0.50	Win	Win	+0.50	Win	Win
	Draw	Lose		Draw	Win
	Lose	Lose		Lose	Lose
-0.75	Win by 1	Half win	+0.75	Win	Win
	Win by 2+	Win		Draw	Win
	Draw	Lose		Lose by 1	Half lose
	Lose	Lose		Lose by 2+	Lose
-1.00	Win by 1	Stake refund	+1.00	Win	Win
	Win by 2+	Win		Draw	Win
	Draw	Lose		Lose by 1	Stake refund
	Lose	Lose		Lose by 2+	Lose
-1.25	Win by 2+	Win	+1.25	Win	Win
	Win by 1	Half lose		Draw	Win
	Draw	Lose		Lose by 1	Half win
	Lose	Lose		Lose by 2+	Lose
-1.50	Win by 2+	Win	+1.50	Win	Win
	Win by 1	Lose		Draw	Win
	Draw	Lose		Lose by 1	Win
	Lose	Lose		Lose by 2+	Lose
-1.75	Win by 3+	Win	+1.75	Win	Win
	Win by 2	Half win		Draw	Win
	Win by 1	Lose		Lose by 1	Win
	Draw	Lose		Lose by 2	Half lose
	Lose	Lose		Lose by 3+	Lose
-2.00	Win by 3+	Win	+2.00	Win	Win
	Win by 2	Stake refund		Draw	Win
	Win by 1	Lose		Lose by 1	Win
	Draw	Lose		Lose by 2	Stake refund
	Lose	Lose		Lose by 3+	Lose

Alternative Handicaps

As well the Asian handicaps, many bookmakers also offer 'alternative handicaps'. The major difference with these bets is that the draw is still included in the equation. Let's have a look at the following examples.

Manchester City v Arsenal

The normal match odds are as follows:

```
Man City 2.0      Draw 3.50     Arsenal 3.60
```

Now, on the alternative handicap market we see a market where Arsenal are given a one goal head start.

Match odds, handicap Arsenal +1 goal

```
Man City -1 goal 3.50   Draw 4.00     Arsenal +1
goal 1.75
```

So in this example you would:

- Back Man City if you think they will win by two goals or more
- Back Arsenal if you think they will either win or draw
- Back the Draw if you think Man City will win by one goal

Another alternative handicap market allows us to bet on the first half only, with Arsenal given a goal head start.

Half-time odds, handicap Arsenal +1 goal

```
Man City -1 goal 9.00   Draw 3.00    Arsenal +1
goal 1.47
```

In this example you would:

- Bet on Man City if you think they will be leading at half time by two goals or more.
- Bet on Arsenal if you think they will either be winning or drawing at half time.
- Bet on the Draw if you think Man City will be winning by one goal at half time.

A further handicap market allows us to bet on the second half only, with Man City given a goal head start.

Second half odds, handicap Man City +1 goal

```
Man City +1 goal 1.22   Draw 5.00    Arsenal -1
goal 12.00
```

Here you would:

- Bet on Man City if you think they will either win or draw the second half.
- Bet on Arsenal if you think they will win the second half by two goals or more.
- Bet on the Draw if you think Arsenal will win the second half by one goal.

Advantages

With these alternative handicap markets, there are advantages and disadvantages with getting involved.

If in a tight match you fancy the favourite to win by the odd goal, remembering that this team are receiving a minus-1 goal start it may be worth backing the draw on the alternative handicap: you will certainly be receiving a far better price than you would by just straight backing the favourite, and in football generally the majority of a winning team's results are by the odd goal, the most common results are either 1-0 or 2-1. They occur between 20% and 25% of the time amongst all results, so we certainly would not look to be backing the draw at anything below 4.0.

Also, as you will have seen by the half-time/full-time stats, winning both halves is incredibly difficult – so this is a market where it certainly could pay to take a contrarian view and oppose the favourite (especially away from home).

Disadvantages

On the match odds, we would certainly avoid backing the team given a goal start (i.e. the unfancied team) as you will undoubtedly get better odds by simply laying the favourite on the betting exchanges. Effectively you will be making the same bet but the odds will be better.

Other Handicaps

There are a few other handicap markets that sharp-eyed punters can take advantage of, and the best place to start looking for these is on the Oddschecker site.

Corner handicaps

As an example, we shall have a look at the Manchester United v Tottenham Hotspur match that took place on Tuesday 1 December 2009 (Fig 7.1). The market we are going to look at is the corner handicap market.

The first thing to do is to evaluate each team's corner rate and how they match up. You can find out the basic corner statistics of each side by looking them up on the Premier Betting site, or by searching for a team's previous match statistics on websites such as bbc.co.uk. In this example, we have looked at both Manchester United's last seven home matches record and Tottenham Hotspur's last seven away matches record. The reason the number of matches we have looked at is seven is because this was the only data available from that season at that point in time. You could extend it to as many matches as you want, going into previous seasons, but for ease and accuracy in this example we decided to stick with data from the same term.

On looking at the Manchester United corner data from their last seven matches, we see they forced 77 corners and conceded 16. So, if we divide the 77 and 16 by the seven matches played, we have 11.00 and 2.28 – which indicates that, on average, Manchester United forced 11.00 corners and conceded 2.28 corners. So it could be said that Manchester United had on average a corner superiority of 11.00 - 2.28 = 8.72 corners per game, against their opposition.

Tottenham Hotspur on the other hand, in their seven away games, forced 38 corners and conceded 49 corners. So if we divide the 38 and 49 by the seven matches played, we have 5.42 and 7.00, indicating that on average Tottenham Hotspur forced 5.42 corners and conceded 7.00 corners. So it could be said that Tottenham Hotspur at this time had on average a corner superiority of 5.42 - 7.00 = -1.58 corners per game, against their opposition.

So, by looking at Manchester United's home record, we have found that they have a far superior corner rate to that of Tottenham – and, just as importantly, we know by how much (this is key for evaluating the significance of specific handicap figures). Now it's time to start looking at odds for this market. With these stats to hand, we'll soon be able to quickly spot value.

Figure 7.1 – Man United v Spurs, corner handicap odds

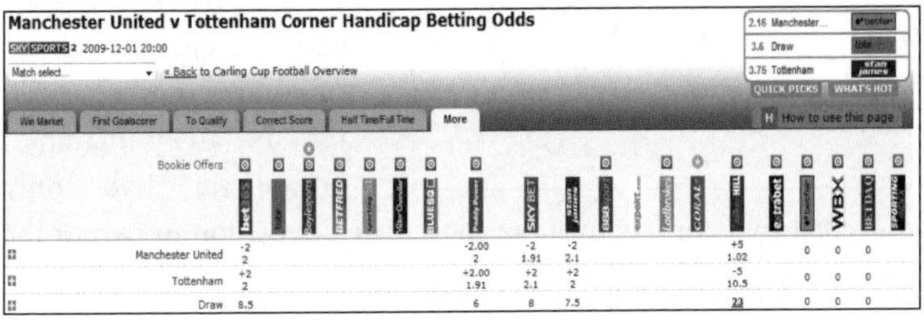

Manchester United v Tottenham Corner Handicap Betting Odds

SKY SPORTS 2 2009-12-01 20:00

Match select « Back to Carling Cup Football Overview

2.16 Manchester... | 3.6 Draw | 3.75 Tottenham

QUICK PICKS | WHAT'S HOT

Win Market | First Goalscorer | To Qualify | Correct Score | Half Time/Full Time | More

How to use this page

Bookie Offers	bet		SKY BET	stan james	HILL		WBX	BETDAQ
Manchester United	-2 2	-2.00 2	-2 1.91	-2 2.1	+5 1.02	0	0	0
Tottenham	+2 2	+2.00 1.91	+2 2.1	+2 2	-5 10.5	0	0	0
Draw	8.5	6	8	7.5	23	0	0	0

Looking at the market, Manchester United with a handicap of -2 corners are priced at 2.10 with Stan James and Tottenham +2 corners are priced at 2.00. You will see that the draw is priced at 7.5 (Fig 7.2).

Figure 7.2 – Man United v Spurs, Stan James' corner handicap odds, Man United -2 corners

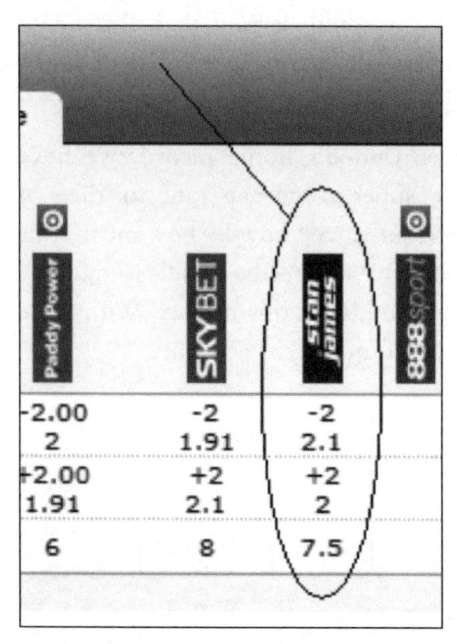

Looking at Manchester United's previous seven home games at the time, we know they had an average corner supremacy of 8.72 and had forced two or more corners than their opposition in six out of seven matches. And in Tottenham's away games, we know they had a negative corner superiority rate of -1.58. Of six away matches, Tottenham had only conceded two corners or more than their opposition in two of the six matches.

So, knowing this, we can immediately see that Manchester United are very good value on this handicap. Their advantage so outweighs it as to make it irrelevant. Their superiority would still be 6.72.

In this simple way, just being armed with corner superiority stats, some good value bets can be struck. The same applies for other stats handicap markets – what you're doing is seeing where bookies have not got their handicaps right. If you look to specialise in this area, some good profits can be secured.

⚽ ⚽ ⚽

Well, this concludes our look at the numerous different football betting markets out there – what they are, how best to approach them and how you can profit from them. Next comes Part II, and the bank of all the stats and analysis you need for evaluating individual teams and bets in the 2010/11 Premier League season.

Part II

The Premier Football Betting Form Book: Teams, Records and Referees

Introduction

Welcome to Part II of *The Premier Football Betting Handbook 2010/11*. This is the 'form book' portion, if you like, but it's no dry list of meaningless facts. Here we've brought together all the most important stats and analysis for betting on any market in the 2010/11 season, along with our professional tips and strategies wherever relevant. Every section is linked in with the betting markets. If you use this simple information – which is not brought together and analysed in one place anywhere else – you need never make a bad bet again. (We're not promising endless victories: you'll still lose, it can't be avoided, but at least you'll no longer lose on unnecessary bets with hopeless odds, and your victories will be even sweeter.)

8 – Grading the Teams

Grading the sides can be a powerful tool when it comes to looking for betting opportunities. Here we break down the 20 Premier League teams of 2010/11 into a hierarchy of A-D based on past form. We then see how the grades got on against each other with last season's stats, providing a quick and accurate method of instantly sizing up the probabilities of any match-up between sides of different (or the same) grades. This really helps to anchor your betting on a given game within dependable boundaries, with key average odds provided for all the win and goal markets, and is the kind of thing often overlooked by average punters. Some of the findings are particularly unexpected – and a good way of getting good value bets. A little information and thought like this can really pay dividends.

The grades awarded in this chapter then come into play again in '10 – The Teams', where, as part of our detailed analysis, we look at their performance last year through the lens of these grades.

9 – Summary of the 2009/10 Season

This chapter provides a team-based breakdown of last season's results, where we can look to see if there are any trends that are worth keeping an eye on in 2010/11.

We look at tables for the following, breaking down in detail:

- the season league table
- half-time/full-time table (home and away)
- match goals (home and away)
- corners (home and away)
- bookings (home and away)
- top scorers
- team scoring record
- match goal times.

10 – The Teams

In this chapter we provide comprehensive stats for every Premier League team, for every betting market in 2010/11:

- their season record
- top scorers (total goals, first, last, each way, anytime)
- scoring (matches, clean sheets, won to nil, both teams scored, 1st half, 2nd half)
- match goal times (for first and last goal, with the percentages and break-even odds)
- half-time/full-time results (home and away, percentages, break-even odds)
- goals (under/over markets, percentages and break-even odds)
- bookings (home and away, percentages and break-even odds)
- corner superiority (home and away, percentages and break-even odds).

We end each team's section by highlighting a number of key stats that we think are worth paying particular attention to in your betting this year.

Top Betting Trends for 2010/11

A brief, but incredibly important final section rounds this out: here we list some of our top betting tips for the 2010/11 season, and the odds you need to have in mind, based on the preceding stats and analysis. These are the bets that are likely to gain the best value prices, and to have the highest chance of giving you a return.

We then have a brief look at highlights of the newly promoted teams' 2009/10 records.

11 – The Referees

Reprising our coverage of Part I, here we do for referees and their records what we do for the teams, providing detailed breakdown and averages of their cards awarded over a season, and the number of times their performances have fallen into one of the three Betfair point brackets. We end each section by giving you our direct insight into what to bear in mind with each ref, as well our value tip for betting on games they officiate over in the 2010/11 season.

⚽ ⚽ ⚽

In our experience, all this can be incredibly powerful information to have on hand. It's what we use as our betting bread and butter. Combined with our introductions to the key betting markets in Part I, it should be the one-stop reference guide for boosting your betting profits over the course of the 2010/11 Premiership season.

8

Grading the Sides

As previously stated, we have broken the teams down and graded them A through to D. Statistics from last season are then mapped onto this hierarchy, so that you can see almost at a glance what sort of parameters the results of any match are likely to fall within, what the average odds are of all the outcomes, and start to hone your betting decisions from the get-go. It also gives you an edge by revealing dependable patterns that otherwise get overlooked, and where you can, accordingly, often find good value at the bookies.

Grade A

Those teams we expect to see fighting for the Champions League places:

Arsenal, Chelsea, Liverpool*, Man United and Man City.

[*Spurs and Liverpool are two sides that came close, in our calculations, to swapping places in this grading for the 2010/11 season. But you really need another season of form, continued along their respectively excellent and disappointing lines of 2009/10, before you can think about doing this.]

Grade B

Those teams we believe are not quite up to the standard of the very best but will certainly be fighting for European places:

Aston Villa, Everton and Spurs*.

Grade C

Those sides we believe will be too good to be embroiled in any relegation battles:

Birmingham, Blackburn, Fulham, Newcastle, Stoke, Sunderland and West Ham.

Grade D

Those teams we believe will be fighting against the drop from day one:

Blackpool, Bolton, West Brom, Wigan and Wolves.

⚽ ⚽ ⚽

This grading might seem obvious, but it's a really important foundation for good betting – there is no doubt about it, teams certainly perform better (and worse) against certain standards of teams, and often in ways you would not expect. There are numerous genuine but unnoticed opportunities out there, and up for grabs, when you analyse games through this filter.

[*See note on p.117]

How the Graded Sides Perform Against Each Other

One of the best ways of pinpointing winners, as said, is to see how certain graded sides perform against each other. When looking to place a bet at Premier Betting, we go through the following procedure with this:

- Firstly, and most importantly, we use the Premier Betting ratings to ensure we are gaining value (you can see these by subscribing to premier-betting.com). You can also adopt or adapt some of the techniques we showed you in Part I. If there is no value we simply do not consider this selection.
- We then see how the specific team with value has performed recently against similar opposition.
- We then look to see the general trend of how similar graded teams have performed against each other.
- When all of these match up to the positive, we know to place our bet.

Below are tables showing last season how the different graded sides got on against each other. Before we get to them, let us show you the kind of excellent, and often unexpected, information these graded comparisons throw up, and which you should be looking for when you use them.

- Although, at times, it seems that the grade A sides are all-conquering, when it came to playing the grade B sides away from home they only won four out of 15 matches.
- When grade C sides faced grade A sides at home, 14 of the 30 matches ended up being a draw and 20 of the 30 matches ended up producing under 2.5 goals. Indeed, the stats for these games certainly indicate that laying the away favourite is the best course of action.

- Grade C sides at home to grade D sides had an amazing 25 wins in 36 matches. 22 of these games produced over 2.5 goals. This is clearly because these teams target those matches as must-win games; so backing the home side in these encounters would, in all probability, prove to be profitable.
- When looking at the reverse fixtures, with grade D sides at home to grade C sides, the grade D sides only won 11 of 36 matches, with 14 of these games ending in a draw. Under 2.5 goals also came in high at 23 games out of 36. The reasons here again will be the grade C sides having targeted these matches and set themselves up not to lose. Hence the high draw and low score count.

As previously stated, this information is very useful – full of the kind of insight that most punters simply don't have access to, and which odds can fail to take into account – and are an important element in ensuring you always give yourself the best opportunity to profit.

GRADE A v GRADE A

Teams	Played	Home	Draw	Away
A v A	20	10	3	7
Percentage	N/A	50	15	35
Odds	N/A	2	6.67	2.86

Teams	Played	Under 2.5	Over 2.5
A v A	20	9	11
Percentage	N/A	45	55
Odds	N/A	2.22	1.82

GRADE A v GRADE B

Teams	Played	Home	Draw	Away
A v B	15	9	2	4
Percentage	N/A	60	13	27
Odds	N/A	1.67	7.5	3.75

Teams	Played	Under 2.5	Over 2.5
A v B	15	3	12
Percentage	N/A	20	80
Odds	N/A	5.00	1.25

GRADE B v GRADE A

Teams	Played	Home	Draw	Away
B v A	15	8	3	4
Percentage	N/A	53	20	27
Odds	N/A	1.88	5.00	3.75

Teams	Played	Under 2.5	Over 2.5
B v A	15	6	9
Percentage	N/A	40	60
Odds	N/A	2.50	1.67

GRADE A v GRADE C

Teams	Played	Home	Draw	Away
A v C	30	26	4	0
Percentage	N/A	87	13	0
Odds	N/A	1.15	7.50	N/A

Teams	Played	Under 2.5	Over 2.5
A v C	30	7	23
Percentage	N/A	23	77
Odds	N/A	4.29	1.30

GRADE C v GRADE A

Teams	Played	Home	Draw	Away
C v A	30	5	14	11
Percentage	N/A	17	47	37
Odds	N/A	5.88	2.14	2.73

Teams	Played	Under 2.5	Over 2.5
C v A	30	20	10
Percentage	N/A	67	33
Odds	N/A	1.50	3.00

GRADE A v GRADE D

Teams	Played	Home	Draw	Away
A v D	30	28	2	0
Percentage	N/A	93	7	0
Odds	N/A	1.07	14.25	N/A

Teams	Played	Under 2.5	Over 2.5
A v D	30	8	22
Percentage	N/A	27	73
Odds	N/A	3.75	1.36

GRADE D v GRADE A

Teams	Played	Home	Draw	Away
D v A	30	6	6	18
Percentage	N/A	20	20	60
Odds	N/A	5.00	5.00	1.67

Teams	Played	Under 2.5	Over 2.5
D v A	30	12	18
Percentage	N/A	40	60
Odds	N/A	2.50	1.67

GRADE B v GRADE B

Teams	Played	Home	Draw	Away
B v B	6	1	5	0
Percentage	N/A	17	83	0
Odds	N/A	5.88	1.20	N/A

Teams	Played	Under 2.5	Over 2.5
B v B	6	3	3
Percentage	N/A	50	50
Odds	N/A	2.00	2.00

GRADE B v GRADE C

Teams	Played	Home	Draw	Away
B v C	18	11	5	2
Percentage	N/A	61	28	11
Odds	N/A	1.64	3.60	9.09

Teams	Played	Under 2.5	Over 2.5
B v C	18	13	5
Percentage	N/A	72	28
Odds	N/A	1.38	3.60

GRADE C v GRADE B

Teams	Played	Home	Draw	Away
C v B	18	4	6	8
Percentage	N/A	22	33	44
Odds	N/A	4.55	3.00	2.25

Teams	Played	Under 2.5	Over 2.5
C v B	18	8	10
Percentage	N/A	44	56
Odds	N/A	2.25	1.80

GRADE B v GRADE D

Teams	Played	Home	Draw	Away
B v D	18	13	3	2
Percentage	N/A	72	17	11
Odds	N/A	1.38	5.90	9.09

Teams	Played	Under 2.5	Over 2.5
B v D	18	7	11
Percentage	N/A	39	61
Odds	N/A	2.56	1.64

GRADE D v GRADE B

Teams	Played	Home	Draw	Away
D v B	18	5	4	9
Percentage	N/A	28	22	50
Odds	N/A	3.57	4.54	2.00

Teams	Played	Under 2.5	Over 2.5
D v B	18	9	9
Percentage	N/A	50	50
Odds	N/A	2.00	2.00

GRADE C v GRADE C

Teams	Played	Home	Draw	Away
C v C	30	18	9	3
Percentage	N/A	60	30	10
Odds	N/A	1.67	3.33	10.00

Teams	Played	Under 2.5	Over 2.5
C v C	30	16	14
Percentage	N/A	53	47
Odds	N/A	1.88	2.14

GRADE C v GRADE D

Teams	Played	Home	Draw	Away
C v D	36	25	7	4
Percentage	N/A	69	19	11
Odds	N/A	1.44	5.14	9.09

Teams	Played	Under 2.5	Over 2.5
C v D	36	14	22
Percentage	N/A	39	61
Odds	N/A	2.57	1.64

GRADE D v GRADE C

Teams	Played	Home	Draw	Away
D v C	36	11	14	11
Percentage	N/A	31	39	31
Odds	N/A	3.27	2.57	3.27

Teams	Played	Under 2.5	Over 2.5
D v C	36	23	13
Percentage	N/A	64	36
Odds	N/A	1.57	2.77

GRADE D v GRADE D

Teams	Played	Home	Draw	Away
D v D	30	13	9	8
Percentage	N/A	43	30	27
Odds	N/A	2.31	3.33	3.75

Teams	Played	Under 2.5	Over 2.5
D v D	30	16	14
Percentage	N/A	53	47
Odds	N/A	1.88	2.14

9

Summary of the 2009/10 Season

In this chapter we present a series of tables that highlight the strengths and weaknesses last season of the 17 teams that will be competing this season. The aim is to give you a top-line overview in areas that we feel are crucial for the main betting markets. We go further into the stats through our in-depth summary of each team in the next chapter, where we'll also have coverage of the three new promoted sides.

League table, 2009/10

			Home					Away						
		Pld	W	D	L	F	A	W	D	L	F	A	GD	PTS
1	Chelsea	38	17	1	1	68	14	10	4	5	35	18	71	86
2	Man United	38	16	1	2	52	12	11	3	5	34	16	58	85
3	Arsenal	38	15	2	2	48	15	8	4	7	35	26	42	75
4	Tottenham	38	14	2	3	40	12	7	5	7	27	29	26	70
5	Man City	38	12	4	3	41	20	6	9	4	32	25	28	67
6	Aston Villa	38	8	8	3	29	16	9	5	5	23	23	13	64
7	Liverpool	38	13	3	3	43	15	5	6	8	18	20	26	63
8	Everton	38	11	6	2	35	21	5	7	7	25	28	11	61
9	Birmingham	38	8	9	2	19	13	5	2	12	19	34	-9	50
10	Blackburn	38	10	6	3	28	18	3	5	11	13	37	-14	50
11	Stoke	38	7	6	6	24	21	4	8	7	10	27	-14	47
12	Fulham	38	11	3	5	27	15	1	7	11	12	31	-7	46
13	Sunderland	38	9	7	3	32	19	2	4	13	16	37	-8	44
14	Bolton	38	6	6	7	26	31	4	3	12	16	36	-25	39
15	Wolverhampton	38	5	6	8	13	22	4	5	10	19	34	-24	38
16	Wigan	38	6	7	6	19	24	3	2	14	18	55	-42	36
17	West Ham	38	7	5	7	30	29	1	6	12	17	37	-19	35
18	Burnley	38	7	5	7	25	30	1	1	17	17	52	-40	30
19	Hull	38	6	6	7	22	29	0	6	13	12	46	-41	30
20	Portsmouth	38	5	3	11	24	32	2	4	13	10	34	-32	19

Top scorers

Player	Team	Started	Goals	First	Last	Each way	Anytime
Didier Drogba	Chelsea	31	29	8	9	17	20
Wayne Rooney	Man United	32	26	10	6	16	18
Darren Bent	Sunderland	38	24	13	7	16	17
Carlos Tévez	Man City	32	23	6	7	14	14
Frank Lampard	Chelsea	36	22	3	8	12	14
Fernando Torres	Liverpool	20	18	8	4	11	12
Jermain Defoe	Tottenham	31	18	7	2	12	12
Cesc Fàbregas	Arsenal	26	15	4	3	9	13
Emmanuel Adebayor	Man City	25	14	6	5	10	12
Gabriel Agbonlahor	Aston Villa	35	13	7	5	11	12
Louis Saha	Everton	26	13	3	5	7	9
Dimitar Berbatov	Man United	25	12	4	2	8	11
Florent Malouda	Chelsea	26	12	3	3	7	9
Nicolas Anelka	Chelsea	31	11	7	2	9	9
Andrei Arshavin	Arsenal	25	10	3	4	5	10
John Carew	Aston Villa	22	10	2	3	9	9
Cameron Jerome	Birmingham	32	10	4	1	8	8
Craig Bellamy	Man City	26	10	0	2	4	8
Carlton Cole	West Ham	26	10	2	1	9	10
Hugo Rodallega	Wigan	38	10	5	5	8	9
Robin van Persie	Arsenal	14	9	5	2	7	8
David Dunn	Blackburn	20	9	4	3	8	8
Steven Gerrard	Liverpool	32	9	4	2	5	8
Dirk Kuyt	Liverpool	35	9	4	2	8	8
Kenwyne Jones	Sunderland	24	9	2	2	6	7
Kevin Doyle	Wolverhampton W	33	9	5	2	7	8

Scoring summary table in alphabetical order

Team	Matches scored in	Clean sheets	Won to nil	Both teams scored	A goal first half	A goal second half
Arsenal	33	14	12	20	31	34
Aston Villa	29	15	11	19	27	28
Birmingham	29	11	7	22	23	29
Blackburn	24	13	6	18	28	28
Bolton	22	5	3	19	32	31
Chelsea	37	18	17	20	35	34
Everton	32	11	9	23	27	31
Fulham	22	12	7	15	27	28
Liverpool	26	16	11	15	23	30
Man City	30	11	8	22	29	29
Man United	32	19	18	14	27	32
Stoke	24	13	7	16	20	29
Sunderland	26	7	5	21	32	28
Tottenham	29	13	10	19	27	31
West Ham	27	8	5	22	27	34
Wigan	25	8	6	19	27	32
Wolverhampton W	21	8	4	17	28	27

Number of matches each team scored in

Team	Matches scored in
Chelsea	37
Arsenal	33
Everton	32
Man United	32
Man City	30
Aston Villa	29
Birmingham	29
Tottenham	29
West Ham	27
Liverpool	26
Sunderland	26
Wigan	25
Blackburn	24
Stoke	24
Bolton	22
Fulham	22
Wolverhampton W	21

Number of clean sheets and matches each team won to nil

Team	Clean sheets	Won to nil
Man United	19	18
Chelsea	18	17
Liverpool	16	11
Aston Villa	15	11
Arsenal	14	12
Tottenham	13	10
Blackburn	13	6
Stoke	13	7
Fulham	12	7
Everton	11	9
Man City	11	8
Birmingham	11	7
West Ham	8	5
Wigan	8	6
Wolverhampton W	8	4
Sunderland	7	5
Bolton	5	3

Number of matches both teams scored

Team	Both teams scored
Everton	23
Man City	22
Birmingham	22
West Ham	22
Sunderland	21
Chelsea	20
Arsenal	20
Aston Villa	19
Tottenham	19
Wigan	19
Bolton	19
Blackburn	18
Wolverhampton W	17
Stoke	16
Liverpool	15
Fulham	15
Man United	14

Number of matches with at least one goal in the first half (scored by any team)

Team	A goal first half
Chelsea	35
Sunderland	32
Bolton	32
Arsenal	31
Man City	29
Blackburn	28
Wolverhampton W	28
Everton	27
West Ham	27
Aston Villa	27
Tottenham	27
Wigan	27
Fulham	27
Man United	27
Birmingham	23
Liverpool	23
Stoke	20

Number of matches with at least one goal in the second half (scored by any team)

Team	A goal second half
Chelsea	34
Arsenal	34
West Ham	34
Wigan	32
Man United	32
Bolton	31
Everton	31
Tottenham	31
Liverpool	30
Man City	29
Birmingham	29
Stoke	29
Sunderland	28
Blackburn	28
Aston Villa	28
Fulham	28
Wolverhampton W	27

Match goal time summary table in alphabetical order

Team	First ten mins	Before 27 mins	After 27 mins	No goals	Before 75 mins	After 75 mins	90+ min goal	No goals
Arsenal	7	18	18	2	8	26	11	4
Aston Villa	7	21	6	11	8	20	6	10
Birmingham	7	13	10	10	8	21	7	9
Blackburn	9	21	7	10	10	18	4	10
Bolton	10	17	15	6	5	25	1	8
Chelsea	8	21	14	3	12	22	13	4
Everton	4	18	9	11	10	21	9	7
Fulham	5	13	10	11	12	16	4	10
Liverpool	6	12	10	15	12	18	9	8
Man City	9	16	13	9	19	20	7	9
Man United	6	11	16	11	5	27	8	6
Stoke	4	14	6	18	10	19	6	6
Sunderland	15	28	4	6	9	19	6	10
Tottenham	10	15	12	11	8	23	8	7
West Ham	6	17	10	11	12	22	7	4
Wigan	7	15	12	11	11	21	12	6
Wolverhampton W	8	17	11	10	14	13	3	11

First goal of the game

Team	First ten mins
Sunderland	15
Bolton	10
Tottenham	10
Blackburn	9
Man City	9
Chelsea	8
Wolverhampton W	8
Arsenal	7
Aston Villa	7
Birmingham	7
Wigan	7
Liverpool	6
Man United	6
West Ham	6
Fulham	5
Everton	4
Stoke	4

First goal of the game

Team	Before 27 mins
Sunderland	28
Blackburn	21
Chelsea	21
Aston Villa	21
Arsenal	18
Everton	18
Bolton	17
Wolverhampton W	17
West Ham	17
Man City	16
Tottenham	15
Wigan	15
Stoke	14
Birmingham	13
Fulham	13
Liverpool	12
Man United	11

First goal of the game

Team	After 27 mins
Arsenal	18
Man United	16
Bolton	15
Chelsea	14
Man City	13
Tottenham	12
Wigan	12
Wolverhampton W	11
West Ham	10
Birmingham	10
Fulham	10
Liverpool	10
Everton	9
Blackburn	7
Aston Villa	6
Stoke	6
Sunderland	4

Number of matches 0-0 at half time

Team	No goals
Stoke	18
Liverpool	15
Man United	11
Tottenham	11
Wigan	11
West Ham	11
Fulham	11
Everton	11
Aston Villa	11
Wolverhampton W	10
Birmingham	10
Blackburn	10
Man City	9
Bolton	6
Sunderland	6
Chelsea	3
Arsenal	2

Last goal of the game

Team	Before 75 mins
Wolverhampton W	14
Liverpool	12
West Ham	12
Fulham	12
Chelsea	12
Wigan	11
Stoke	10
Everton	10
Blackburn	10
Man City	9
Sunderland	9
Tottenham	8
Aston Villa	8
Birmingham	8
Arsenal	8
Man United	5
Bolton	5

Last goal of the game

Team	After 75 mins
Man United	27
Arsenal	26
Bolton	25
Tottenham	23
West Ham	22
Chelsea	22
Wigan	21
Everton	21
Birmingham	21
Man City	20
Aston Villa	20
Stoke	19
Sunderland	19
Liverpool	18
Blackburn	18
Fulham	16
Wolverhampton W	13

Number of matches with full-time score same as half-time score (no further goals)

Team	No goals
Wolverhampton W	11
Aston Villa	10
Sunderland	10
Blackburn	10
Fulham	10
Birmingham	9
Man City	9
Liverpool	8
Bolton	8
Everton	7
Tottenham	7
Wigan	6
Man United	6
Stoke	6
Chelsea	4
Arsenal	4
West Ham	4

Number of matches each team was involved in when there was a goal scored in time added on (90+ minutes)

Team	90+ min goal
Chelsea	13
Wigan	12
Arsenal	11
Everton	9
Liverpool	9
Man United	8
Tottenham	8
West Ham	7
Birmingham	7
Man City	7
Aston Villa	6
Stoke	6
Sunderland	6
Blackburn	4
Fulham	4
Wolverhampton W	3
Bolton	1

Half time/full time abbreviations

H/H = Home side leading at both half time and full time.

H/D = Home side leading at half time; a draw at full time.

H/A = Home side leading at half time; away side win at full time.

D/H = A draw at half time; a home win at full time.

D/D = A draw at half time; a draw at full time.

D/A = A draw at half time; an away win at full time.

A/H = Away side leading at half time; home side win at full time.

A/D = Away side leading at half time; a draw at full time.

A/A = Away side leading at half time; away win at full time.

Half-time/full-time table – home

This is in order of the teams that won their home matches and were also leading at half time (H/H).

		HOME – Half-time/full-time results								
	TEAM	H/H	H/D	H/A	D/H	D/D	D/A	A/H	A/D	A/A
1	Tottenham	13	0	0	1	2	1	0	0	2
2	Chelsea	12	0	0	4	1	1	1	0	0
3	Arsenal	11	0	0	3	2	0	1	0	2
4	Liverpool	10	0	1	3	2	0	0	1	2
5	Man City	10	1	0	2	2	2	0	1	1
6	Man United	9	0	0	6	0	0	1	1	2
7	Blackburn	7	0	0	2	5	0	1	1	3
8	Fulham	6	0	0	2	2	2	3	1	3
9	Sunderland	6	3	1	3	2	0	0	2	2
10	West Ham	6	2	0	1	2	3	0	1	4
11	Birmingham	5	1	0	2	7	1	1	1	1
12	Bolton	5	2	0	1	4	1	0	0	6
13	Stoke	5	1	0	2	5	5	0	0	0
14	Aston Villa	4	2	0	4	4	2	0	2	1
15	Everton	4	2	0	6	4	0	1	0	2
16	Wolverhampton	4	0	0	1	4	2	0	2	6
17	Wigan	2	2	1	3	4	3	1	1	2

Half-time/full-time table – away

This is in order of the teams that won their away matches and were also leading at half time (A/A).

		AWAY – Half-time/full-time results								
	TEAM	H/H	H/D	H/A	D/H	D/D	D/A	A/H	A/D	A/A
1	Chelsea	2	1	1	3	2	1	0	1	8
2	Aston Villa	3	2	0	2	3	3	0	0	6
3	Man United	2	1	0	3	2	5	0	0	5
4	Man City	3	3	0	1	6	1	0	0	5
5	Arsenal	3	0	1	2	3	3	2	1	4
6	Tottenham	5	1	0	1	4	3	1	0	4
7	Everton	5	1	0	1	4	1	1	2	4
8	Wolverhampton	7	2	0	2	2	0	1	1	4
9	Bolton	9	0	1	2	1	0	1	2	3
10	Birmingham	8	0	1	3	1	2	1	1	2
11	Blackburn	9	0	0	2	3	1	0	2	2
12	Sunderland	9	0	0	4	2	0	0	2	2
13	Liverpool	4	0	0	4	6	4	0	0	1
14	Wigan	10	0	0	3	1	2	1	1	1
15	Fulham	8	1	0	1	6	0	2	0	1
16	West Ham	7	2	0	5	3	0	0	1	1
17	Stoke	5	1	1	1	6	3	1	1	0

Match goals – home

This is in order of teams whose home matches produced the most games with over 2.5 goals.

		Home – Match goals				
	TEAM	1 or more	Ov. 1.5	Ov. 2.5	Ov. 3.5	Ov. 4.5
1	Man United	19	17	16	6	3
2	Chelsea	19	17	15	9	8
3	Arsenal	18	16	13	9	3
4	Liverpool	18	11	13	8	3
5	Tottenham	18	14	12	5	3
6	West Ham	18	17	12	7	3
7	Bolton	18	14	11	10	3
8	Blackburn	15	14	10	5	2
9	Everton	19	18	10	6	3
10	Man City	18	15	10	8	5
11	Fulham	17	13	9	2	0
12	Stoke	17	14	9	4	1
13	Sunderland	17	14	9	7	2
14	Aston Villa	17	13	7	4	3
15	Wigan	17	11	7	5	3
16	Birmingham	15	10	6	1	0
17	Wolverhampton	16	12	5	1	1

Match goals – away

This is in order of teams whose away matches produced the most games with over 2.5 goals.

		Away – Match goals				
	TEAM	1 or more	Ov. 1.5	Ov. 2.5	Ov. 3.5	Ov. 4.5
1	Wigan	19	18	15	9	4
2	Birmingham	19	15	13	5	2
3	Everton	17	13	13	10	7
4	Arsenal	18	16	12	7	5
5	Chelsea	18	18	12	4	1
6	Tottenham	17	16	12	6	2
7	West Ham	17	15	11	7	2
8	Wolverhampton	18	13	11	8	2
9	Blackburn	16	14	10	4	3
10	Bolton	18	15	10	4	3
11	Fulham	16	14	9	4	1
12	Man City	17	16	9	5	4
13	Man United	18	13	9	8	2
14	Aston Villa	17	14	8	3	1
15	Sunderland	19	13	8	5	2
16	Liverpool	15	10	6	4	2
17	Stoke	15	12	5	2	1

Corners – home

This table is in order of home teams who won in corner superiority.

		Corner supremacy			Corner numbers		
	TEAM	Won	Draw	Lost	0–9	10–12	13+
1	Arsenal	17	0	2	9	6	4
2	Man City	16	0	3	4	7	8
3	Man United	15	2	2	5	6	8
4	Liverpool	15	1	3	5	7	7
5	Chelsea	14	0	5	7	5	7
6	Fulham	12	3	4	9	8	2
7	Everton	12	0	7	5	7	7
8	Tottenham	11	1	7	4	7	8
9	Aston Villa	10	2	7	3	6	10
10	Blackburn	10	2	7	9	6	4
11	Stoke	9	2	8	9	3	7
12	Wigan	8	3	8	7	5	7
13	Wolverhampton	8	3	8	7	5	7
14	West Ham	8	2	9	8	6	5
15	Birmingham	7	1	11	9	2	8
16	Sunderland	5	3	11	7	5	7
17	Bolton	3	3	13	5	5	9

Corners – away

This table is in order of away teams who won in corner superiority.

		Corner supremacy			Corner numbers		
	TEAM	Won	Draw	Lost	0–9	10–12	13+
1	Arsenal	15	2	3	7	7	5
2	Chelsea	13	2	4	4	5	10
3	Man United	13	0	6	8	5	6
4	Liverpool	12	2	5	10	4	5
5	Tottenham	9	2	8	7	6	6
6	Sunderland	8	4	7	7	6	6
7	Everton	8	1	10	7	6	6
8	Wolverhampton	8	1	10	4	6	9
9	Wigan	8	0	11	10	6	3
10	Blackburn	7	3	9	11	3	5
11	Fulham	5	2	12	6	6	7
12	Birmingham	5	1	13	4	11	4
13	Aston Villa	5	0	14	4	3	12
14	West Ham	5	0	14	4	9	6
15	Man City	4	3	12	6	9	4
16	Stoke	3	3	13	6	6	7
17	Bolton	3	0	16	7	5	7

Bookings – home

This table is in order of home teams who received the most yellow cards.

		Yellow cards		Red cards		Betfair points		
	TEAM	F	A	F	A	0–5	6–8	9 +
1	Sunderland	42	43	2	3	2	7	10
2	Birmingham	36	35	1	3	3	8	8
3	Bolton	34	28	2	1	5	8	6
4	Stoke	30	39	3	1	4	7	8
5	Blackburn	28	38	1	1	4	9	6
6	West Ham	27	43	1	5	5	5	9
7	Wigan	27	38	0	2	4	9	6
8	Tottenham	26	40	0	2	6	5	8
9	Arsenal	24	40	1	1	6	7	6
10	Wolverhampton	24	26	1	3	8	7	4
11	Aston Villa	23	35	0	1	5	10	3
12	Man United	23	31	0	1	12	3	4
13	Man City	21	47	0	2	6	7	6
14	Liverpool	20	43	2	3	7	5	7
15	Everton	20	38	1	4	7	4	8
16	Chelsea	17	28	2	1	11	3	5
17	Fulham	15	19	0	2	13	4	2

Bookings – away

This table is in order of away teams who received the most yellow cards.

		Yellow cards		Red cards		Betfair points		
	TEAM	F	A	F	A	0–5	6–8	9 +
1	Bolton	41	20	2	1	6	6	7
2	Sunderland	40	19	7	2	5	7	7
3	Wolverhampton	40	14	3	0	8	6	5
4	Chelsea	39	29	3	1	4	7	8
5	West Ham	39	28	2	3	6	5	8
6	Wigan	37	34	3	1	6	7	6
7	Everton	37	24	1	1	8	5	6
8	Fulham	37	24	1	1	8	5	6
9	Birmingham	36	19	0	0	6	10	3
10	Blackburn	36	19	0	0	6	10	3
11	Stoke	36	16	0	2	8	7	4
12	Liverpool	34	32	3	1	6	4	9
13	Arsenal	32	41	0	3	3	9	7
14	Tottenham	31	32	1	2	8	4	7
15	Aston Villa	30	17	2	3	3	4	6
16	Man City	30	38	2	4	5	4	10
17	Man United	28	33	3	2	6	6	7

10

The Teams

ARSENAL (Grade A)

Season record

	Home					Away						
Pld	Won	Draw	Lost	F	A	Won	Draw	Lost	F	A	GD	Points
38	15	2	2	48	15	8	4	7	35	26	42	75

Top Scorers

Player	Started	Goals	First	Last	Each Way	Anytime
Cesc Fàbregas	26	15	4	3	9	13
Andrey Arshavin	25	10	3	4	5	10
Robin van Persie	14	9	5	2*	7	8
Thomas Vermaelen	33	7	1	2	3	5
Nicklas Bendtner	13	6	1	5	5	6
Abou Diaby	26	6	2	3*	5	5

***Last Scorer** – Abou Diaby, 1-0 victory at home to Liverpool; Robin van Persie, 1-0 victory away at Fulham.

Scoring

	Matches Scored In	Clean Sheets	Won to Nil	Both Teams Scored	A Goal 1st Half	A Goal 2nd Half
Home	17	11	10	7	15	18
Away	16	3	2	14	15	16
Total	33	14	12	21	30	34

Match goal times

	First Goal of Match			
	1st 10 mins	Before 27 mins	After 27 mins	No Goals
Home	3	10	9	1
Away	4	8	9	1
Total	7	18	18	2
%	18.42	47.37	47.37	5.26
Break-Even Odds	5.43	2.11	2.11	19.00

	Last Goal of Match			
	Before 75 mins	After 75 mins	90+ min Goal	No Goals
Home	3	15	6	1
Away	5	11	5	3
Total	8	26	11	4
%	21.05	68.42	28.95	10.53
Break-Even Odds	4.75	1.46	3.45	9.50

Half time/full time

	Half Time / Full Time Results								
	H/H	H/D	H/A	D/H	D/D	D/A	A/H	A/D	A/A
Home	11	0	0	3	2	0	1	0	2
%	57.89	0.00	0.00	15.79	10.53	0.00	5.26	0.00	10.53
Break-Even Odds	1.73	N/A	N/A	6.33	9.50	N/A	19.00	N/A	9.50
Away	3	0	1	2	3	3	2	1	4
%	15.79	0.00	5.26	10.53	15.79	15.79	10.53	5.26	21.05
Break-Even Odds	6.33	N/A	19.00	9.50	6.33	6.33	9.50	19.00	4.75

Goals

	Match goals				
	1 or More	Ov. 1.5	Ov. 2.5	Ov. 3.5	Ov. 4.5
Home	18	16	13	9	3
Away	18	16	12	7	5
Total	36	32	25	16	8
%	94.74	84.21	65.79	42.11	21.05
Break-Even Odds	1.06	1.19	1.52	2.38	4.75

Bookings

	Yellow Cards		Red Cards		Betfair Points		
	F	A	F	A	0-5	6-8	9+
Home	24	40	1	1	6	7	6
%	N/A	N/A	N/A	N/A	31.58	36.84	31.58
Break-Even Odds	N/A	N/A	N/A	N/A	3.17	2.71	3.17
Away	32	41	0	3	3	9	7
%	N/A	N/A	N/A	N/A	15.79	47.37	36.84
Break-Even Odds	N/A	N/A	N/A	N/A	6.33	2.11	2.71

Corner superiority

	Corner Supremacy			Corner Numbers		
	Won	Draw	Lost	0-9	10-12	13+
Home	17	0	2	9	6	4
%	89.47	0.00	10.53	47.37	31.58	21.05
Break-Even Odds	1.12	N/A	9.50	2.11	3.17	4.75
Away	15	2	2	7	7	5
%	78.95	10.53	10.53	36.84	36.84	26.32
Break-Even Odds	1.27	9.50	9.50	2.71	2.71	3.80

Summary

- The last goal of the match was scored after 75 minutes in (68%, odds 1.47) of all of Arsenal's matches.
- 25 Arsenal matches out of 38 (65% / odds 1.53) finished with three or more goals; backing over 2.5 goals at above 1.52 would have yielded a level stake profit last season.
- Just two Arsenal matches were 0-0 at half-time (5.26% / odds 19.00) in all games played.
- A total of 11 of their games (28.95% / odds 3.45) had a goal in the 90+ injury time window.
- In the 18 matches Arsenal led at half-time, they went on to win the game in 15 of them (83.33% / odds 1.20).
- Only nine of their matches (23.68% / odds 4.22) featured two or less bookings.
- Corner supremacy was won by Arsenal in 32 out 38 games (84.21% / odds 1.19).
- 13+ corners occurred in only nine of Arsenal's matches (23.68% / odds 4.22).

Home (graded analysis)

	Home Record					
Team	Won	Draw	Lost	F	A	Pts
A	1	1	2	2	6	4
B	2	1	0	8	2	7
C	6	0	0	19	3	18
D	6	0	0	19	4	18
Total	15	2	2	48	15	47
%	78.95	10.53	10.53			
Odds	1.27	9.50	9.50			

	Half Time / Full Time Results								
Team	H/H	H/D	H/A	D/H	D/D	D/A	A/H	A/D	A/A
A	0	0	0	1	1	0	0	0	2
B	1	0	0	1	1	0	0	0	0
C	6	0	0	0	0	0	0	0	0
D	4	0	0	1	0	0	1	0	0
Total	11	0	0	3	2	0	1	0	2
%	57.89	0.00	0.00	15.79	10.53	0.00	5.26	0.00	10.53
Odds	1.73	N/A	N/A	6.33	9.50	N/A	19.00	N/A	9.50

Goals

	Match goals				
Team	1 or More	Ov. 1.5	Ov. 2.5	Ov. 3.5	Ov. 4.5
A	3	2	2	1	0
B	3	3	3	1	0
C	6	6	3	3	1
D	6	5	5	4	2
Total	18	16	13	9	3
%	94.74	84.21	68.42	47.37	15.79
Odds	1.06	1.19	1.46	2.11	6.33

	Clean Sheet		Scored	
Team	Yes	No	Yes	No
A	2	2	2	2
B	2	1	3	0
C	4	2	6	0
D	3	3	6	0
Total	11	8	17	2
%	57.89	42.11	89.47	10.53
Odds	1.73	2.38	1.12	9.50

	Won By			Draw	Lost By		
Team	+3	2	1	0	1	2	+3
A	0	0	1	1	0	1	1
B	2	0	0	1	0	0	0
C	2	4	0	0	0	0	0
D	3	2	1	0	0	0	0
Total	7	6	2	2	0	1	1
%	36.84	31.58	5.26	10.53	0.00	5.26	5.26
Odds	2.71	3.17	19.00	9.50	N/A	19.00	19.00

Bookings

	Yellow Cards		Red Cards		Betfair Points		
Team	F	A	F	A	0-5	6-8	9+
A	10	6	0	0	1	1	2
B	3	5	0	0	2	1	0
C	6	14	1	0	2	2	2
D	5	15	0	1	1	3	2
Total	24	40	1	1	6	7	6
				%	31.58	36.84	31.58
				Odds	3.17	2.71	3.17

Corners

	Corner Supremacy			Corner Numbers		
Team	Won	Draw	Lost	0-9	10-12	13+
A	3	0	1	3	0	1
B	2	0	1	1	0	2
C	6	0	0	4	2	0
D	6	0	0	1	4	1
Total	17	0	2	9	6	4
%	89.47	0.00	10.53	47.37	31.58	21.05
Odds	1.12	N/A	9.50	2.11	3.17	4.75

Summary

- Ten of 12 Arsenal home matches (83%) against grade C and D sides finished with a H/H half-time/full-time result; this equates to odds of 1.20.
- Arsenal had a perfect home record against grade C and D sides.
- 13 of their home matches finished in over 2.5 goals (68%), which equates to odds of 1.47.
- They kept a clean sheet seven times at home (58%) against grade C and D sides. This equates to odds of 1.71.
- In 15 home games against grade B, C and D sides, Arsenal won by at least two goals 13 times (86%). This equates to odds of 1.15.
- Only three of Arsenal's 12 home matches (25%) against grade C and D sides featured two bookings or less. This equates to odds of 4.0.
- Arsenal had a superior corner count for all but two of their home matches.
- They had a superiority of four corners or more on 12 home occasions.
- Against grade C and D sides, in particular, they had a superiority of four corners or more in eight of 12 home matches. In seven of these 12 matches, this was a superiority of six or more.

Away (graded analysis)

	Away Record					
Team	Won	Draw	Lost	F	A	Pts
A	1	0	3	5	9	3
B	1	1	1	7	3	4
C	2	2	2	8	7	8
D	4	1	1	15	7	13
Total	8	4	7	35	26	28
%	42.11	21.05	36.84			
Odds	2.38	4.75	2.71			

	Half Time / Full Time Results								
Team	H/H	H/D	H/A	D/H	D/D	D/A	A/H	A/D	A/A
A	2	0	1	0	0	0	1	0	0
B	1	0	0	0	1	0	0	0	1
C	0	0	0	2	1	2	0	1	0
D	0	0	0	0	1	1	1	0	3
Total	3	0	1	2	3	3	2	1	4
%	15.79	0.00	5.26	10.53	15.79	15.79	10.53	5.26	21.05
Odds	6.33	N/A	19.00	9.50	6.33	6.33	9.50	19.00	4.75

Goals

	Match goals				
Team	1 or More	Ov. 1.5	Ov. 2.5	Ov. 3.5	Ov. 4.5
A	4	4	3	1	1
B	2	2	2	1	1
C	6	4	3	2	0
D	6	6	4	3	3
Total	18	16	12	7	5
%	94.74	84.21	63.16	36.84	26.32
Odds	1.06	1.19	1.58	2.71	3.80

	Clean Sheet		Scored	
Team	Yes	No	Yes	No
A	0	4	3	1
B	1	2	2	1
C	1	5	5	1
D	1	5	6	0
Total	3	16	16	3
%	15.79	84.21	84.21	15.79
Odds	6.33	1.19	1.19	6.33

	Won By			Draw	Lost By		
Team	+3	2	1	0	1	2	+3
A	0	0	1	0	1	2	0
B	1	0	0	1	1	0	0
C	0	1	1	2	2	0	0
D	2	1	1	1	1	0	0
Total	3	2	3	4	5	2	0
%	15.79	10.53	15.79	21.05	26.32	10.53	0.00
Odds	6.33	9.50	6.33	4.75	3.80	9.50	N/A

Bookings

	Yellow Cards		Red Cards		Betfair Points		
Team	F	A	F	A	0-5	6-8	9+
A	13	11	0	0	0	1	3
B	3	5	0	0	1	2	0
C	8	14	0	2	0	4	2
D	8	11	0	1	2	2	2
Total	32	41	0	3	3	9	7
				%	15.79	47.37	36.84
				Odds	6.33	2.11	2.71

Corners

	Corner Supremacy			Corner Numbers		
Team	Won	Draw	Lost	0-9	10-12	13+
A	3	0	1	3	0	1
B	2	0	1	1	0	2
C	6	0	0	4	2	0
D	6	0	0	1	4	1
Total	17	0	2	9	6	4
%	89.47	0.00	10.53	47.37	31.58	21.05
Odds	1.12	N/A	9.50	2.11	3.17	4.75

Summary

- 12 of Arsenal's away matches finished with over 2.5 goals (63%) last year, which equates to odds of 1.58.
- Back Arsenal NOT to keep a clean sheet away against grade C and D opposition. This happened 53% last season equalling odds of 1.89.
- Away against grade C and D sides, A/A result was achieved in only three matches in 12 (25%). This equates to odds of 4.00.
- Only three Arsenal away games (16%) featured five or less points on the Betfair bookings markets. This equates to odds of 6.30.
- Against sides graded A, B or C, only one Arsenal away game in 13 (8%) featured five or less points on the Betfair bookings markets. This equates to odds of 12.50.
- Arsenal won three of four away matches (75%) in corner superiority against fellow grade A opposition, which equals odds of 1.33.

ASTON VILLA (Grade B)

Season record

	Home					Away						
Pld	Won	Draw	Lost	F	A	Won	Draw	Lost	F	A	GD	Points
38	8	8	3	29	16	9	5	5	23	23	13	64

Top Scorers

Player	Started	Goals	First	Last	Each Way	Anytime
Gabriel Agbonlahor	35	13	7	5*	11	12
John Carew	22	10	2	3*	9	9
James Milner	36	7	2	4*	7	7

***Last scorer** – Gabriel Agbonlahor, 1-0 victories away to Liverpool and Manchester United; John Carew, 1-0 victory home to Fulham; James Milner, 1-0 victory home to Birmingham.

Scoring

	Matches Scored In	Clean Sheets	Won to Nil	Both Teams Scored	A Goal 1st Half	A Goal 2nd Half
	14	7	5	9	13	14
Away	16	8	6	10	14	14
Total	30	15	11	19	27	28

Match Goal Times

	First Goal of Match			
	1st 10 mins	Before 27 mins	After 27 mins	No Goals
Home	4	11	2	6
Away	3	10	4	5
Total	7	21	6	11
%	18.42	55.26	15.79	28.95
Break-Even Odds	5.43	1.81	6.33	3.45

	Last Goal of Match			
	Before 75 mins	After 75 mins	90+ min Goal	No Goals
Home	5	9	3	5
Away	3	11	3	5
Total	8	20	6	10
%	21.05	52.63	15.79	26.32
Break-Even Odds	4.75	1.90	6.33	3.80

Half Time/Full time

	Half Time / Full Time Results								
	H/H	H/D	H/A	D/H	D/D	D/A	A/H	A/D	A/A
Home	4	2	0	4	4	2	0	2	1
%	21.05	10.53	0.00	21.05	21.05	10.53	0.00	10.53	5.26
Break-Even Odds	4.75	9.50	N/A	4.75	4.75	9.50	N/A	9.50	19.00
Away	3	2	0	2	3	3	0	0	6
%	15.79	10.53	0.00	10.53	15.79	15.79	0.00	0.00	31.58
Break-Even Odds	6.33	9.50	N/A	9.50	6.33	6.33	N/A	N/A	3.17

Goals

	Match goals				
	1 or More	Ov. 1.5	Ov. 2.5	Ov. 3.5	Ov. 4.5
Home	17	13	6	4	2
Away	17	14	8	3	1
Total	34	27	14	7	3
%	89.47	71.05	36.84	18.42	7.89
Break-Even Odds	1.12	1.41	2.71	5.43	12.67

Bookings

	Yellow Cards		Red Cards		Betfair Points		
	F	A	F	A	0-5	6-8	9+
Home	23	35	0	1	5	10	3
%	N/A	N/A	N/A	N/A	26.32	57.89	15.79
Break-Even Odds	N/A	N/A	N/A	N/A	3.80	1.73	6.33
Away	38	24	2	3	5	8	6
%	N/A	N/A	N/A	N/A	26.32	42.11	31.58
Break-Even Odds	N/A	N/A	N/A	N/A	3.80	2.38	3.17

Corner Superiority

	Corner Supremacy			Corner Numbers		
	Won	Draw	Lost	0-9	10-12	13+
Home	10	2	7	3	6	10
%	52.63	10.53	36.84	15.79	31.58	52.63
Break-Even Odds	1.90	9.50	2.71	6.33	3.17	1.90
Away	5	0	14	3	3	13
%	26.32	0.00	73.68	15.79	15.79	68.42
Break-Even Odds	3.80	N/A	1.36	6.33	6.33	1.46

Summary

- In 18 out of 38 Aston Villa matches (47.37%), no further goals were scored after 75 minutes.
- Only 14 of their matches out of 38 (36.84%) finished with three or more goals; backing under 2.5 goals at above 1.65 would have yielded a level stake profit last season.
- 11 of all Villa's matches were 0-0 at H-T (28.95%) in all games played.
- In the 12 matches Aston Villa led at half-time, they went on win the match in ten of them (83.33%), including all six away matches that fall into this category.
- Only ten of their matches (26.32%) had two or less bookings.
- They had corner supremacy in 15 matches (39.47%).
- 13+ corners occurred in 23 of all 38 matches (60.53%).
- Nine or less corners occurred in six matches (15.79%).

Home (Graded Analysis)

	Home Record					
Team	Won	Draw	Lost	F	A	Pts
A	1	3	1	4	4	6
B	0	2	0	3	3	2
C	3	2	1	5	2	11
D	4	1	1	17	7	13
Total	8	8	3	29	16	32
%	42.11	42.11	15.79			
Odds	2.38	2.38	6.33			

	Half Time / Full Time Results								
Team	H/H	H/D	H/A	D/H	D/D	D/A	A/H	A/D	A/A
A	0	1	0	1	2	1	0	0	0
B	0	1	0	0	0	0	0	1	0
C	1	0	0	2	2	1	0	0	0
D	3	0	0	1	0	0	0	1	1
Total	4	2	0	4	4	2	0	2	1
%	21.05	10.53	0.00	21.05	21.05	10.53	0.00	10.53	5.26
Odds	4.75	9.50	N/A	4.75	4.75	9.50	N/A	9.50	19.00

Goals

	Match goals				
Team	1 or More	Ov. 1.5	Ov. 2.5	Ov. 3.5	Ov. 4.5
A	4	3	2	0	0
B	2	2	1	1	0
C	5	2	0	0	0
D	6	6	4	3	3
Total	17	13	7	4	3
%	89.47	68.42	36.84	21.05	15.79
Odds	1.12	1.46	2.71	4.75	6.33

	Clean Sheet		Scored	
Team	Yes	No	Yes	No
A	1	4	3	2
B	0	2	2	0
C	4	2	4	2
D	2	4	5	1
Total	7	12	14	5
%	36.84	63.16	73.68	26.32
Odds	2.71	1.58	1.36	3.80

	Won By			Draw	Lost By		
Team	+3	2	1	0	1	2	+3
A	0	0	0	3	1	0	0
B	0	0	0	2	0	0	0
C	0	1	2	2	1	0	0
D	3	1	0	1	0	1	0
Total	3	2	2	8	2	1	0
%	15.79	10.53	10.53	42.11	10.53	5.26	0.00
Odds	6.33	9.50	9.50	2.38	9.50	19.00	N/A

Bookings

	Yellow Cards		Red Cards		Betfair Points		
Team	F	A	F	A	0-5	6-8	9+
A	6	7	0	1	1	4	0
B	2	3	0	0	1	1	0
C	5	11	0	0	2	3	1
D	10	14	0	0	1	2	2
Total	23	35	0	1	5	10	3
				%	26.32	52.63	15.79
				Odds	3.80	1.90	6.33

Corners

	Corner Supremacy			Corner Numbers		
Team	Won	Draw	Lost	0-9	10-12	13+
A	0	2	3	1	1	3
B	1	0	1	0	0	2
C	4	0	2	1	1	4
D	5	0	1	1	4	1
Total	10	2	7	3	6	10
%	52.63	10.53	36.84	15.79	31.58	52.63
Odds	1.90	9.50	2.71	6.33	3.17	1.90

Summary

- Only four of their 12 home games (33% / odds 3.00) against grade C and D sides finished half-time/full-time H/H.
- 13 of their 19 home games (68% / odds 1.47) finished in under 2.5 goals.
- In six of seven home games (86% / odds 1.16) against grade A and B opposition, Villa failed to keep a clean sheet.
- In four of six home matches (66% / odds 1.51) against grade D opposition, Villa won by two goals or more.
- Only three matches (16% / odds 6.25) played at Villa Park featured more than 9 Betfair booking points.
- Ten of their home matches (53% / odds 1.88) featured 13 or more corners.
- At home, Aston Villa had a superior corner count against C and D grade sides nine (75%) out of 12 matches played.

Away (Graded Analysis)

	Away Record					
Team	Won	Draw	Lost	F	A	Pts
A	2	0	3	6	14	6
B	0	2	0	1	1	2
C	3	1	2	7	4	10
D	4	2	0	9	4	14
Total	9	5	5	23	23	32
%	47.37	26.32	26.32			
Odds	2.11	3.80	3.80			

	Half Time / Full Time Results								
Team	H/H	H/D	H/A	D/H	D/D	D/A	A/H	A/D	A/A
A	2	0	0	1	0	0	0	0	2
B	0	1	0	0	1	0	0	0	0
C	1	0	0	1	1	1	0	0	2
D	0	1	0	0	1	2	0	0	2
Total	3	2	0	2	3	3	0	0	6
%	15.79	10.53	0.00	10.53	15.79	15.79	0.00	0.00	31.58
Odds	6.33	9.50	N/A	9.50	6.33	6.33	N/A	N/A	3.17

Goals

	Match goals				
Team	1 or More	Ov. 1.5	Ov. 2.5	Ov. 3.5	Ov. 4.5
A	5	4	4	3	1
B	1	1	0	0	0
C	5	4	2	0	0
D	6	5	2	0	0
Total	17	14	8	3	1
%	89.47	73.68	42.11	15.79	5.26
Odds	1.12	1.36	2.38	6.33	19.00

	Clean Sheet		Scored	
Team	Yes	No	Yes	No
A	1	4	4	1
B	1	1	1	1
C	4	2	5	1
D	2	4	6	0
Total	8	11	16	3
%	42.11	57.89	84.21	15.79
Odds	2.38	1.73	1.19	6.33

	Won By			Draw	Lost By		
Team	+3	2	1	0	1	2	+3
A	0	1	1	0	0	1	2
B	0	0	0	2	0	0	0
C	0	2	1	1	2	0	0
D	0	1	3	2	0	0	0
Total	0	4	5	5	2	1	2
%	0.00	21.05	26.32	26.32	10.53	5.26	10.53
Odds	N/A	4.75	3.80	3.80	9.50	19.00	9.50

Bookings

	Yellow Cards		Red Cards		Betfair Points		
Team	F	A	F	A	0-5	6-8	9+
A	10	9	0	0	1	2	2
B	3	1	1	1	1	0	1
C	17	7	1	2	1	2	3
D	8	7	0	0	2	4	0
Total	38	24	2	3	5	8	6
				%	26.31	42.10	31.58
				Odds	3.80	2.37	3.17

Corners

	Corner Supremacy			Corner Numbers		
Team	Won	Draw	Lost	0-9	10-12	13+
A	0	0	5	1	0	4
B	1	0	1	1	0	1
C	1	0	5	2	2	2
D	3	0	3	0	1	5
Total	5	0	14	4	3	12
%	26.32	0.00	73.68	21.05	15.79	63.16
Odds	3.80	N/A	1.36	4.75	6.33	1.58

Summary

- Four of their 12 away matches (33% / odds 3.00) against grade C and D opposition were won A/A.
- 11 of their away games (58% / odds 1.72) finished with under 2.5 goals.
- Villa kept a clean sheet in six of 12 away matches (50% / odds 2.00) at grade C and D sides.
- Villa lost three of five away matches (60% / odds 1.66) against grade A opposition by two goals or more.
- Only five away matches (26% / odds 3.80) featured two or less bookings.
- In corner superiority against grade A, B and C opposition, Villa lost 11 of 13 away matches (85% / odds 1.18).
- Villa went on to win all six away matches they were leading at half-time.

BIRMINGHAM CITY (Grade C)

Season record

	Home					Away						
Pld	Won	Draw	Lost	F	A	Won	Draw	Lost	F	A	GD	Points
38	8	9	2	19	13	5	2	12	19	34	-9	50

Top Scorers

Player	Started	Goals	First	Last	Each Way	Anytime
Cameron Jerome	32	10	4	1*	8	8

*Last Scorer – 1-0 victory away to Stoke.

Scoring

	Matches Scored In	Clean Sheets	Won to Nil	Both Teams Scored	A Goal 1st Half	A Goal 2nd Half
Home	14	8	4	10	9	13
Away	15	3	3	12	14	16
Total	29	11	7	22	23	29

Match Goal Times

	First Goal of Match			
	1st 10 mins	Before 27 mins	After 27 mins	No Goals
Home	1	4	5	5
Away	6	9	5	5
Total	7	13	10	10
%	18.42	34.21	26.32	26.32
Break-Even Odds	5.43	2.92	3.80	3.80

	Last Goal of Match			
	Before 75 mins	After 75 mins	90+ min Goal	No Goals
Home	5	8	2	6
Away	3	13	5	3
Total	8	21	7	9
%	21.05	55.26	18.42	23.68
Break-Even Odds	4.75	1.81	5.43	4.22

Half Time/Full time

	Half Time / Full Time Results								
	H/H	H/D	H/A	D/H	D/D	D/A	A/H	A/D	A/A
Home	5	1	0	2	7	1	1	1	1
%	26.32	5.26	0.00	10.53	36.84	5.26	5.26	5.26	5.26
Break-Even Odds	3.80	19.00	N/A	9.50	2.71	19.00	19.00	19.00	19.00
Away	8	0	1	3	1	2	1	1	2
%	42.11	0.00	5.26	15.79	5.26	10.53	5.26	5.26	10.53
Break-Even Odds	2.38	N/A	19.00	6.33	19.00	9.50	19.00	19.00	9.50

Goals

	Match goals				
	1 or More	Ov. 1.5	Ov. 2.5	Ov. 3.5	Ov. 4.5
Home	15	10	6	1	0
Away	19	14	12	5	2
Total	34	24	18	6	2
%	89.47	63.16	47.37	15.79	5.26
Break-Even Odds	1.12	1.58	2.11	6.33	19.00

Bookings

	Yellow Cards		Red Cards		Betfair Points		
	F	A	F	A	0-5	6-8	9+
Home	36	35	1	3	3	8	8
%	N/A	N/A	N/A	N/A	15.79	42.11	42.11
Break-Even Odds	N/A	N/A	N/A	N/A	6.33	2.38	2.38
Away	38	19	0	0	6	10	3
%	N/A	N/A	N/A	N/A	31.58	52.63	15.79
Break-Even Odds	N/A	N/A	N/A	N/A	3.17	1.90	6.33

Corner Superiority

	Corner Supremacy			Corner Numbers		
	Won	Draw	Lost	0-9	10-12	13+
Home	7	1	11	9	2	8
%	36.84	5.26	57.89	47.37	10.53	42.11
Break-Even Odds	2.71	19.00	1.73	2.11	9.50	2.38
Away	5	1	13	4	11	4
%	26.32	5.26	68.42	21.05	57.89	21.05
Break-Even Odds	3.80	19.00	1.46	4.75	1.73	4.75

Summary

- Both teams scored in 22 (57.89%) of all matches.
- Ten matches were 0-0 at H-T (26.32%) in all games played.
- In the 16 matches where Birmingham were drawing at half-time, they went on win the match in just four of them (25%).
- Only nine matches (21.68%) had two or less bookings.
- Lost corner supremacy in 24 matches (63.16%).

Home (Graded Analysis)

	Home Record					
Team	Won	Draw	Lost	F	A	Pts
A	0	5	0	3	3	5
B	0	2	1	3	4	2
C	4	1	0	6	2	13
D	4	1	1	7	4	13
Total	8	9	2	19	13	33
%	42.11	47.37	10.53			
Odds	2.38	2.11	9.50			

	Half Time / Full Time Results								
Team	H/H	H/D	H/A	D/H	D/D	D/A	A/H	A/D	A/A
A	0	1	0	0	4	0	0	0	0
B	0	0	0	0	1	1	0	1	0
C	3	0	0	1	1	0	0	0	0
D	2	0	0	1	1	0	1	0	1
Total	5	1	0	2	7	1	1	1	1
%	26.32	5.26	0.00	10.53	36.84	5.26	5.26	5.26	5.26
Odds	3.80	19.00	N/A	9.50	2.71	19.00	19.00	19.00	19.00

Goals

	Match goals				
Team	1 or More	Ov. 1.5	Ov. 2.5	Ov. 3.5	Ov. 4.5
A	3	3	0	0	0
B	3	2	1	1	0
C	4	2	2	0	0
D	5	3	3	0	0
Total	15	10	6	1	0
%	78.95	52.63	31.58	5.26	0.00
Odds	1.27	1.90	3.17	19.00	N/A

	Clean Sheet		Scored	
Team	Yes	No	Yes	No
A	2	3	3	2
B	0	3	2	1
C	3	2	4	1
D	3	3	5	1
Total	8	11	14	5
%	42.11	57.89	73.68	26.32
Odds	2.38	1.73	1.36	3.80

	Won By			Draw	Lost By		
Team	+3	2	1	0	1	2	+3
A	0	0	0	5	0	0	0
B	0	0	0	2	1	0	0
C	0	0	4	1	0	0	0
D	0	0	4	1	1	0	0
Total	0	0	8	9	2	0	0
%	0.00	0.00	42.10	47.37	10.53	0.00	0.00
Odds	N/A	N/A	2.37	2.11	9.50	N/A	N/A

Bookings

	Yellow Cards		Red Cards		Betfair Points		
Team	F	A	F	A	0-5	6-8	9+
A	11	7	1	2	0	1	4
B	6	5	0	0	1	1	1
C	9	10	0	1	1	3	1
D	10	13	0	0	1	3	2
Total	36	35	1	3	3	8	8
				%	15.79	42.11	42.11
				Odds	6.33	2.38	2.38

Corners

	Corner Supremacy			Corner Numbers		
Team	Won	Draw	Lost	0-9	10-12	13+
A	1	0	4	2	1	2
B	2	0	1	2	0	1
C	1	1	3	2	0	3
D	3	0	3	3	1	2
Total	7	1	11	9	2	8
%	36.84	5.26	57.89	47.37	10.53	42.11
Odds	2.71	19.00	1.73	2.11	9.50	2.38

Summary

- Five of 11 home games (45% / odds 2.22) against grade C and D sides finished half-time/full-time H/H.
- 13 of 19 home games (68% / odds 1.47) finished under 2.5 goals.
- Birmingham kept a clean sheet in six of 11 home games (54% / odds 1.85) against grade C and D opposition.
- Only three home matches (16% / odds 6.25) played at St Andrew's featured 0-5 Betfair booking points.
- 8 home matches (42% / odds 2.38) featured 13 or more corners.

Away (Graded Analysis)

	Away Record					
Team	Won	Draw	Lost	F	A	Pts
A	0	1	4	4	14	1
B	0	1	2	2	4	1
C	1	0	4	4	9	3
D	4	0	2	9	7	12
Total	5	2	12	19	34	17
%	26.32	10.53	63.16			
Odds	3.80	9.50	1.58			

	Half Time / Full Time Results								
Team	H/H	H/D	H/A	D/H	D/D	D/A	A/H	A/D	A/A
A	4	0	0	0	0	0	0	1	0
B	0	0	0	2	1	0	0	0	0
C	3	0	0	0	0	1	1	0	0
D	1	0	1	1	0	1	0	0	2
Total	8	0	1	3	1	2	1	1	2
%	42.11	0.00	5.26	15.79	5.26	10.53	5.26	5.26	10.53
Odds	2.38	N/A	19.00	6.33	19.00	9.50	19.00	19.00	9.50

Goals

	Match goals				
Team	1 or More	Ov. 1.5	Ov. 2.5	Ov. 3.5	Ov. 4.5
A	5	5	5	3	1
B	3	2	1	0	0
C	5	4	3	1	0
D	6	4	4	1	1
Total	19	15	13	5	2
%	100.00	78.95	68.42	26.32	10.53
Odds	1.00	1.27	1.46	3.80	9.50

	Clean Sheet		Scored	
Team	Yes	No	Yes	No
A	0	5	3	2
B	0	3	2	1
C	1	4	4	1
D	2	4	6	0
Total	3	16	15	4
%	15.79	84.21	78.95	21.05
Odds	6.33	1.19	1.27	4.75

	Won By			Draw	Lost By		
Team	+3	2	1	0	1	2	+3
A	0	0	0	1	1	1	2
B	0	0	0	1	2	0	0
C	0	0	1	0	2	2	0
D	0	0	4	0	2	0	0
Total	0	0	5	2	7	3	2
%	0.00	0.00	26.32	10.53	36.84	15.79	10.53
Odds	N/A	N/A	3.80	9.50	2.71	6.33	9.50

Bookings

	Yellow Cards		Red Cards		Betfair Points		
Team	F	A	F	A	0-5	6-8	9+
A	8	3	0	0	2	3	0
B	7	3	0	0	0	2	1
C	8	6	0	0	2	2	1
D	13	7	0	0	2	3	1
Total	36	19	0	0	6	10	3
				%	31.58	52.63	15.79
				Odds	3.17	1.90	6.33

Corners

	Corner Supremacy			Corner Numbers		
Team	Won	Draw	Lost	0-9	10-12	13+
A	0	0	5	0	4	1
B	0	0	3	0	3	0
C	3	0	2	2	1	2
D	2	1	3	2	3	1
Total	5	1	13	4	11	4
%	26.32	5.26	68.42	21.05	57.89	21.05
Odds	3.80	19.00	1.46	4.75	1.73	4.75

Summary

- In eight of 19 away matches (42% / odds 2.37) Birmingham lost half time/full time H/H.
- They scored in five of eight away matches (62% / odds 1.60) against grade A and B opposition.
- Birmingham lost five of 19 matches (26% / odds 3.80) by two goals or more.
- Only three of their away matches (16% / odds 6.25) featured five or more bookings.
- They only won five of 11 away matches (45% / odds 2.20) in terms of corner superiority against grade C and D opposition

BLACKBURN ROVERS (Grade C)

Season record

	Home					Away						
Pld	Won	Draw	Lost	F	A	Won	Draw	Lost	F	A	GD	Points
38	10	6	3	28	18	3	5	11	13	37	-14	50

Top Scorers

Player	Started	Goals	First	Last	Each Way	Anytime
David Dunn	20	9	4	3*	8	8

Scoring

	Matches Scored In	Clean Sheets	Won to Nil	Both Teams Scored	A Goal 1st Half	A Goal 2nd Half
Home	13	7	3	10	14	14
Away	11	6	3	8	14	14
Total	24	13	6	18	28	28

***Last Scorer** – David Dunn, 1-0 victory away to Burnley.

Match Goal Times

	First Goal of Match			
	1st 10 mins	Before 27 mins	After 27 mins	No Goals
Home	6	12	2	5
Away	3	9	5	5
Total	9	21	7	10
%	23.68	55.26	18.42	26.32
Break-Even Odds	4.22	1.81	5.43	3.80

	Last Goal of Match			
	Before 75 mins	After 75 mins	90+ min Goal	No Goals
Home	4	10	3	5
Away	6	8	1	5
Total	10	18	4	10
%	26.32	47.37	10.53	26.32
Break-Even Odds	3.80	2.11	9.50	3.80

Half Time/Full time

	Half Time / Full Time Results								
	H/H	H/D	H/A	D/H	D/D	D/A	A/H	A/D	A/A
Home	7	0	0	2	5	0	1	1	3
%	36.84	0.00	0.00	10.53	26.32	0.00	5.26	5.26	15.79
Break-Even Odds	2.71	N/A	N/A	9.50	3.80	N/A	19.00	19.00	6.33
Away	9	0	0	2	3	1	0	2	2
%	47.37	0.00	0.00	10.53	15.79	5.26	0.00	10.53	10.53
Break-Even Odds	2.11	N/A	N/A	9.50	6.33	19.00	N/A	9.50	9.50

Goals

	Match goals				
	1 or More	Ov. 1.5	Ov. 2.5	Ov. 3.5	Ov. 4.5
Home	15	14	10	5	2
Away	16	14	10	4	3
Total	31	28	20	9	5
%	81.58	73.68	52.63	23.68	13.16
Break-Even Odds	1.23	1.36	1.90	4.22	7.60

Bookings

	Yellow Cards		Red Cards		Betfair Points		
	F	A	F	A	0-5	6-8	9+
Home	28	38	1	1	4	9	6
%	N/A	N/A	N/A	N/A	21.05	47.37	31.58
Break-Even Odds	N/A	N/A	N/A	N/A	4.75	2.11	3.17
Away	31	22	1	1	8	6	5
%	N/A	N/A	N/A	N/A	42.11	31.58	26.32
Break-Even Odds	N/A	N/A	N/A	N/A	2.38	3.17	3.80

Corner Superiority

	Corner Supremacy			Corner Numbers		
	Won	Draw	Lost	0-9	10-12	13+
Home	10	2	7	9	6	4
%	52.63	10.53	36.84	47.37	31.58	21.05
Break-Even Odds	1.90	9.50	2.71	2.11	3.17	4.75
Away	6	3	10	11	3	5
%	31.58	15.79	52.63	57.89	15.79	26.32
Break-Even Odds	3.17	6.33	1.90	1.73	6.33	3.80

Summary

- In 20 out of their 38 (52.63%) matches, no further goals were scored after 75 minutes.
- Ten of their matches were 0-0 at H-T (26.32%), out of all games played.
- In the 13 matches Blackburn were drawing at half-time, they went on win the match in just three of them (23.08%).
- Only nine of their total matches (23.68%) had 13+ corners.
- 20 out of 38 of their matches (52.63%) had nine or less corners in the match.
- Nine out of their 38 matches (24%) had four or more goals.

Home (Graded Analysis)

	Home Record					
Team	Won	Draw	Lost	F	A	Pts
A	1	3	1	3	4	6
B	1	0	2	4	6	3
C	2	3	0	6	3	9
D	6	0	0	15	5	18
Total	10	6	3	28	18	36
%	52.63	31.58	15.79			
Odds	1.90	3.17	6.33			

	Half Time / Full Time Results								
Team	H/H	H/D	H/A	D/H	D/D	D/A	A/H	A/D	A/A
A	0	0	0	1	2	0	0	1	1
B	0	0	0	1	0	0	0	0	2
C	2	0	0	0	3	0	0	0	0
D	5	0	0	0	0	0	1	0	0
Total	7	0	0	2	5	0	1	1	3
%	36.84	0.00	0.00	10.53	26.32	0.00	5.26	5.26	15.79
Odds	2.71	N/A	N/A	9.50	3.80	N/A	19.00	19.00	6.33

Goals

	Match goals				
Team	1 or More	Ov. 1.5	Ov. 2.5	Ov. 3.5	Ov. 4.5
A	3	3	1	0	0
B	3	3	2	1	1
C	3	3	2	1	0
D	6	5	5	3	1
Total	15	14	10	5	2
%	78.95	73.68	52.63	26.32	10.53
Odds	1.27	1.36	1.90	3.80	9.50

	Clean Sheet		Scored	
Team	Yes	No	Yes	No
A	2	3	2	3
B	0	3	2	1
C	3	2	3	2
D	2	4	6	0
Total	7	12	13	6
%	36.84	63.16	68.42	31.58
Odds	2.71	1.58	1.46	3.17

	Won By			Draw	Lost By		
Team	+3	2	1	0	1	2	+3
A	0	0	1	3	0	1	0
B	0	0	1	1	1	1	0
C	0	1	1	2	0	0	0
D	1	2	3	0	0	0	0
Total	1	3	6	6	1	2	0
%	5.26	15.79	31.58	26.32	5.26	10.53	0.00
Odds	19.00	6.33	3.17	3.80	19.00	9.50	N/A

Bookings

	Yellow Cards		Red Cards		Betfair Points		
Team	F	A	F	A	0-5	6-8	9 +
A	6	6	0	0	2	3	0
B	5	6	1	0	1	0	2
C	6	13	0	0	0	4	1
D	11	13	0	1	1	2	3
Total	28	38	1	1	4	9	6
				%	21.05	47.37	31.58
				Odds	4.75	2.11	3.17

Corners

	Corner Supremacy			Corner Numbers		
Team	Won	Draw	Lost	0-9	10-12	13+
A	1	0	4	3	0	2
B	3	0	0	2	1	0
C	2	1	2	3	2	0
D	4	1	1	1	3	2
Total	10	2	7	9	6	4
%	52.63	10.53	36.84	47.37	31.58	21.05
Odds	1.90	9.50	2.71	2.11	3.17	4.75

Summary

- Blackburn did not lose at home to grade C or D opposition.
- Seven of 11 home games (64% / odds 1.56) against grade C and D sides finished half-time/full-time H/H.
- They kept a clean sheet in five of 13 home games (38% / odds 2.63) against grade A, B and C sides.
- Only one game in 11 at home (9% / odds 11.10) against grade C and D sides featured 0-5 Betfair booking points.
- Won corner superiority in nine of 14 home matches (64% / odds 1.56) against grade B, C and D sides.
- Won all seven home matches against grade C and D sides when leading at half-time.

Away (Graded Analysis)

	Away Record					
Team	Won	Draw	Lost	F	A	Pts
A	0	0	5	4	19	0
B	1	0	2	2	6	3
C	0	1	4	2	10	1
D	2	4	0	5	2	10
Total	3	5	11	13	37	14
%	15.79	26.32	57.89			
Odds	6.33	3.80	1.73			

	Half Time / Full Time Results								
Team	H/H	H/D	H/A	D/H	D/D	D/A	A/H	A/D	A/A
A	4	0	0	1	0	0	0	0	0
B	2	0	0	0	0	1	0	0	0
C	3	0	0	1	1	0	0	0	0
D	0	0	0	0	2	0	0	2	2
Total	9	0	0	2	3	1	0	2	2
%	47.37	0.00	0.00	10.53	15.79	5.26	0.00	10.53	10.53
Odds	2.11	N/A	N/A	9.50	6.33	19.00	N/A	9.50	9.50

Goals

	Match goals				
Team	1 or More	Ov. 1.5	Ov. 2.5	Ov. 3.5	Ov. 4.5
A	5	5	4	3	3
B	3	2	2	1	0
C	4	4	4	0	0
D	4	3	0	0	0
Total	16	14	10	4	3
%	84.21	73.68	52.63	21.05	15.79
Odds	1.19	1.36	1.90	4.75	6.33

	Clean Sheet		Scored	
Team	Yes	No	Yes	No
A	0	5	3	2
B	1	2	2	1
C	1	4	2	3
D	4	2	4	2
Total	6	13	11	8
%	31.58	68.42	57.89	42.11
Odds	3.17	1.46	1.73	2.38

	Won By			Draw	Lost By		
Team	+3	2	1	0	1	2	+3
A	0	0	0	0	1	1	3
B	0	0	1	0	0	1	1
C	0	0	0	1	2	0	2
D	0	1	1	4	0	0	0
Total	0	1	2	5	3	2	6
%	0.00	5.26	10.53	26.32	15.79	10.53	31.58
Odds	N/a	19.00	9.50	3.80	6.33	9.50	3.17

Bookings

	Yellow Cards		Red Cards		Betfair Points		
Team	F	A	F	A	0–5	6–8	9+
A	10	3	0	0	4	0	1
B	3	3	0	0	1	2	0
C	7	6	1	0	2	2	1
D	11	10	0	1	1	2	3
Total	31	22	1	1	8	6	5
				%	42.11	31.58	26.32
				Odds	2.38	3.17	3.80

Corners

	Corner Supremacy			Corner Numbers		
Team	Won	Draw	Lost	0–9	10–12	13+
A	1	0	4	5	0	0
B	1	0	2	1	1	1
C	3	1	1	1	1	3
D	2	2	2	4	1	1
Total	7	3	9	11	3	5
%	36.84	15.79	47.37	57.89	15.79	26.32
Odds	2.71	6.33	2.11	1.73	6.33	3.80

Summary

- Blackburn lost H/H nine of 13 away matches (69% / odds 1.44) against grade A, B and C opposition.
- All seven games away to grade D sides finished with under 2.5 goals.
- Blackburn lost eight of 13 home matches (62% / odds 1.6) against grade A, B and C opposition by two goals or more.
- Only two of 13 home matches against grade A, B and C sides (15% / odds 6.67) featured nine or more Betfair booking points.
- 11 of their total 19 away matches (58% / odds 1.73) featured under ten corners.

BOLTON WANDERERS (Grade D)

Season record

	Home					Away						
Pld	Won	Draw	Lost	F	A	Won	Draw	Lost	F	A	GD	Points
38	6	6	7	26	31	4	3	12	16	36	-25	39

Top Scorers

Player	Started	Goals	First	Last	Each Way	Anytime
Ivan Klasnic	12	8	4	1	6	7
Matt Taylor	29	8	1	4	7	7
Kevin Davies	37	7	3	0	7	7

Scoring

	Matches Scored In	Clean Sheets	Won to Nil	Both Teams Scored	A Goal 1st Half	A Goal 2nd Half
Home	12	4	3	9	16	14
Away	10	1	0	10	16	16
Total	22	5	3	19	32	30

Match Goal Times

	First Goal of Match			
	1st 10 mins	Before 27 mins	After 27 mins	No Goals
Home	3	8	8	3
Away	7	9	7	3
Total	10	17	15	6
%	26.32	44.74	39.47	15.79
Break-Even Odds	3.80	2.24	2.53	6.33

	Last Goal of Match			
	Before 75 mins	After 75 mins	90+ min Goal	No Goals
Home	2	12	1	5
Away	3	13	0	3
Total	5	25	1	8
%	13.16	65.79	2.63	21.05
Break-Even Odds	7.60	1.52	38.02	4.75

Half Time/Full time

	Half Time / Full Time Results								
	H/H	H/D	H/A	D/H	D/D	D/A	A/H	A/D	A/A
Home	5	2	0	1	4	1	0	0	6
%	26.32	10.53	0.00	5.26	21.05	5.26	0.00	0.00	31.58
Break-Even Odds	3.80	9.50	N/A	19.00	4.75	19.00	N/A	N/A	3.17
Away	9	0	1	2	1	0	1	2	3
%	47.37	0.00	5.26	10.53	5.26	0.00	5.26	10.53	15.79
Break-Even Odds	2.11	N/A	19.00	9.50	19.00	N/A	19.00	9.50	6.33

Goals

	Match goals				
	1 or More	Ov. 1.5	Ov. 2.5	Ov. 3.5	Ov. 4.5
Home	18	14	11	10	3
Away	18	15	10	4	3
Total	36	29	21	14	6
%	94.74	76.32	55.26	36.84	15.79
Break-Even Odds	1.06	1.31	1.81	2.71	6.33

Bookings

	Yellow Cards		Red Cards		Betfair Points		
	F	A	F	A	0-5	6-8	9+
Home	34	28	2	1	5	8	6
%	N/A	N/A	N/A	N/A	26.32	42.11	31.58
Break-Even Odds	N/A	N/A	N/A	N/A	3.80	2.38	3.17
Away	41	20	3	0	6	6	7
%	N/A	N/A	N/A	N/A	31.58	31.58	36.84
Break-Even Odds	N/A	N/A	N/A	N/A	3.17	3.17	2.71

Corner Superiority

	Corner Supremacy			Corner Numbers		
	Won	Draw	Lost	0-9	10-12	13+
Home	3	3	13	5	5	9
%	15.79	15.79	68.42	26.32	26.32	47.37
Break-Even Odds	6.33	6.33	1.46	3.80	3.80	2.11
Away	3	0	16	7	5	7
%	15.79	0.00	84.21	36.84	26.32	36.84
Break-Even Odds	6.33	N/A	1.19	2.71	3.80	2.71

Summary

- The last goal of the match was scored after 75 minutes in 63.16% of all of Bolton's matches.
- Bolton only kept five clean sheets (13.16%) all season.
- 14 matches out of their full 38 (36.84%) finished with four or more goals; backing over 3.5 goals at above 2.75 would have yielded a level stake profit last season.
- 36 out their 38 matches (94.74%) contained at least one goal.
- In the 13 matches Bolton were winning at half-time, they went on win the match in eight (61.54%) of them.
- Only nine of their matches (21.68%) had two or less bookings.
- They lost corner supremacy in 29 matches (76.32%).

Home (Graded Analysis)

	Home Record					
Team	Won	Draw	Lost	F	A	Pts
A	0	1	4	5	16	1
B	1	1	1	5	5	4
C	2	2	2	6	6	8
D	3	2	0	10	4	11
Total	6	6	7	26	31	24
%	31.58	31.58	36.84			
Odds	3.17	3.17	2.71			

	Half Time / Full Time Results								
Team	H/H	H/D	H/A	D/H	D/D	D/A	A/H	A/D	A/A
A	0	0	0	0	1	1	0	0	3
B	1	0	0	0	1	0	0	0	1
C	1	0	0	1	2	0	0	0	2
D	3	2	0	0	0	0	0	0	0
Total	5	2	0	1	4	1	0	0	6
%	26.32	10.53	0.00	5.26	21.05	5.26	0.00	0.00	31.58
Odds	3.80	9.50	N/A	19.00	4.75	19.00	N/A	N/A	3.17

Goals

	Match goals				
Team	1 or More	Ov. 1.5	Ov. 2.5	Ov. 3.5	Ov. 4.5
A	5	5	4	4	2
B	3	2	2	2	1
C	5	4	2	1	0
D	5	3	3	3	0
Total	18	14	11	10	3
%	94.74	73.68	57.89	52.63	15.79
Odds	1.06	1.36	1.73	1.90	6.33

	Clean Sheet		Scored	
Team	Yes	No	Yes	No
A	0	5	2	3
B	0	3	2	1
C	1	5	3	3
D	3	2	5	0
Total	4	15	12	7
%	21.05	78.95	63.16	36.84
Odds	4.75	1.27	1.58	2.71

	Won By			Draw	Lost By		
Team	+3	2	1	0	1	2	+3
A	0	0	0	1	1	1	2
B	0	0	1	1	1	0	0
C	0	1	1	2	1	1	0
D	1	0	2	2	0	0	0
Total	1	1	4	6	3	2	2
%	5.26	5.26	21.05	31.58	15.79	10.53	10.53
Odds	19.00	19.00	4.75	3.17	6.33	9.50	9.50

Bookings

	Yellow Cards		Red Cards		Betfair Points		
Team	F	A	F	A	0–5	6–8	9+
A	8	7	2	1	1	1	3
B	7	2	0	0	1	2	0
C	13	10	0	0	1	3	2
D	6	9	0	0	2	2	1
Total	34	28	2	1	5	8	6
				%	26.32	42.11	31.58
				Odds	3.80	2.38	3.17

Corners

	Corner Supremacy			Corner Numbers		
Team	Won	Draw	Lost	0–9	10–12	13+
A	1	0	4	1	0	4
B	0	1	2	1	1	1
C	1	1	4	2	3	1
D	1	1	3	1	1	3
Total	3	3	13	5	5	9
%	15.79	15.79	68.42	26.32	26.32	47.37
Odds	6.33	6.33	1.46	3.80	3.80	2.11

Summary

- Bolton were undefeated at home against grade D sides.
- They lost four of eight home games (50% / odds 2.00) against grade A and B sides half-time/full-time A/A.
- Nine of their 13 home games (69% / odds 1.58) against grade A, B and D sides featured over 3.5 goals.
- Only five of their 19 home matches (26% / odds 3.80) featured two or less bookings.
- They lost corner superiority in ten of 14 home matches (71% / odds 1.40) against grade A, B and C sides.

Away (Graded Analysis)

	Away Record					
Team	Won	Draw	Lost	F	A	Pts
A	0	0	5	3	11	0
B	0	0	3	1	8	0
C	3	1	2	7	11	10
D	1	2	2	5	6	5
Total	4	3	12	16	36	15
%	21.05	15.79	63.16			
Odds	4.75	6.33	1.58			

	Half Time / Full Time Results								
Team	H/H	H/D	H/A	D/H	D/D	D/A	A/H	A/D	A/A
A	4	0	0	0	0	0	1	0	0
B	2	0	0	1	0	0	0	0	0
C	2	0	1	0	0	0	0	1	2
D	1	0	0	1	1	0	0	1	1
Total	9	0	1	2	1	0	1	2	3
%	47.37	0.00	5.26	10.53	5.26	0.00	5.26	10.53	15.79
Odds	2.11	N/A	19.00	9.50	19.00	N/A	19.00	9.50	6.33

Goals

	Match goals				
Team	1 or More	Ov. 1.5	Ov. 2.5	Ov. 3.5	Ov. 4.5
A	5	4	2	1	1
B	3	2	1	1	1
C	6	6	5	1	0
D	4	3	2	1	1
Total	18	15	10	4	3
%	94.74	78.95	52.63	21.05	15.79
Odds	1.06	1.27	1.90	4.75	6.33

	Clean Sheet		Scored	
Team	Yes	No	Yes	No
A	0	5	2	3
B	0	3	1	2
C	0	6	4	2
D	1	4	3	2
Total	1	18	10	9
%	5.26	94.74	52.63	47.37
Odds	19.00	1.06	1.90	2.11

	Won By			Draw	Lost By		
Team	+3	2	1	0	1	2	+3
A	0	0	0	0	2	3	0
B	0	0	0	0	1	1	1
C	0	0	3	1	0	0	2
D	0	0	1	2	2	0	0
Total	0	0	4	3	5	4	3
%	0.00	0.00	21.05	15.79	26.32	21.05	15.79
Odds	N/A	N/A	4.75	6.33	3.80	4.75	6.33

Bookings

	Yellow Cards		Red Cards		Betfair Points		
Team	F	A	F	A	0-5	6-8	9 +
A	12	3	0	0	2	2	1
B	8	2	0	1	0	1	2
C	17	8	2	0	1	2	3
D	4	7	0	0	3	1	1
Total	41	20	2	1	6	6	7
				%	31.58	31.58	36.84
				Odds	3.17	3.17	2.71

Corners

	Corner Supremacy			Corner Numbers		
Team	Won	Draw	Lost	0-9	10-12	13+
A	0	0	5	2	1	2
B	0	0	3	2	0	1
C	1	0	5	3	2	1
D	2	0	3	0	2	3
Total	3	0	16	7	5	7
%	15.79	0.00	84.21	36.84	26.32	36.84
Odds	6.33	N/A	1.19	2.71	3.80	2.71

Summary

- Nine of their 14 away matches (64% / odds 1.56) against grade A, B and C sides were lost H/H.
- They kept only one clean sheet in 19 away games.
- They lost five of eight away matches (62% / odds 1.60) against grade A and B opposition by two goals or more.
- Only three of their 14 away matches against grade A, B and C sides (21% / odds 4.65) featured two or less bookings.
- They won only one of 14 away matches (7% / odds 14.00) in the corner superiority market against sides graded A, B and C.

CHELSEA (Grade A)

Season record

	Home					Away						
Pld	Won	Draw	Lost	F	A	Won	Draw	Lost	F	A	GD	Points
38	17	1	1	68	14	10	4	5	35	18	71	86

Top Scorers

Player	Started	Goals	First	Last	Each Way	Anytime
Didier Drogba	31	29	8	9	17	20
Frank Lampard	36	22	3	8	12	14
Florent Malouda	26	12	3	3	7	9
Nicolas Anelka	31	11	7	2*	9	9

Scoring

	Matches Scored In	Clean Sheets	Won to Nil	Both Teams Scored	A Goal 1st Half	A Goal 2nd Half
Home	19	11	11	8	17	17
Away	18	7	6	12	18	17
Total	37	18	17	20	35	34

***Last Scorer** – Nicolas Anelka, 1-0 victory at home to Bolton.

Match Goal Times

	First Goal of Match			
	1st 10 mins	Before 27 mins	After 27 mins	No Goals
Home	6	12	5	2
Away	2	9	9	1
Total	8	21	14	3
%	21.05	55.26	36.84	7.89
Break-Even Odds	4.75	1.81	2.71	12.67

	Last Goal of Match			
	Before 75 mins	After 75 mins	90+ min Goal	No Goals
Home	5	12	8	2
Away	7	10	5	2
Total	12	22	13	4
%	31.58	57.89	34.21	10.53
Break-Even Odds	3.17	1.73	2.92	9.50

Half Time/Full time

	Half Time / Full Time Results								
	H/H	H/D	H/A	D/H	D/D	D/A	A/H	A/D	A/A
Home	12	0	0	4	1	1	1	0	0
%	63.16	0.00	0.00	21.05	5.26	5.26	5.26	0.00	0.00
Break-Even Odds	1.58	N/A	N/A	4.75	19.00	19.00	19.00	N/A	N/A
Away	2	1	1	3	2	1	0	1	8
%	10.53	5.26	5.26	15.79	10.53	5.26	0.00	5.26	42.11
Break-Even Odds	9.50	19.00	19.00	6.33	9.50	19.00	N/A	19.00	2.38

Goals

	Match goals				
	1 or More	Ov. 1.5	Ov. 2.5	Ov. 3.5	Ov. 4.5
Home	19	17	15	9	8
Away	18	18	12	4	1
Total	37	35	27	13	9
%	97.37	92.11	71.05	34.21	23.68
Break-Even Odds	1.03	1.09	1.41	2.92	4.22

Bookings

	Yellow Cards		Red Cards		Betfair Points		
	F	A	F	A	0-5	6-8	9+
Home	17	30	2	1	11	3	5
%	N/A	N/A	N/A	N/A	57.89	15.79	26.32
Break-Even Odds	N/A	N/A	N/A	N/A	1.73	6.33	3.80
Away	39	29	3	1	4	7	8
%	N/A	N/A	N/A	N/A	21.05	36.84	42.11
Break-Even Odds	N/A	N/A	N/A	N/A	4.75	2.71	2.38

Corner Superiority

	Corner Supremacy			Corner Numbers		
	Won	Draw	Lost	0-9	10-12	13+
Home	14	0	5	7	5	7
%	73.68	0.00	26.32	36.84	26.32	36.84
Break-Even Odds	1.36	N/A	3.80	2.71	3.80	2.71
Away	13	2	4	4	5	10
%	68.42	10.53	21.05	21.05	26.32	52.63
Break-Even Odds	1.46	9.50	4.75	4.75	3.80	1.90

Summary

- The last goal of the match was scored after 75 minutes in 57.89% of all of Chelsea's matches.
- 27 matches out of Chelsea's full 38 (71.05%) finished with three or more goals; backing over 2.5 goals at above 1.41 would have yielded a level stake profit last season.
- Just three of all their matches were 0-0 at half-time (7.9%).
- A total of 13 games out of their full 38 (34.21%) had a goal in the 90+ injury time bracket.
- In the 21 matches Chelsea led at half time, they went on to win the match in 20 of them (95.23%).
- They achieved corner supremacy in 27 out their 38 games (71.05%).
- Nine or less corners occurred in just 11 of their matches (28.95%).

Home (Graded Analysis)

	Home Record					
Team	Won	Draw	Lost	F	A	Pts
A	3	0	1	7	4	9
B	2	1	0	13	4	7
C	6	0	0	28	4	18
D	6	0	0	20	2	18
Total	17	1	1	68	14	52
%	89.47	5.26	5.26			
Odds	1.12	19.00	19.00			

	Half Time / Full Time Results								
Team	H/H	H/D	H/A	D/H	D/D	D/A	A/H	A/D	A/A
A	1	0	0	2	0	1	0	0	0
B	2	0	0	0	1	0	0	0	0
C	4	0	0	1	0	0	1	0	0
D	5	0	0	1	0	0	0	0	0
Total	12	0	0	4	1	1	1	0	0
%	63.16	0.00	0.00	21.05	5.26	5.26	5.26	0.00	0.00
Odds	1.58	N/A	N/A	4.75	19.00	19.00	19.00	N/A	N/A

Goals

	Match goals				
Team	1 or More	Ov. 1.5	Ov. 2.5	Ov. 3.5	Ov. 4.5
A	4	3	1	1	1
B	3	3	3	2	2
C	6	6	6	4	4
D	6	5	5	2	1
Total	19	17	15	9	8
%	100.00	89.47	78.95	47.37	42.11
Odds	1.00	1.12	1.27	2.11	2.38

	Clean Sheet		Scored	
Team	Yes	No	Yes	No
A	3	1	4	0
B	1	2	3	0
C	3	3	6	0
D	4	2	6	0
Total	11	8	19	0
%	57.89	42.11	100.00	0.00
Odds	1.73	2.38	1.00	N/A

	Won By			Draw	Lost By		
Team	+3	2	1	0	1	2	+3
A	0	2	1	0	0	1	0
B	2	0	0	1	0	0	0
C	5	0	1	0	0	0	0
D	3	0	3	0	0	0	0
Total	10	2	5	1	0	1	0
%	52.63	10.53	26.32	5.26	0.00	5.26	0.00
Odds	1.90	9.50	3.80	19.00	N/A	19.00	N/A

Bookings

	Yellow Cards		Red Cards		Betfair Points		
Team	F	A	F	A	0-5	6-8	9+
A	9	7	2	0	1	1	2
B	3	5	0	0	2	0	1
C	1	7	0	0	5	1	0
D	4	9	0	1	3	1	2
Total	17	28	2	1	11	3	5
				%	57.89	15.79	26.32
				Odds	1.73	6.33	3.80

Corners

	Corner Supremacy			Corner Numbers		
Team	Won	Draw	Lost	0-9	10-12	13+
A	1	0	3	2	1	1
B	3	0	0	1	0	2
C	6	0	0	2	2	2
D	4	0	2	2	2	2
Total	14	0	5	7	5	7
%	73.68	0.00	26.32	36.84	26.32	36.84
Odds	1.36	N/A	3.80	2.71	3.80	2.71

Summary

- 11 of Chelsea's 15 home games (73% / odds 1.36) against grade B, C and D sides finished half-time/full-time H/H.
- 14 of their 15 home matches (93% / odds 1.07) against grade B, C and D sides finished with over 2.5 goals.
- They kept a clean sheet in eight of their 15 home matches (53% / odds 1.88) against grade B, C and D sides.
- They won by three goals or more in ten of their 15 home matches (67% / odds 1.50) against grade B, C and D sides.
- Ten of 15 home matches (67% / odds 1.50) against grade B, C and D sides featured two bookings or less.
- They won corner superiority in 14 of their total of 19 home matches (74% / odds 1.36).

Away (Graded Analysis)

	Away Record					
Team	Won	Draw	Lost	F	A	Pts
A	3	0	1	8	3	9
B	0	0	3	3	6	0
C	3	3	0	9	4	12
D	4	1	1	15	5	13
Total	10	4	5	35	18	34
%	52.63	21.05	26.32			
Odds	1.90	4.75	3.80			

	Half Time / Full Time Results								
Team	H/H	H/D	H/A	D/H	D/D	D/A	A/H	A/D	A/A
A	0	0	0	1	0	0	0	0	3
B	1	0	0	2	0	0	0	0	0
C	0	1	1	0	1	1	0	1	1
D	1	0	0	0	1	0	0	0	4
Total	2	1	1	3	2	1	0	1	8
%	10.53	5.26	5.26	15.79	10.53	5.26	0.00	5.26	42.11
Odds	9.50	19.00	19.00	6.33	9.50	19.00	N/A	19.00	2.38

Goals

	Match goals				
Team	1 or More	Ov. 1.5	Ov. 2.5	Ov. 3.5	Ov. 4.5
A	4	4	3	0	0
B	3	3	3	0	0
C	5	5	2	1	0
D	6	6	4	3	1
Total	18	18	12	4	1
%	94.74	94.74	63.16	21.05	5.26
Odds	1.06	1.06	1.58	4.75	19.00

	Clean Sheet		Scored	
Team	Yes	No	Yes	No
A	2	2	4	0
B	0	3	3	0
C	2	4	5	1
D	3	3	6	0
Total	7	12	18	1
%	36.84	63.16	94.74	5.26
Odds	2.71	1.58	1.06	19.00

	Won By			Draw	Lost By		
Team	+3	2	1	0	1	2	+3
A	1	1	1	0	1	0	0
B	0	0	0	0	3	0	0
C	0	2	1	3	0	0	0
D	2	1	1	1	0	1	0
Total	3	4	3	4	4	1	0
%	15.79	21.05	15.79	21.05	21.05	5.26	0.00
Odds	6.33	4.75	6.33	4.75	4.75	19.00	N/A

Bookings

	Yellow Cards		Red Cards		Betfair Points		
Team	F	A	F	A	0-5	6-8	9 +
A	11	7	0	0	0	3	1
B	7	5	1	0	0	2	1
C	11	10	1	0	2	1	3
D	10	7	1	1	2	1	3
Total	39	29	3	1	4	7	8
				%	21.05	36.84	42.11
				Odds	4.75	2.71	2.38

Corners

	Corner Supremacy			Corner Numbers		
Team	Won	Draw	Lost	0-9	10-12	13+
A	0	1	3	2	0	2
B	2	0	1	0	1	2
C	5	1	0	0	2	4
D	6	0	0	2	2	2
Total	13	2	4	4	5	10
%	68.42	10.53	21.05	21.05	26.32	52.63
Odds	1.46	9.50	4.75	4.75	3.80	1.90

Summary

- Chelsea won A/A three out of four away matches against grade A sides.
- Ten of their 13 away matches (77% / 1.30) against sides graded A, B and D featured over 2.5 goals.
- They drew three of six matches away to grade C sides.
- Zero out of seven away matches against grade A and B sides featured two bookings or less.
- In the corner superiority markets, 13 of their 15 away matches (87% / 1.15) were won against grade B, C and D sides.

EVERTON (Grade B)

Season record

	Home					Away						
Pld	Won	Draw	Lost	F	A	Won	Draw	Lost	F	A	GD	Points
38	11	6	2	35	21	5	7	7	25	28	11	61

Top Scorers

Player	Started	Goals	First	Last	Each Way	Anytime
Louis Saha	26	13	3	5	7	9
Tim Cahill	33	8	4	2	4	6
Mikel Arteta	11	6	3	2	5	5
Diniyar Bilyaletdinov	16	6	4	2*	6	6

Scoring

	Matches Scored In	Clean Sheets	Won to Nil	Both Teams Scored	A Goal 1st Half	A Goal 2nd Half
Home	18	6	6	12	12	16
Away	14	5	3	11	15	15
Total	32	11	9	23	27	31

***Last Scorer** – Diniyar Bilyaletdinov, 1-0 victory at home to Portsmouth.

Match Goal Times

	First Goal of Match			
	1st 10 mins	Before 27 mins	After 27 mins	No Goals
Home	2	9	3	7
Away	2	9	6	4
Total	4	18	9	11
%	10.53	47.37	23.68	28.95
Break-Even Odds	9.50	2.11	4.22	3.45

	Last Goal of Match			
	Before 75 mins	After 75 mins	90+ min Goal	No Goals
Home	3	13	6	3
Away	7	8	3	4
Total	10	21	9	7
%	26.32	55.26	23.68	18.42
Break-Even Odds	3.80	1.81	4.22	5.43

Half Time/Full time

	Half Time / Full Time Results								
	H/H	H/D	H/A	D/H	D/D	D/A	A/H	A/D	A/A
Home	4	2	0	6	4	0	1	0	2
%	21.05	10.53	0.00	31.58	21.05	0.00	5.26	0.00	10.53
Break-Even Odds	4.75	9.50	N/A	3.17	4.75	N/A	19.00	N/A	9.50
Away	5	1	0	1	4	1	1	2	4
%	26.32	5.26	0.00	5.26	21.05	5.26	5.26	10.53	21.05
Break-Even Odds	3.80	19.00	N/A	19.00	4.75	19.00	19.00	9.50	4.75

Goals

	Match goals				
	1 or More	Ov. 1.5	Ov. 2.5	Ov. 3.5	Ov. 4.5
Home	19	18	9	5	2
Away	17	13	11	7	4
Total	36	31	20	12	6
%	94.74	81.58	52.63	31.58	15.79
Break-Even Odds	1.06	1.23	1.90	3.17	6.33

Bookings

	Yellow Cards		Red Cards		Betfair Points		
	F	A	F	A	0-5	6-8	9+
Home	20	38	1	4	7	4	8
%	N/A	N/A	N/A	N/A	36.84	21.05	42.11
Break-Even Odds	N/A	N/A	N/A	N/A	2.71	4.75	2.38
Away	37	24	1	1	8	5	6
%	N/A	N/A	N/A	N/A	42.11	26.32	31.58
Break-Even Odds	N/A	N/A	N/A	N/A	2.38	3.80	3.17

Corner Superiority

	Corner Supremacy			Corner Numbers		
	Won	Draw	Lost	0-9	10-12	13+
Home	12	0	7	5	7	7
%	63.16	0.00	36.84	26.32	36.84	36.84
Break-Even Odds	1.58	N/A	2.71	3.80	2.71	2.71
Away	8	2	9	7	6	6
%	42.11	10.53	47.37	36.84	31.58	31.58
Break-Even Odds	2.38	9.50	2.11	2.71	3.17	3.17

Summary

- 20 matches out of Everton's full 38 (52.63%) finished with three or more goals; backing over 2.5 goals at above 1.55 would have yielded a level stake profit last season.
- 12 matches out of Everton's full 38 (31.58%) finished with four or more goals; backing over 3.5 goals at above 2.40 would have yielded a level stake profit last season.
- Both teams scored in the match in 23 (60.53%) out of Everton's 38 matches, the highest rate in the Premier League last season.
- Just four of their total matches (10.53%) had a goal in the first ten minutes of the match, joint lowest in the Premier League last season.
- A total of nine Everton games (23.68%) had a goal in the 90+ injury time window.
- 15 of Everton's total matches (39.47%) had two or less bookings.

Home (Graded Analysis)

	Home Record					
Team	Won	Draw	Lost	F	A	Pts
A	3	0	2	8	10	9
B	0	2	0	3	3	2
C	3	3	0	11	5	12
D	5	1	0	13	3	16
Total	11	6	2	35	21	39
%	57.89	31.58	10.53			
Odds	1.73	3.17	9.50			

	Half Time / Full Time Results								
Team	H/H	H/D	H/A	D/H	D/D	D/A	A/H	A/D	A/A
A	1	0	0	2	0	0	0	0	2
B	0	1	0	0	1	0	0	0	0
C	2	1	0	0	2	0	1	0	0
D	1	0	0	4	1	0	0	0	0
Total	4	2	0	6	4	0	1	0	2
%	21.05	10.53	0.00	31.58	21.05	0.00	5.26	0.00	10.53
Odds	4.75	9.50	N/A	3.17	4.75	N/A	19.00	N/A	9.50

Goals

	Match goals				
Team	1 or More	Ov. 1.5	Ov. 2.5	Ov. 3.5	Ov. 4.5
A	5	5	3	2	1
B	2	2	1	1	0
C	6	6	3	1	0
D	6	5	3	2	2
Total	19	18	10	6	3
%	100.00	94.74	52.63	31.58	15.79
Odds	1.00	1.06	1.90	3.17	6.33

	Clean Sheet		Scored	
Team	Yes	No	Yes	No
A	1	4	4	1
B	0	2	2	0
C	2	4	6	0
D	3	3	6	0
Total	6	13	18	1
%	31.58	68.42	94.74	5.26
Odds	3.17	1.46	1.06	19.00

	Won By			Draw	Lost By		
Team	+3	2	1	0	1	2	+3
A	0	2	1	0	0	1	1
B	0	0	0	2	0	0	0
C	1	1	1	3	0	0	0
D	1	2	2	1	0	0	0
Total	2	5	4	6	0	1	1
%	10.53	26.32	21.05	31.58	0.00	5.26	5.26
Odds	9.50	3.80	4.75	3.17	N/A	19.00	19.00

Bookings

	Yellow Cards		Red Cards		Betfair Points		
Team	F	A	F	A	0–5	6–8	9+
A	7	3	0	0	3	1	1
B	5	7	1	1	0	0	2
C	4	13	0	0	2	3	1
D	4	15	0	3	2	0	4
Total	20	38	1	4	7	4	8
				%	36.84	21.05	42.11
				Odds	2.71	4.75	2.38

Corners

	Corner Supremacy			Corner Numbers		
Team	Won	Draw	Lost	0–9	10–12	13+
A	2	0	3	0	2	3
B	0	0	2	2	0	0
C	4	0	2	1	4	1
D	6	0	0	2	1	3
Total	12	0	7	5	7	7
%	63.16	0.00	36.84	26.32	36.84	36.84
Odds	1.58	N/A	2.71	3.80	2.71	2.71

Summary

- Four out of Everton's six home games (67% / odds 1.50) against grade D sides finished half-time/full-time D/H.
- They only kept one clean sheet in seven home matches (14% / odds 7.10) against grade A and B sides.
- Everton won by two goals or more in five of 12 home matches (42% / odds 2.40) against grades C and D sides.
- Three of their five home matches against grade A sides featured two bookings or less.
- They won ten of 12 matches (84% / odds 1.20) in corner superiority markets against grade C and D sides.

Away (Graded Analysis)

	Away Record					
Team	Won	Draw	Lost	F	A	Pts
A	1	2	2	7	9	5
B	0	1	1	3	4	1
C	2	3	1	9	8	9
D	2	1	3	6	7	7
Total	5	7	7	25	28	22
%	26.32	36.84	36.84			
Odds	3.80	2.71	2.71			

	Half Time / Full Time Results								
Team	H/H	H/D	H/A	D/H	D/D	D/A	A/H	A/D	A/A
A	1	0	0	1	2	0	0	0	1
B	1	0	0	0	0	0	0	1	0
C	0	1	0	0	1	0	1	1	2
D	3	0	0	0	1	1	0	0	1
Total	5	1	0	1	4	1	1	2	4
%	26.32	5.26	0.00	5.26	21.05	5.26	5.26	10.53	21.05
Odds	3.80	19.00	N/A	19.00	4.75	19.00	19.00	9.50	4.75

Goals

	Match goals				
Team	1 or More	Ov. 1.5	Ov. 2.5	Ov. 3.5	Ov. 4.5
A	5	4	4	4	3
B	2	2	2	1	0
C	5	5	5	3	2
D	5	2	2	2	2
Total	17	13	13	10	7
%	89.47	68.42	68.42	52.63	36.84
Odds	1.12	1.46	1.46	1.90	2.71

	Clean Sheet		Scored	
Team	Yes	No	Yes	No
A	1	4	3	2
B	0	2	2	0
C	1	5	5	1
D	3	3	4	2
Total	5	14	14	5
%	26.32	73.68	73.68	26.32
Odds	3.80	1.36	1.36	3.80

	Won By			Draw	Lost By		
Team	+3	2	1	0	1	2	+3
A	0	1	0	2	1	0	1
B	0	0	0	1	1	0	0
C	0	0	2	3	1	0	0
D	0	0	2	1	3	0	0
Total	0	1	4	7	6	0	1
%	0.00	5.26	21.05	36.84	31.58	0.00	5.26
Odds	N/A	19.00	4.75	2.71	3.17	N/A	19.00

Bookings

	Yellow Cards		Red Cards		Betfair Points		
Team	F	A	F	A	0-5	6-8	9 +
A	9	9	1	1	2	1	2
B	6	3	0	0	0	1	1
C	11	6	0	0	3	1	2
D	11	6	0	0	3	2	1
Total	37	24	1	1	8	5	6
				%	42.11	26.32	31.58
				Odds	2.38	3.80	3.17

Corners

	Corner Supremacy			Corner Numbers		
Team	Won	Draw	Lost	0-9	10-12	13+
A	1	1	3	1	1	3
B	1	0	1	0	0	2
C	1	0	5	4	1	1
D	5	0	1	2	4	0
Total	8	1	10	7	6	6
%	42.11	5.26	52.63	36.84	31.58	31.58
Odds	2.38	19.00	1.90	2.71	3.17	3.17

Summary

- Everton lost three out of six away matches against grade D sides.
- 11 of their 13 away matches (85% / 1.18) at grade A, B and C sides featured over 2.5 goals.
- They only won one away game by two goals or more.
- They only lost one away game by three goals or more.
- Two of their seven away matches (29% / odds 3.50) against grade A and B sides featured two or less bookings.
- Five of their seven away matches (71% / 1.40) against grade A and B sides featured over 13 corners.

FULHAM (Grade C)

Season record

	Home					Away						
Pld	Won	Draw	Lost	F	A	Won	Draw	Lost	F	A	GD	Points
38	11	3	5	27	15	1	7	11	12	31	-7	46

Top Scorers

Player	Started	Goals	First	Last	Each Way	Anytime
Bobby Zamora	27	8	5	2	8	8
Clint Dempsey	27	7	1	5	3	6
Damien Duff	30	6	0	3	4	5

Scoring

	Matches Scored In	Clean Sheets	Won to Nil	Both Teams Scored	A Goal 1st Half	A Goal 2nd Half
Home	13	8	6	7	14	15
Away	9	4	1	8	13	13
Total	22	12	7	15	27	28

Match Goal Times

	First Goal of Match			
	1st 10 mins	Before 27 mins	After 27 mins	No Goals
Home	3	6	8	5
Away	2	11	2	6
Total	5	17	10	11
%	13.16	44.74	26.32	28.95
Break-Even Odds	7.60	2.24	3.80	3.45

	Last Goal of Match			
	Before 75 mins	After 75 mins	90+ min Goal	No Goals
Home	5	10	2	4
Away	7	6	2	6
Total	12	16	4	10
%	31.58	42.11	10.53	26.32
Break-Even Odds	3.17	2.38	9.50	3.80

Half Time/Full time

	Half Time / Full Time Results								
	H/H	H/D	H/A	D/H	D/D	D/A	A/H	A/D	A/A
Home	6	0	0	2	2	2	3	1	3
%	31.58	0.00	0.00	10.53	10.53	10.53	15.79	5.26	15.79
Break-Even Odds	3.17	N/A	N/A	9.50	9.50	9.50	6.33	19.00	6.33
Away	8	1	0	1	6	0	2	0	1
%	42.11	5.26	0.00	5.26	31.58	0.00	10.53	0.00	5.26
Break-Even Odds	2.38	19.00	N/A	19.00	3.17	N/A	9.50	N/A	19.00

Goals

	Match goals				
	1 or More	Ov. 1.5	Ov. 2.5	Ov. 3.5	Ov. 4.5
Home	17	13	9	2	1
Away	16	14	8	4	1
Total	33	27	17	6	2
%	86.84	71.05	44.74	15.79	5.26
Break-Even Odds	1.15	1.41	2.24	6.33	19.00

Bookings

	Yellow Cards		Red Cards		Betfair Points		
	F	A	F	A	0-5	6-8	9+
Home	15	19	0	2	13	4	2
%	N/A	N/A	N/A	N/A	68.42	21.05	10.53
Break-Even Odds	N/A	N/A	N/A	N/A	1.46	4.75	9.50
Away	31	24	1	0	10	5	4
%	N/A	N/A	N/A	N/A	52.63	26.32	21.05
Break-Even Odds	N/A	N/A	N/A	N/A	1.90	3.80	4.75

Corner Superiority

	Corner Supremacy			Corner Numbers		
	Won	Draw	Lost	0-9	10-12	13+
Home	12	3	4	9	8	2
%	63.16	15.79	21.05	47.37	42.11	10.53
Break-Even Odds	1.58	6.33	4.75	2.11	2.38	9.50
Away	5	2	12	6	6	7
%	26.32	10.53	63.16	31.58	31.58	36.84
Break-Even Odds	3.80	9.50	1.58	3.17	3.17	2.71

Summary

- Fulham only scored in 22 of all their matches (57.89%), the second lowest record in the Premier League last season.
- Both teams scored in the match in 15 (39.47%) out of Fulham's total 38 matches, the lowest in the Premier League last season.
- 11 of their matches were 0-0 at half-time (28.95%).
- In the nine matches Fulham led at half-time, they went on win the match in seven of them (77.78%).
- 23 of their total 38 matches (60.53%) had two or less bookings.
- Only six of all their matches (15.79%) contained four or more goals; backing under 3.5 at 1.20 or higher would have yielded a profit.

Home (Graded Analysis)

	Home Record					
Team	Won	Draw	Lost	F	A	Pts
A	2	0	3	7	6	6
B	1	1	1	2	3	4
C	4	0	1	9	4	12
D	4	2	0	9	2	14
Total	11	3	5	27	15	36
%	57.89	15.79	26.32			
Odds	1.73	6.33	3.80			

	Half Time / Full Time Results								
Team	H/H	H/D	H/A	D/H	D/D	D/A	A/H	A/D	A/A
A	1	0	0	1	0	1	0	0	2
B	0	0	0	0	1	0	1	0	1
C	3	0	0	0	0	1	1	0	0
D	2	0	0	1	1	0	1	1	0
Total	6	0	0	2	2	2	3	1	3
%	31.58	0.00	0.00	10.53	10.53	10.53	15.79	5.26	15.79
Odds	3.17	N/A	N/A	9.50	9.50	9.50	6.33	19.00	6.33

Goals

	Match goals				
Team	1 or More	Ov. 1.5	Ov. 2.5	Ov. 3.5	Ov. 4.5
A	5	4	3	1	0
B	2	2	1	0	0
C	5	3	3	1	0
D	5	4	2	0	0
Total	17	13	9	2	0
%	89.47	68.42	47.37	10.53	0.00
Odds	1.12	1.46	2.11	9.50	N/A

	Clean Sheet		Scored	
Team	Yes	No	Yes	No
A	1	4	3	2
B	1	2	1	2
C	2	3	4	1
D	4	2	5	1
Total	8	11	13	6
%	42.11	57.89	68.42	31.58
Odds	2.38	1.73	1.46	3.17

	Won By			Draw	Lost By		
Team	+3	2	1	0	1	2	+3
A	1	1	0	0	2	1	0
B	0	0	1	1	0	1	0
C	1	0	3	0	1	0	0
D	1	1	2	2	0	0	0
Total	3	2	6	3	3	2	0
%	15.79	10.53	31.58	15.79	15.79	10.53	0.00
Odds	6.33	9.50	3.17	6.33	6.33	9.50	N/A

Bookings

	Yellow Cards		Red Cards		Betfair Points		
Team	F	A	F	A	0–5	6–8	9 +
A	5	1	0	2	3	1	1
B	2	2	0	0	3	0	0
C	3	6	0	0	3	2	0
D	5	10	0	0	4	1	1
Total	15	19	0	2	13	4	2
				%	68.42	21.05	10.53
				Odds	1.46	4.75	9.50

Corners

	Corner Supremacy			Corner Numbers		
Team	Won	Draw	Lost	0–9	10–12	13+
A	2	1	2	3	2	0
B	3	0	0	2	1	0
C	3	1	1	2	3	0
D	4	1	1	2	2	2
Total	12	3	4	9	8	2
%	63.16	15.79	21.05	47.37	42.11	10.53
Odds	1.58	6.33	4.75	2.11	2.38	9.50

Summary

- Five of Fulham's 11 home games (45% / odds 2.20) against grade C and D sides finished half-time/full-time H/H.
- They conceded in nine of 13 home matches (69% / odds 1.45) against grade A, B and C sides.
- They only won three home matches in 11 (25% / odds 4.00) by two goals or more against grade C and D sides.
- 13 of all 19 Fulham home matches (68% / odds 1.47) featured two bookings or less.
- Only two of their 19 home matches (11% / odds 9.50) featured over 13 corners.

Away (Graded Analysis)

	Away Record					
Team	Won	Draw	Lost	F	A	Pts
A	0	2	3	3	11	2
B	0	0	3	1	6	0
C	0	2	3	4	8	2
D	1	3	2	4	6	6
Total	1	7	11	12	31	10
%	5.26	36.84	57.89			
Odds	19.00	2.71	1.73			

	Half Time / Full Time Results								
Team	H/H	H/D	H/A	D/H	D/D	D/A	A/H	A/D	A/A
A	1	0	0	1	2	0	1	0	0
B	2	0	0	0	0	0	1	0	0
C	3	1	0	0	1	0	0	0	0
D	2	0	0	0	3	0	0	0	1
Total	8	1	0	1	6	0	2	0	1
%	42.11	5.26	0.00	5.26	31.58	0.00	10.53	0.00	5.26
Odds	2.38	19.00	N/A	19.00	3.17	N/A	9.50	N/A	19.00

Goals

	Match goals				
Team	1 or More	Ov. 1.5	Ov. 2.5	Ov. 3.5	Ov. 4.5
A	4	4	4	2	0
B	3	3	1	0	0
C	4	3	2	2	1
D	5	4	2	0	0
Total	16	14	9	4	1
%	84.21	73.68	47.37	21.05	5.26
Odds	1.19	1.36	2.11	4.75	19.00

	Clean Sheet		Scored	
Team	Yes	No	Yes	No
A	1	4	2	3
B	0	3	1	2
C	1	4	2	3
D	2	4	4	2
Total	4	15	9	10
%	21.05	78.95	47.37	52.63
Odds	4.75	1.27	2.11	1.90

	Won By			Draw	Lost By		
Team	+3	2	1	0	1	2	+3
A	0	0	0	2	1	0	2
B	0	0	0	0	1	2	0
C	0	0	0	2	2	1	0
D	0	0	1	3	1	1	0
Total	0	0	1	7	5	4	2
%	0.00	0.00	5.26	36.84	26.32	21.05	10.53
Odds	N/A	N/A	19.00	2.71	3.80	4.75	9.50

Bookings

	Yellow Cards		Red Cards		Betfair Points		
Team	F	A	F	A	0-5	6-8	9 +
A	9	5	0	0	3	2	0
B	4	2	0	0	2	1	0
C	8	9	1	0	2	1	2
D	10	8	0	0	3	1	2
Total	31	24	1	0	10	5	4
				%	52.63	26.32	21.05
				Odds	1.90	3.80	4.75

Corners

	Corner Supremacy			Corner Numbers		
Team	Won	Draw	Lost	0-9	10-12	13+
A	0	0	5	1	2	2
B	0	0	3	0	1	2
C	3	1	1	3	1	1
D	2	1	3	2	2	2
Total	5	2	12	6	6	7
%	26.32	10.53	63.16	31.58	31.58	36.84
Odds	3.80	9.50	1.58	3.16	3.16	2.72

Summary

- Seven of Fulham's 14 away matches (50% / odds 2.00) against grade B, C and D sides were lost half-time/full-time H/H.
- They only scored in five of 13 away matches (38% / odds 2.65) against sides graded A, B and C.
- They only won one game away all season.
- Ten of their total 19 away matches (53% / odds 1.90) featured two or less bookings.
- Fulham lost corner superiority in all eight away matches against grade A and B sides.

LIVERPOOL (Grade A)

Season record

	Home					Away						
Pld	Won	Draw	Lost	F	A	Won	Draw	Lost	F	A	GD	Points
38	13	3	3	43	15	5	6	8	18	20	26	63

Top Scorers

Player	Started	Goals	First	Last	Each Way	Anytime
Fernando Torres	20	18	8	4	11	12
Steven Gerrard	32	9	4	2	5	8
Dirk Kuyt	35	9	4	2	8	8
Yossi Benayoun	19	6	2	3	3	4

Scoring

	Matches Scored In	Clean Sheets	Won to Nil	Both Teams Scored	A Goal 1st Half	A Goal 2nd Half
Home	17	10	9	8	14	17
Away	10	7	3	7	9	13
Total	27	17	12	15	23	30

Match Goal Times

	First Goal of Match			
	1st 10 mins	Before 27 mins	After 27 mins	No Goals
Home	4	9	5	5
Away	2	4	5	10
Total	6	13	10	15
%	15.79	34.21	26.32	39.47
Break-Even Odds	6.33	2.92	3.80	2.53

	Last Goal of Match			
	Before 75 mins	After 75 mins	90+ min Goal	No Goals
Home	8	9	5	2
Away	4	9	4	6
Total	12	18	9	8
%	31.58	47.37	23.68	21.05
Break-Even Odds	3.17	2.11	4.22	4.75

Half Time/Full time

	Half Time / Full Time Results								
	H/H	H/D	H/A	D/H	D/D	D/A	A/H	A/D	A/A
Home	10	0	1	3	2	0	0	1	2
%	52.63	0.00	5.26	15.79	10.53	0.00	0.00	5.26	10.53
Break-Even Odds	1.90	N/A	19.00	6.33	9.50	N/A	N/A	19.00	9.50
Away	4	0	0	4	6	4	0	0	1
%	21.05	0.00	0.00	21.05	31.58	21.05	0.00	0.00	5.26
Break-Even Odds	4.75	N/A	N/A	4.75	3.17	4.75	N/A	N/A	19.00

Goals

	Match goals				
	1 or More	Ov. 1.5	Ov. 2.5	Ov. 3.5	Ov. 4.5
Home	18	17	12	7	2
Away	15	11	6	4	2
Total	33	28	18	11	4
%	86.84	73.68	47.37	28.95	10.53
Break-Even Odds	1.15	1.36	2.11	3.45	9.50

Bookings

	Yellow Cards		Red Cards		Betfair Points		
	F	A	F	A	0-5	6-8	9+
Home	22	43	2	3	7	5	7
%	N/A	N/A	N/A	N/A	36.84	26.32	36.84
Break-Even Odds	N/A	N/A	N/A	N/A	2.71	3.80	2.71
Away	34	32	3	1	6	4	9
%	N/A	N/A	N/A	N/A	31.58	21.05	47.37
Break-Even Odds	N/A	N/A	N/A	N/A	3.17	4.75	2.11

Corner Superiority

	Corner Supremacy			Corner Numbers		
	Won	Draw	Lost	0-9	10-12	13+
Home	15	1	3	5	7	7
%	78.95	5.26	15.79	26.32	36.84	36.84
Break-Even Odds	1.27	19.00	6.33	3.80	2.71	2.71
Away	12	2	5	10	4	5
%	63.16	10.53	26.32	52.63	21.05	26.32
Break-Even Odds	1.58	9.50	3.80	1.90	4.75	3.80

Summary

- Liverpool only scored in 27 of all their matches (71.05%), the lowest of the Grade A sides in the Premier League last season.
- Both teams scored in the match in 15 (39.47%) out of Liverpool's total 38 matches, the lowest in the Premier League last season.
- 15 of all their matches were 0-0 at half-time (39.47%), the second highest number in the Premier League last season.
- In the 12 matches Liverpool led at half-time, they went on to win the match in 11 of them (91.67%).
- They achieved corner supremacy in 27 out of all 38 games (71.05%).

Home (Graded Analysis)

	Home Record					
Team	Won	Draw	Lost	F	A	Pts
A	1	1	2	5	6	4
B	2	0	1	4	3	6
C	4	2	0	14	3	14
D	6	0	0	20	3	18
Total	13	3	3	43	15	42
%	68.42	15.79	15.79			
Odds	1.46	6.33	6.33			

	Half Time / Full Time Results								
Team	H/H	H/D	H/A	D/H	D/D	D/A	A/H	A/D	A/A
A	0	0	1	1	1	0	0	0	1
B	1	0	0	1	0	0	0	0	1
C	4	0	0	0	1	0	0	1	0
D	5	0	0	1	0	0	0	0	0
Total	10	0	1	3	2	0	0	1	2
%	52.63	0.00	5.26	15.79	10.53	0.00	0.00	5.26	10.53
Odds	1.90	N/A	19.00	6.33	9.50	N/A	N/A	19.00	9.50

Goals

	Match goals				
Team	1 or More	Ov. 1.5	Ov. 2.5	Ov. 3.5	Ov. 4.5
A	4	4	2	1	0
B	3	2	2	2	1
C	5	5	5	2	0
D	6	6	4	3	2
Total	18	17	13	8	3
%	94.74	89.47	68.42	42.11	15.79
Odds	1.06	1.12	1.46	2.38	6.33

	Clean Sheet		Scored	
Team	Yes	No	Yes	No
A	1	3	3	1
B	2	1	3	0
C	4	2	5	1
D	3	3	6	0
Total	10	9	17	2
%	52.63	47.37	89.47	10.53
Odds	1.90	2.11	1.12	9.50

	Won By			Draw	Lost By		
Team	+3	2	1	0	1	2	+3
A	0	1	0	1	1	1	0
B	0	1	1	0	0	1	0
C	3	0	1	2	0	0	0
D	3	2	1	0	0	0	0
Total	6	4	3	3	1	2	0
%	31.58	21.05	15.79	15.79	5.26	10.53	0.00
Odds	3.17	4.75	6.33	6.33	19.00	9.50	N/A

Bookings

	Yellow Cards		Red Cards		Betfair Points		
Team	F	A	F	A	0-5	6-8	9+
A	8	8	1	1	1	1	2
B	6	8	1	1	0	0	3
C	3	14	0	0	3	2	1
D	3	13	0	1	3	2	1
Total	20	43	2	3	7	5	7
				%	36.84	26.32	36.84
				Odds	2.71	3.80	2.71

Corners

	Corner Supremacy			Corner Numbers		
Team	Won	Draw	Lost	0-9	10-12	13+
A	3	0	1	2	1	1
B	1	1	1	1	0	2
C	5	0	1	1	4	1
D	6	0	0	1	2	3
Total	15	1	3	5	7	7
%	78.95	5.26	15.79	26.32	36.84	36.84
Odds	1.27	19.00	6.33	3.80	2.71	2.71

Summary

- Nine of Liverpool's 12 home games (75% / odds 1.33) against grade C and D sides finished half-time/full-time H/H.
- Nine of their 12 home games (75% / odds 1.33) against grade C and D sides featured over 2.5 goals.
- Eight of their 12 home games (67% / 1.50) against grade C and D sides were won by two goals or more.
- Only two of their 12 home games (17% / odds 6.00) against grade C and D sidesfeatured nine or more Betfair booking points.
- They won corner superiority in 15 of their 19 home games (79% / odds 1.27).

Away (Graded Analysis)

Team	Away Record					
	Won	Draw	Lost	F	A	Pts
A	0	1	3	1	5	1
B	2	0	1	4	2	6
C	1	3	2	6	8	6
D	2	2	2	7	5	8
Total	5	6	8	18	20	21
%	26.32	31.58	42.11			
Odds	3.80	3.17	2.38			

Team	Half Time / Full Time Results								
	H/H	H/D	H/A	D/H	D/D	D/A	A/H	A/D	A/A
A	0	0	0	3	1	0	0	0	0
B	1	0	0	0	0	1	0	0	1
C	1	0	0	1	3	1	0	0	0
D	2	0	0	0	2	2	0	0	0
Total	4	0	0	4	6	4	0	0	1
%	21.05	0.00	0.00	21.05	31.58	21.05	0.00	0.00	5.26
Odds	4.75	N/A	N/A	4.75	3.17	4.75	N/A	N/A	19.00

Goals

	Match goals				
Team	1 or More	Ov. 1.5	Ov. 2.5	Ov. 3.5	Ov. 4.5
A	3	2	1	0	0
B	3	2	1	0	0
C	5	4	2	2	1
D	4	3	2	2	1
Total	15	11	6	4	2
%	78.95	57.89	31.58	21.05	10.53
Odds	1.27	1.73	3.17	4.75	9.50

	Clean Sheet		Scored	
Team	Yes	No	Yes	No
A	1	3	1	3
B	2	1	3	0
C	1	5	4	2
D	3	3	2	4
Total	7	12	10	9
%	36.84	63.16	52.63	47.37
Odds	2.71	1.58	1.90	2.11

	Won By			Draw	Lost By		
Team	+3	2	1	0	1	2	+3
A	0	0	0	1	2	1	0
B	0	1	1	0	1	0	0
C	0	0	1	3	1	1	0
D	1	0	1	2	1	1	0
Total	1	1	3	6	5	3	0
%	5.26	5.26	15.79	31.58	26.32	15.79	0.00
Odds	19.00	19.00	6.33	3.17	3.80	6.33	N/A

Bookings

	Yellow Cards		Red Cards		Betfair Points		
Team	F	A	F	A	0–5	6–8	9+
A	12	7	0	0	1	0	3
B	4	5	0	0	2	0	1
C	7	10	2	0	1	3	2
D	11	10	1	1	2	1	3
Total	34	32	3	1	6	4	9
				%	31.58	21.05	47.37
				Odds	3.17	4.75	2.11

Corners

	Corner Supremacy			Corner Numbers		
Team	Won	Draw	Lost	0–9	10–12	13+
A	3	0	1	2	0	2
B	1	0	2	0	2	1
C	2	2	2	5	1	0
D	6	0	0	3	1	2
Total	12	2	5	10	4	5
%	63.16	10.53	26.32	52.63	21.05	26.32
Odds	1.58	9.50	3.80	1.90	4.75	3.80

Summary

- Five of Liverpool's 12 away games (42% / odds 2.40) against C and D sides finished in half-time/full-time result of D/D.
- 13 of their 19 away matches (68% / odds 1.46) finished with under 2.5 goals.
- Five of their 12 away matches (42% / odds 2.40) against grade C and D sides finished in a draw.
- Three of their four away matches against grade A sides featured nine or more Betfair booking points.
- Liverpool won corner superiority in 12 of their 19 away matches (63% / odds 1.58).

MANCHESTER CITY (Grade A)

Season record

	Home					Away						
Pld	Won	Draw	Lost	F	A	Won	Draw	Lost	F	A	GD	Points
38	12	4	3	41	20	6	9	4	32	25	28	67

Top Scorers

Player	Started	Goals	First	Last	Each Way	Anytime
Carlos Tévez	32	23	6	7	14	14
Emmanuel Adebayor	25	14	6	5*	10	12
Craig Bellamy	26	10	0	2	4	8

***Last scorer** – Emmanuel Adebayor in a 1-0 victory at home to Wolverhampton and 1-0 victory away to Portsmouth.

Scoring

	Matches Scored In	Clean Sheets	Won to Nil	Both Teams Scored	A Goal 1st Half	A Goal 2nd Half
Home	15	6	5	10	14	15
Away	15	5	3	12	15	14
Total	30	11	8	22	29	29

Match Goal Times

	First Goal of Match			
	1st 10 mins	Before 27 mins	After 27 mins	No Goals
Home	4	8	6	5
Away	5	8	7	4
Total	9	16	13	9
%	23.68	42.11	34.21	23.68
Break-Even Odds	4.22	2.38	2.92	4.22

	Last Goal of Match			
	Before 75 mins	After 75 mins	90+ min Goal	No Goals
Home	5	10	2	4
Away	4	10	5	5
Total	9	20	7	9
%	23.68	52.63	18.42	23.68
Break-Even Odds	4.22	1.90	5.43	4.22

Half Time/Full time

	Half Time / Full Time Results								
	H/H	H/D	H/A	D/H	D/D	D/A	A/H	A/D	A/A
Home	10	1	0	2	2	2	0	1	1
%	52.63	5.26	0.00	10.53	10.53	10.53	0.00	5.26	5.26
Break-Even Odds	1.90	19.00	N/A	9.50	9.50	9.50	N/A	19.00	19.00
Away	3	3	0	1	6	1	0	0	5
%	15.79	15.79	0.00	5.26	31.58	5.26	0.00	0.00	26.32
Break-Even Odds	6.33	6.33	N/A	19.00	3.17	19.00	N/A	N/A	3.80

Goals

	Match goals				
	1 or More	Ov. 1.5	Ov. 2.5	Ov. 3.5	Ov. 4.5
Home	18	15	10	8	5
Away	17	16	9	5	4
Total	35	31	19	13	9
%	92.11	81.58	50.00	34.21	23.68
Break-Even Odds	1.09	1.23	2.00	2.92	4.22

Bookings

	Yellow Cards		Red Cards		Betfair Points		
	F	A	F	A	0-5	6-8	9+
Home	21	47	0	2	6	7	6
%	N/A	N/A	N/A	N/A	31.58	36.84	31.58
Break-Even Odds	N/A	N/A	N/A	N/A	3.17	2.71	3.17
Away	30	38	2	4	5	4	10
%	N/A	N/A	N/A	N/A	26.32	21.05	52.63
Break-Even Odds	N/A	N/A	N/A	N/A	3.80	4.75	1.90

Corner Superiority

	Corner Supremacy			Corner Numbers		
	Won	Draw	Lost	0-9	10-12	13+
Home	16	0	3	3	7	9
%	84.21	0.00	15.79	15.79	36.84	47.37
Break-Even Odds	1.19	N/A	6.33	6.33	2.71	2.11
Away	7	3	9	6	9	4
%	36.84	15.79	47.37	31.58	47.37	21.05
Break-Even Odds	2.71	6.33	2.11	3.17	2.11	4.75

Summary

- 13 of Man City's total matches (34.21%) contained four or more goals in the game and backing over 3.5 goals at odds over 3.0 would have yielded a level stake profit last season.
- Both teams scored in 22 of Man City's total matches (57.89%), the second highest number in the Premier League last season.
- In the 16 matches Man City led at half-time they went on win the match in 15 of them (93.75%).
- Only 11 of their 38 matches (28.95%) had two or less bookings.
- Only nine of their total matches (23.68%) featured nine or less corners.
- Man City won corner supremacy in 20 matches (52.63%), the lowest of the grade A sides.

Home (Graded Analysis)

	Home Record					
Team	Won	Draw	Lost	F	A	Pts
A	2	1	1	6	4	7
B	1	0	2	3	4	3
C	5	1	0	20	8	16
D	4	2	0	12	4	14
Total	12	4	3	41	20	40
%	63.16	21.05	15.79			
Odds	1.58	4.75	6.33			

	Half Time / Full Time Results								
Team	H/H	H/D	H/A	D/H	D/D	D/A	A/H	A/D	A/A
A	1	0	0	1	1	1	0	0	0
B	1	0	0	0	0	1	0	0	1
C	5	0	0	0	1	0	0	0	0
D	3	1	0	1	0	0	0	1	0
Total	10	1	0	2	2	2	0	1	1
%	52.63	5.26	0.00	10.53	10.53	10.53	0.00	5.26	5.26
Odds	1.90	19.00	N/A	9.50	9.50	9.50	N/A	19.00	19.00

Goals

	Match goals				
Team	1 or More	O 1.5	O 2.5	O 3.5	O 4.5
A	3	2	2	1	1
B	3	2	1	1	0
C	6	6	5	5	3
D	6	5	2	1	1
Total	18	15	10	8	5
%	94.74	78.95	52.63	42.11	26.32
Odds	1.06	1.27	1.90	2.38	3.80

	Clean Sheet		Scored	
Team	Yes	No	Yes	No
A	1	3	2	2
B	0	3	1	2
C	1	5	6	0
D	4	2	6	0
Total	6	13	15	4
%	31.58	68.42	78.95	21.05
Odds	3.17	1.46	1.27	4.75

	Won By			Draw	Lost By		
Team	+3	2	1	0	1	2	+3
A	0	1	1	1	1	0	0
B	0	1	0	0	1	1	0
C	2	2	1	1	0	0	0
D	1	2	1	2	0	0	0
Total	3	6	3	4	2	1	0
%	15.79	31.58	15.79	21.05	10.53	5.26	0.00
Odds	6.33	3.17	6.33	4.75	9.50	19.00	N/A

Bookings

	Yellow Cards		Red Cards		Betfair Points		
Team	F	A	F	A	0-5	6-8	9+
A	7	15	0	0	0	1	3
B	4	7	0	0	0	2	1
C	4	11	0	1	4	1	1
D	6	14	0	1	2	3	1
Total	21	47	0	2	6	7	6
				%	31.58	36.84	31.58
				Odds	3.17	2.71	3.17

Corners

	Corner Supremacy			Corner Numbers		
Team	Won	Draw	Lost	0-9	10-12	13+
A	3	0	1	0	1	3
B	3	0	0	1	1	1
C	6	0	0	1	2	3
D	4	0	2	2	3	1
Total	16	0	3	4	7	8
%	84.21	0.00	15.79	21.05	36.84	42.11
Odds	1.19	N/A	6.33	4.75	2.71	2.38

Summary

- Eight of Man City's 12 home games (67% / odds 1.50) against grade C and D sides finished half-time/full-time H/H.
- They kept only two clean sheets in 13 home matches (15% / odds 6.50) against A, B and C sides.
- Seven of their home 12 games (58% / 1.71) against grade C and D sides were won by two goals or more.
- Only two of their 12 home games (17% / odds 6.00) against grade C and D sides featured five or more bookings.
- They won corner superiority in 16 of 19 home games (84% / odds 1.19).

Away (Graded Analysis)

	Away Record					
Team	Won	Draw	Lost	F	A	Pts
A	1	2	1	9	8	5
B	0	1	2	1	6	1
C	2	4	0	7	4	10
D	3	2	1	15	7	11
Total	6	9	4	32	25	27
%	31.58	47.37	21.05			
Odds	3.17	2.11	4.75			

	Half Time / Full Time Results								
Team	H/H	H/D	H/A	D/H	D/D	D/A	A/H	A/D	A/A
A	0	0	0	1	2	1	0	0	0
B	2	1	0	0	0	0	0	0	0
C	0	1	0	0	3	0	0	0	2
D	1	1	0	0	1	0	0	0	3
Total	3	3	0	1	6	1	0	0	5
%	15.79	15.79	0.00	5.26	31.58	5.26	0.00	0.00	26.32
Odds	6.33	6.33	N/A	19.00	3.17	19.00	N/A	N/A	3.80

Goals

	Match goals				
Team	1 or More	Ov. 1.5	Ov. 2.5	Ov. 3.5	Ov. 4.5
A	3	3	3	3	2
B	3	3	1	0	0
C	5	5	1	0	0
D	6	5	4	2	2
Total	17	16	9	5	4
%	89.47	84.21	47.37	26.32	21.05
Odds	1.12	1.19	2.11	3.80	4.75

	Clean Sheet		Scored	
Team	Yes	No	Yes	No
A	1	3	3	1
B	0	3	1	2
C	2	4	5	1
D	2	4	6	0
Total	5	14	15	4
%	26.32	73.68	78.95	21.05
Odds	3.80	1.36	1.27	4.75

	Won By			Draw	Lost By		
Team	+3	2	1	0	1	2	+3
A	0	1	0	2	1	0	0
B	0	0	0	1	0	1	1
C	0	1	1	4	0	0	0
D	2	0	1	2	1	0	0
Total	2	2	2	9	2	1	1
%	10.53	10.53	10.53	47.37	10.53	5.26	5.26
Odds	9.50	9.50	9.50	2.11	9.50	19.00	19.00

Bookings

	Yellow Cards		Red Cards		Betfair Points		
Team	F	A	F	A	0-5	6-8	9+
A	5	11	0	2	1	1	2
B	5	3	0	0	1	1	1
C	9	12	0	2	2	1	3
D	11	12	2	0	1	1	4
Total	30	38	2	4	5	4	10
				%	26.32	21.05	52.63
				Odds	3.80	4.75	1.90

Corners

	Corner Supremacy			Corner Numbers		
Team	Won	Draw	Lost	0-9	10-12	13+
A	0	0	4	2	2	0
B	1	1	1	0	2	1
C	2	1	3	4	2	0
D	1	1	4	0	3	3
Total	4	3	12	6	9	4
%	21.05	15.79	63.16	31.58	47.37	21.05
Odds	4.75	6.33	1.58	3.17	2.11	4.75

Summary

- Five of Man City's 12 away games (42% / odds 2.40) against C and D sides finished in a half-time/full-time result of A/A.
- Seven of their nine away matches (78% / odds 1.29) against grade B and C sides finished in under 2.5 goals.
- Nine of their 19 away matches (47% / odds 2.11) finished in a draw.
- Seven of their 12 away matches (58% / odds 1.71) against grade C and D sides featured five or more bookings.
- Man City lost corner superiority in 12 of 19 away matches (63% / odds 1.58).

MANCHESTER UNITED (Grade A)

Season record

	Home					Away						
Pld	Won	Draw	Lost	F	A	Won	Draw	Lost	F	A	GD	Points
38	16	1	2	52	12	11	3	5	34	16	58	85

Top Scorers

Player	Started	Goals	First	Last	Each Way	Anytime
Wayne Rooney	32	26	10	6*	16	18
Dimitar Berbatov	25	12	4	2	8	11

Last scorer – Wayne Rooney in a 1-0 victory at home to Birmingham.

Scoring

	Matches Scored In	Clean Sheets	Won to Nil	Both Teams Scored	A Goal 1st Half	A Goal 2nd Half
Home	18	11	11	7	15	17
Away	14	8	7	7	12	15
Total	32	19	18	14	27	32

Match Goal Times

	First Goal of Match			
	1st 10 mins	Before 27 mins	After 27 mins	No Goals
Home	5	7	8	4
Away	1	4	8	7
Total	6	11	16	11
%	15.79	28.95	42.11	28.95
Break-Even Odds	6.33	3.45	2.38	3.45

	Last Goal of Match			
	Before 75 mins	After 75 mins	90+ min Goal	No Goals
Home	3	14	4	2
Away	2	13	4	4
Total	5	27	8	6
%	13.16	71.05	21.05	15.79
Break-Even Odds	7.60	1.41	4.75	6.33

Half Time/Full time

	Half Time / Full Time Results								
	H/H	H/D	H/A	D/H	D/D	D/A	A/H	A/D	A/A
Home	9	0	0	6	0	0	1	1	2
%	47.37	0.00	0.00	31.58	0.00	0.00	5.26	5.26	10.53
Break-Even Odds	2.11	N/A	N/A	3.17	N/A	N/A	19.00	19.00	9.50
Away	2	1	0	3	2	5	0	0	6
%	10.53	5.26	0.00	15.79	10.53	26.32	0.00	0.00	31.58
Break-Even Odds	9.50	19.00	N/A	6.33	9.50	3.80	N/A	N/A	3.17

Goals

	Match goals				
	1 or More	Ov. 1.5	Ov. 2.5	Ov. 3.5	Ov. 4.5
Home	19	17	16	7	3
Away	18	13	9	8	2
Total	37	30	25	15	5
%	97.37	78.95	65.79	39.47	13.16
Break-Even Odds	1.03	1.27	1.52	2.53	7.60

Bookings

	Yellow Cards		Red Cards		Betfair Points		
	F	A	F	A	0-5	6-8	9+
Home	23	31	0	1	12	3	4
%	N/A	N/A	N/A	N/A	63.16	15.79	21.05
Break-Even Odds	N/A	N/A	N/A	N/A	1.58	6.33	4.75
Away	28	33	4	1	6	6	7
%	N/A	N/A	N/A	N/A	31.58	31.58	36.84
Break-Even Odds	N/A	N/A	N/A	N/A	3.17	3.17	2.71

Corner Superiority

	Corner Supremacy			Corner Numbers		
	Won	Draw	Lost	0-9	10-12	13+
Home	15	2	2	5	6	8
%	78.95	10.53	10.53	26.32	31.58	42.11
Break-Even Odds	1.27	9.50	9.50	3.80	3.17	2.38
Away	13	0	6	8	5	6
%	68.42	0.00	31.58	42.11	26.32	31.58
Break-Even Odds	1.46	N/A	3.17	2.38	3.80	3.17

Summary

- The last goal of the match was scored after 75 minutes in 71.05% of all Man United's matches, the highest in the Premier League last season.
- 25 matches out of Man United's 38 (65.79%) finished with three or more goals; backing over 2.5 goals at above 1.52 would have yielded a level stake profit last season.
- Man United kept a total of 19 clean sheets (50%), the highest in the Premier League last season. In only 14 matches (36.84%) both teams scored in the game, the lowest in the Premier League last season.
- A total of eight Man United games (21.05%) had a goal in the 90+ injury time window.
- In the 15 matches Man United led at half time, they went on to win on all 15 occasions (100%).
- 18 of all Man United's matches (47.37%) had two or less bookings.
- Man United achieved corner supremacy in 28 out of 38 games (73.68%).

Home (Graded Analysis)

Team	Home Record					
	Won	Draw	Lost	F	A	Pts
A	3	0	1	9	7	9
B	2	0	1	6	2	6
C	5	1	0	15	2	16
D	6	0	0	22	1	18
Total	16	1	2	52	12	49
%	84.21	5.26	10.53			
Odds	1.19	19.00	9.50			

Team	Half Time / Full Time Results								
	H/H	H/D	H/A	D/H	D/D	D/A	A/H	A/D	A/A
A	0	0	0	2	0	0	1	0	1
B	1	0	0	1	0	0	0	0	1
C	3	0	0	2	0	0	0	1	0
D	5	0	0	1	0	0	0	0	0
Total	9	0	0	6	0	0	1	1	2
%	47.37	0.00	0.00	31.58	0.00	0.00	5.26	5.26	10.53
Odds	2.11	N/A	N/A	3.17	N/A	N/A	19.00	19.00	9.50

Goals

	Match goals				
Team	1 or More	Ov. 1.5	Ov. 2.5	Ov. 3.5	Ov. 4.5
A	4	4	4	1	1
B	3	2	2	1	0
C	6	5	4	1	0
D	6	6	6	3	2
Total	19	17	16	6	3
%	100.00	89.47	84.21	31.58	15.79
Odds	1.00	1.12	1.19	3.17	6.33

	Clean Sheet		Scored	
Team	Yes	No	Yes	No
A	0	4	4	0
B	1	2	2	1
C	5	1	6	0
D	5	1	6	0
Total	11	8	18	1
%	57.89	42.10	94.73	5.26
Odds	1.73	2.71	1.12	19.00

	Won By			Draw	Lost By		
Team	+3	2	1	0	1	2	+3
A	0	0	3	0	1	0	0
B	1	1	0	0	1	0	0
C	3	1	1	1	0	0	0
D	5	0	1	0	0	0	0
Total	9	2	5	1	2	0	0
%	47.37	10.53	26.32	5.26	10.53	0.00	0.00
Odds	2.11	9.50	3.80	19.00	9.50	N/A	N/A

Bookings

	Yellow Cards		Red Cards		Betfair Points		
Team	F	A	F	A	0-5	6-8	9+
A	10	12	0	0	0	2	2
B	4	3	0	0	2	1	0
C	6	8	0	1	5	0	1
D	3	8	0	0	5	0	1
Total	23	31	0	1	12	3	4
				%	63.16	15.79	21.05
				Odds	1.58	6.33	4.75

Corners

	Corner Supremacy			Corner Numbers		
Team	Won	Draw	Lost	0-9	10-12	13+
A	2	1	1	2	2	0
B	2	1	0	1	0	2
C	5	0	1	1	2	3
D	6	0	0	1	2	3
Total	15	2	2	5	6	8
%	78.95	10.53	10.53	26.32	31.58	42.11
Odds	1.27	9.50	9.50	3.80	3.17	2.38

Summary

- Eight out of 12 Man United home games (67% / odds 1.50) against grade C and D sides finished half-time/full-time H/H.
- Man United kept ten clean sheets in 12 home matches (83% / odds 1.20) against grade C and D sides.
- In nine of 12 Man United home games (75% / 1.33) against grade C and D sides, United won by two goals or more.
- 12 of their 15 home games (80% / odds 1.25) against grade B, C and D sides featured two or less bookings.
- Man United won corner superiority in 15 of 19 home games (79% / odds 1.27).

Away (Graded Analysis)

	Away Record					
Team	Won	Draw	Lost	F	A	Pts
A	2	0	2	4	4	6
B	1	1	1	5	5	4
C	3	2	1	8	4	11
D	5	0	1	17	3	15
Total	11	3	5	34	16	36
%	57.89	15.79	26.32			
Odds	1.73	6.33	3.80			

	Half Time / Full Time Results								
Team	H/H	H/D	H/A	D/H	D/D	D/A	A/H	A/D	A/A
A	0	0	0	2	0	1	0	0	1
B	0	0	0	1	1	0	0	0	1
C	1	1	0	0	1	1	0	0	1
D	1	0	0	0	0	3	0	0	2
Total	2	1	0	3	2	5	0	0	6
%	10.53	5.26	0.00	15.79	10.53	26.32	0.00	0.00	31.58
Odds	9.50	19.00	N/A	6.33	9.50	3.80	N/A	N/A	3.17

Goals

	Match goals				
Team	1 or More	Ov. 1.5	Ov. 2.5	Ov. 3.5	Ov. 4.5
A	4	2	1	1	0
B	3	3	2	2	0
C	5	4	2	1	0
D	6	4	4	4	2
Total	18	13	9	8	2
%	94.74	68.42	47.37	42.11	10.53
Odds	1.06	1.46	2.11	2.38	9.50

	Clean Sheet		Scored	
Team	Yes	No	Yes	No
A	1	3	2	2
B	0	3	3	0
C	4	2	4	2
D	3	3	5	1
Total	8	11	14	5
%	42.11	57.89	73.68	26.32
Odds	2.38	1.73	1.36	3.80

	Won By			Draw	Lost By		
Team	+3	2	1	0	1	2	+3
A	0	1	1	0	1	1	0
B	0	1	0	1	0	1	0
C	1	1	1	2	0	0	1
D	3	1	1	0	1	0	0
Total	4	4	3	3	2	2	1
%	21.05	21.05	15.79	15.79	10.53	10.53	5.26
Odds	4.75	4.75	6.33	6.33	9.50	9.50	19.00

Bookings

	Yellow Cards		Red Cards		Betfair Points		
Team	F	A	F	A	0-5	6-8	9+
A	7	8	1	1	1	1	2
B	4	8	2	0	0	1	2
C	8	7	0	1	3	1	2
D	9	10	0	0	2	3	1
Total	28	33	3	2	6	6	7
				%	31.58	31.58	36.84
				Odds	3.17	3.17	2.71

Corners

	Corner Supremacy			Corner Numbers		
Team	Won	Draw	Lost	0-9	10-12	13+
A	1	0	3	2	1	1
B	3	0	0	1	1	1
C	4	0	2	3	1	2
D	5	0	1	2	2	2
Total	13	0	6	8	5	6
%	68.42	0.00	31.58	42.11	26.32	31.58
Odds	1.46	N/A	3.17	2.38	3.80	3.17

Summary

- Three out of Man United's seven away games (43% / odds 2.34) against grade A and B sides finished in a half-time/full-time result of losing D/H.
- Six of their 12 away matches (50% / odds 2.00) against grade C and D sides finished in under 2.5 goals.
- In six of their 12 away matches (50% / odds 2.00) against grade C and D sides, they won by two or more goals.
- Only one of their seven away matches (14% / odds 7.00) against grade A and B sides featured two bookings or less.
- They won corner superiority in 12 of 15 away matches (80% / odds 1.25) against grade B, C and D sides.

STOKE CITY (Grade C)

Season record

	Home					Away						
Pld	Won	Draw	Lost	F	A	Won	Draw	Lost	F	A	GD	Points
38	7	6	6	24	21	4	8	7	10	27	-14	47

Top Scorers

No Stoke player scored six or more goals last season.

Scoring

	Matches Scored In	Clean Sheets	Won to Nil	Both Teams Scored	A Goal 1st Half	A Goal 2nd Half
Home	15	7	5	10	11	15
Away	9	7	3	6	9	14
Total	24	14	8	16	20	29

Match Goal Times

	First Goal of Match			
	1st 10 mins	Before 27 mins	After 27 mins	No Goals
Home	3	9	2	8
Away	1	5	4	10
Total	4	14	6	18
%	10.53	36.84	15.79	47.37
Break-Even Odds	9.50	2.71	6.33	2.11

	Last Goal of Match			
	Before 75 mins	After 75 mins	90+ min Goal	No Goals
Home	6	9	3	4
Away	4	10	3	5
Total	10	19	6	9
%	26.32	50.00	15.79	23.68
Break-Even Odds	3.80	2.00	6.33	4.22

Half Time/Full time

	Half Time / Full Time Results								
	H/H	H/D	H/A	D/H	D/D	D/A	A/H	A/D	A/A
Home	5	1	1	2	5	5	0	0	0
%	26.32	5.26	5.26	10.53	26.32	26.32	0.00	0.00	0.00
Break-Even Odds	3.80	19.00	19.00	9.50	3.80	3.80	N/A	N/A	N/A
Away	5	1	1	1	6	3	1	1	0
%	26.32	5.26	5.26	5.26	31.58	15.79	5.26	5.26	0.00
Break-Even Odds	3.80	19.00	19.00	19.00	3.17	6.33	19.00	19.00	N/A

Goals

	Match goals				
	1 or More	Ov. 1.5	Ov. 2.5	Ov. 3.5	Ov. 4.5
Home	17	14	9	4	1
Away	15	11	5	3	1
Total	32	25	14	7	2
%	84.21	65.79	36.84	18.42	5.26
Break-Even Odds	1.19	1.52	2.71	5.43	19.00

Bookings

	Yellow Cards		Red Cards		Betfair Points		
	F	A	F	A	0-5	6-8	9+
Home	30	39	3	1	4	7	8
%	N/A	N/A	N/A	N/A	21.05	36.84	42.11
Break-Even Odds	N/A	N/A	N/A	N/A	4.75	2.71	2.38
Away	36	16	2	0	8	7	4
%	N/A	N/A	N/A	N/A	42.11	36.84	21.05
Break-Even Odds	N/A	N/A	N/A	N/A	2.38	2.71	4.75

Corner Superiority

	Corner Supremacy			Corner Numbers		
	Won	Draw	Lost	0-9	10-12	13+
Home	9	3	7	9	3	7
%	47.37	15.79	36.84	47.37	15.79	36.84
Break-Even Odds	2.11	6.33	2.71	2.11	6.33	2.71
Away	3	3	13	6	6	7
%	15.79	15.79	68.42	31.58	31.58	36.84
Break-Even Odds	6.33	6.33	1.46	3.17	3.17	2.71

Summary

- 14 matches out of Stoke's 38 (36.84%) finished with three or more goals; backing under 2.5 goals at above 1.58 would have yielded a level stake profit last season.
- 18 of all Stoke's matches were 0-0 at H-T (47.37%), the highest number in the Premier League last season.
- 22 (57.89%) out of 38 matches were drawn at half-time, with Stoke going on to win just five (22.73%).
- 34 matches (89.47%) didn't have a goal scored against them in the first 10 minutes of the game, the best record in the Premier League last season.
- Stoke lost corner supremacy in 20 out of their 38 games (52.63%).
- There were only 13+ corners in 14 of their matches (36.84%).

Home (Graded Analysis)

Team	Won	Draw	Lost	F	A	Pts
	Home Record					
A	0	2	3	4	9	2
B	0	2	1	1	2	2
C	4	0	1	9	4	12
D	3	2	1	10	6	11
Total	7	6	6	24	21	27
%	36.84	31.58	31.58			
Odds	2.71	3.17	3.17			

Team	H/H	H/D	H/A	D/H	D/D	D/A	A/H	A/D	A/A
	Half Time / Full Time Results								
A	0	0	0	0	2	3	0	0	0
B	0	0	0	0	2	1	0	0	0
C	3	0	0	1	0	1	0	0	0
D	2	1	1	1	1	0	0	0	0
Total	5	1	1	2	5	5	0	0	0
%	26.32	5.26	5.26	10.53	26.32	26.32	0.00	0.00	0.00
Odds	3.80	19.00	19.00	9.50	3.80	3.80	N/A	N/A	N/A

Goals

	Match goals				
Team	1 or More	Ov. 1.5	Ov. 2.5	Ov. 3.5	Ov. 4.5
A	5	5	2	1	0
B	1	1	1	0	0
C	5	3	3	1	1
D	6	5	3	2	0
Total	17	14	9	4	1
%	89.47	73.68	47.37	21.05	5.26
Odds	1.12	1.36	2.11	4.75	19.00

	Clean Sheet		Scored	
Team	Yes	No	Yes	No
A	0	5	4	1
B	2	1	1	2
C	2	3	4	1
D	3	3	6	0
Total	7	12	15	4
%	36.84	63.16	78.95	21.05
Odds	2.71	1.58	1.27	4.75

	Won By			Draw	Lost By		
Team	+3	2	1	0	1	2	+3
A	0	0	0	2	1	2	0
B	0	0	0	2	1	0	0
C	1	0	3	0	1	0	0
D	0	2	1	2	1	0	0
Total	1	2	4	6	4	2	0
%	5.26	10.53	21.05	31.58	21.05	10.53	0.00
Odds	19.00	9.50	4.75	3.17	4.75	9.50	N/A

Bookings

	Yellow Cards		Red Cards		Betfair Points		
Team	F	A	F	A	0–5	6–8	9+
A	8	10	2	0	1	2	2
B	2	6	1	0	1	1	1
C	8	11	0	1	2	0	3
D	12	12	0	0	0	4	2
Total	30	39	3	1	4	7	8
				%	21.05	36.84	42.11
				Odds	4.75	2.71	2.38

Corners

	Corner Supremacy			Corner Numbers		
Team	Won	Draw	Lost	0–9	10–12	13+
A	1	1	3	3	1	1
B	2	0	1	0	1	2
C	2	1	2	0	1	4
D	4	0	2	6	0	0
Total	9	2	8	9	3	7
%	47.37	10.53	42.11	47.37	15.79	36.84
Odds	2.11	9.50	2.38	2.11	6.33	2.71

Summary

- Stoke were drawn at half time in 12 of their 19 home games (63% / odds 1.58).
- Five of their eight home matches (62% /1.60) against grade A and B sides finished in under 2.5 goals.
- They lost three home matches in 14 against grade B, C and D sides by no more than one goal.
- Only two of eight home matches (25% / odds 4.00) against grade A and B sides featured two bookings or less.
- All six home matches against grade D opponents featured under ten corners.

Away (Graded Analysis)

	Away Record					
Team	Won	Draw	Lost	F	A	Pts
A	0	0	5	0	19	0
B	1	1	1	2	2	4
C	2	3	0	2	0	9
D	1	4	1	6	6	7
Total	4	8	7	10	27	20
%	21.05	42.11	36.84			
Odds	4.75	2.38	2.71			

	Half Time / Full Time Results								
Team	H/H	H/D	H/A	D/H	D/D	D/A	A/H	A/D	A/A
A	5	0	0	0	0	0	0	0	0
B	0	0	0	1	1	1	0	0	0
C	0	0	0	0	3	2	0	0	0
D	0	1	1	0	2	0	1	1	0
Total	5	1	1	1	6	3	1	1	0
%	26.32	5.26	5.26	5.26	31.58	15.79	5.26	5.26	0.00
Odds	3.80	19.00	19.00	19.00	3.17	6.33	19.00	19.00	N/A

Goals

	Match goals				
Team	1 or More	Ov. 1.5	Ov. 2.5	Ov. 3.5	Ov. 4.5
A	5	5	3	2	1
B	3	1	0	0	0
C	2	1	0	0	0
D	5	5	2	0	0
Total	15	12	5	2	1
%	78.95	63.16	26.32	10.53	5.26
Odds	1.27	1.58	3.80	9.50	19.00

	Clean Sheet		Scored	
Team	Yes	No	Yes	No
A	0	5	0	5
B	1	2	2	1
C	5	0	2	3
D	1	5	5	1
Total	7	12	9	10
%	36.84	63.16	47.37	52.63
Odds	2.71	1.58	2.11	1.90

	Won By			Draw	Lost By		
Team	+3	2	1	0	1	2	+3
A	0	0	0	0	0	2	3
B	0	0	1	1	1	0	0
C	0	0	2	3	0	0	0
D	0	0	1	4	1	0	0
Total	0	0	4	8	2	2	3
%	0.00	0.00	21.05	42.11	10.53	10.53	15.79
Odds	N/A	N/A	4.75	2.38	9.50	9.50	6.33

Bookings

	Yellow Cards		Red Cards		Betfair Points		
Team	F	A	F	A	0-5	6-8	9+
A	6	2	0	0	4	1	0
B	7	1	0	0	1	2	0
C	13	4	0	0	1	3	1
D	10	9	0	2	2	1	3
Total	36	16	0	2	8	7	4
				%	42.11	36.84	21.05
				Odds	2.38	2.71	4.75

Corners

	Corner Supremacy			Corner Numbers		
Team	Won	Draw	Lost	0-9	10-12	13+
A	0	0	5	1	2	2
B	1	0	2	2	0	1
C	1	1	3	1	3	1
D	1	2	3	2	1	3
Total	3	3	13	6	6	7
%	15.79	15.79	68.42	31.58	31.58	36.84
Odds	6.33	6.33	1.46	3.17	3.17	2.71

Summary

- Stoke lost all five away games against grade A sides with a half-time/full-time result of H/H.
- Stoke did not score in all five away games against grade A opposition.
- Eight of their 14 away matches (57% / odds 1.75) against grade B, C and D sides finished in a draw.
- Only four of their 19 away matches (21% / odds 4.76) featured over five bookings.
- They lost corner superiority in ten of their 13 away matches (77% / odds 1.30) against grade A, B and C sides.

SUNDERLAND (Grade C)

Season record

	Home					Away						
Pld	Won	Draw	Lost	F	A	Won	Draw	Lost	F	A	GD	Points
38	9	7	3	32	19	2	4	13	16	37	-8	44

Top Scorers

Player	Started	Goals	First	Last	Each Way	Anytime
Darren Bent	38	24	13	7*	16	17
Kenwyne Jones	24	9	2	2	6	7

***Last scorer** – Darren Bent (four times), 1-0 victory away to Bolton, home to Liverpool, home to Arsenal, and away to Burnley.

Scoring

	Matches Scored In	Clean Sheets	Won to Nil	Both Teams Scored	A Goal 1st Half	A Goal 2nd Half
Home	15	5	3	12	16	15
Away	11	2	2	9	16	13
Total	26	7	5	21	32	28

Match Goal Times

	First Goal of Match			
	1st 10 mins	Before 27 mins	After 27 mins	No Goals
Home	6	14	2	3
Away	9	14	2	3
Total	15	28	4	6
%	39.47	73.68	10.53	15.79
Break-Even Odds	2.53	1.36	9.50	6.33

	Last Goal of Match			
	Before 75 mins	After 75 mins	90+ min Goal	No Goals
Home	5	10	2	4
Away	4	9	4	6
Total	9	19	6	10
%	23.68	50.00	15.79	26.32
Break-Even Odds	4.22	2.00	6.33	3.80

Half-Time/Full-time

	Half Time / Full Time Results								
	H/H	H/D	H/A	D/H	D/D	D/A	A/H	A/D	A/A
Home	6	3	1	3	2	0	0	2	2
%	31.58	15.79	5.26	15.79	10.53	0.00	0.00	10.53	10.53
Break-Even Odds	3.17	6.33	19.00	6.33	9.50	N/A	N/A	9.50	9.50
Away	9	0	0	4	2	0	0	2	2
%	47.37	0.00	0.00	21.05	10.53	0.00	0.00	10.53	10.53
Break-Even Odds	2.11	N/A	N/A	4.75	9.50	N/A	N/A	9.50	9.50

Goals

	Match goals				
	1 or More	Ov. 1.5	Ov. 2.5	Ov. 3.5	Ov. 4.5
Home	17	14	9	7	2
Away	19	13	8	5	2
Total	36	27	17	12	4
%	94.74	71.05	44.74	31.58	10.53
Break-Even Odds	1.06	1.41	2.24	3.17	9.50

Bookings

	Yellow Cards		Red Cards		Betfair Points		
	F	A	F	A	0-5	6-8	9+
Home	42	43	2	3	2	7	10
%	N/A	N/A	N/A	N/A	10.53	36.84	52.63
Break Even Odds	N/A	N/A	N/A	N/A	9.50	2.71	1.90
Away	40	19	7	2	5	7	7
%	N/A	N/A	N/A	N/A	26.32	36.84	36.84
Break Even Odds	N/A	N/A	N/A	N/A	3.80	2.71	2.71

Corner Superiority

	Corner Supremacy			Corner Numbers		
	Won	Draw	Lost	0-9	10-12	13+
Home	5	3	11	7	5	7
%	26.32	15.79	57.89	36.84	26.32	36.84
Break-Even Odds	3.80	6.33	1.73	2.71	3.80	2.71
Away	8	4	7	7	6	6
%	42.11	21.05	36.84	36.84	31.58	31.58
Break-Even Odds	2.38	4.75	2.71	2.71	3.17	3.17

Summary

- 15 of Sunderland's total 38 matches (39.47%) contained a goal in the first 10 minutes, the highest number in the Premier League last season.
- In 28 Sunderland matches out of 38 (73.68%), the first goal of the match came before the 27th minute.
- Six of Sunderland's matches were 0-0 at H-T (15.79%) in all games played.
- In the 13 matches Sunderland were losing at half-time, they didn't win any: losing 11 (84.62%) and drawing two.
- Sunderland only kept seven clean sheets last season.
- Just seven of their 38 matches (18.42%) featured two or less bookings.

Home (Graded Analysis)

	Home Record					
Team	Won	Draw	Lost	F	A	Pts
A	2	1	2	4	5	7
B	1	1	1	4	4	4
C	2	3	0	7	4	9
D	4	2	0	17	6	14
Total	9	7	3	32	19	34
%	47.37	36.84	15.79			
Odds	2.11	2.71	6.33			

	Half Time / Full Time Results								
Team	H/H	H/D	H/A	D/H	D/D	D/A	A/H	A/D	A/A
A	1	1	1	1	0	0	0	0	1
B	1	1	0	0	0	0	0	0	1
C	1	0	0	1	2	0	0	1	0
D	3	1	0	1	0	0	0	1	0
Total	6	3	1	3	2	0	0	2	2
%	31.58	15.79	5.26	15.79	10.53	0.00	0.00	10.53	10.53
Odds	3.17	6.33	19.00	6.33	9.50	N/A	N/A	9.50	9.50

Goals

	Match goals				
Team	1 or More	Ov. 1.5	Ov. 2.5	Ov. 3.5	Ov. 4.5
A	5	2	1	1	0
B	3	3	1	1	0
C	3	3	3	2	0
D	6	6	4	3	2
Total	17	14	9	7	2
%	89.47	73.68	47.37	36.84	10.53
Odds	1.12	1.36	2.11	2.71	9.50

	Clean Sheet		Scored	
Team	Yes	No	Yes	No
A	2	3	4	1
B	0	3	2	1
C	2	3	3	2
D	1	5	6	0
Total	5	14	15	4
%	26.32	73.68	78.95	21.05
Odds	3.80	1.36	1.27	4.75

	Won By			Draw	Lost By		
Team	+3	2	1	0	1	2	+3
A	0	0	2	1	1	1	0
B	0	1	0	1	0	1	0
C	0	1	1	3	0	0	0
D	3	0	1	2	0	0	0
Total	3	2	4	7	1	2	0
%	15.79	10.53	21.05	36.84	5.26	10.53	0.00
Odds	6.33	9.50	4.75	2.71	19.00	9.50	N/A

Bookings

	Yellow Cards		Red Cards		Betfair Points		
Team	F	A	F	A	0–5	6–8	9+
A	11	10	0	0	0	3	2
B	5	5	1	0	1	1	1
C	10	11	1	1	1	1	3
D	16	17	0	2	0	2	4
Total	42	43	2	3	2	7	10
				%	10.53	36.84	52.63
				Odds	9.50	2.71	1.90

Corners

	Corner Supremacy			Corner Numbers		
Team	Won	Draw	Lost	0–9	10–12	13+
A	1	0	4	2	1	2
B	1	1	1	1	1	1
C	2	1	2	1	3	1
D	1	1	4	3	0	3
Total	5	3	11	7	5	7
%	26.32	15.79	57.89	36.84	26.32	36.84
Odds	3.80	6.33	1.73	2.71	3.80	2.71

Summary

- Three out of Sunderland's six home victories (50% / odds 2.00) against grade D sides finished in a half-time/full-time result of H/H.
- Six out of eight Sunderland home matches (75% / odds 1.33) against grade A and B sides finished in under 2.5 goals.
- Five of 11 Sunderland home games (45% / odds 2.20) against C and D opposition ended in draws.
- Seven of Sunderland's 11 home matches (64% / odds 1.57) against grade C and D sides featured five or more bookings.
- Sunderland lost 11 of 19 home matches (58% / 1.72) in corner superiority.

Away (Graded Analysis)

Away Record						
Team	Won	Draw	Lost	F	A	Pts
A	0	1	4	7	18	1
B	0	1	2	1	5	1
C	0	1	4	3	7	1
D	2	1	3	5	7	7
Total	2	4	13	16	37	10
%	10.53	21.05	68.42			
Odds	9.50	4.75	1.46			

Half Time / Full Time Results									
Team	H/H	H/D	H/A	D/H	D/D	D/A	A/H	A/D	A/A
A	4	0	0	0	0	0	0	1	0
B	2	0	0	0	1	0	0	0	0
C	3	0	0	1	1	0	0	0	0
D	0	0	0	3	0	0	0	1	2
Total	9	0	0	4	2	0	0	2	2
%	47.37	0.00	0.00	21.05	10.53	0.00	0.00	10.53	10.53
Odds	2.11	N/A	N/A	4.75	9.50	N/A	N/A	9.50	9.50

Goals

	Match goals				
Team	1 or More	Ov. 1.5	Ov. 2.5	Ov. 3.5	Ov. 4.5
A	5	5	4	3	2
B	3	3	0	0	0
C	5	2	2	1	0
D	6	3	2	1	0
Total	19	13	8	5	2
%	100.00	68.42	42.11	26.32	10.53
Odds	1.00	1.46	2.38	3.80	9.50

	Clean Sheet		Scored	
Team	Yes	No	Yes	No
A	0	5	3	2
B	0	3	1	2
C	0	5	2	3
D	2	4	5	1
Total	2	17	11	8
%	10.53	89.47	57.89	42.11
Odds	9.50	1.12	1.73	2.38

	Won By			Draw	Lost By		
Team	+3	2	1	0	1	2	+3
A	0	0	0	1	1	1	2
B	0	0	0	1	0	2	0
C	0	0	0	1	4	0	0
D	0	0	2	1	2	1	0
Total	0	0	2	4	7	4	2
%	0.00	0.00	10.53	21.05	36.84	21.05	10.53
Odds	N/A	N/A	9.50	4.75	2.71	4.75	9.50

Bookings

	Yellow Cards		Red Cards		Betfair Points		
Team	F	A	F	A	0-5	6-8	9+
A	12	5	2	0	2	0	3
B	3	1	0	0	2	1	0
C	12	6	0	0	1	3	1
D	13	7	5	2	0	3	3
Total	40	19	7	2	5	7	7
				%	26.32	36.84	36.84
				Odds	3.80	2.71	2.71

Corners

	Corner Supremacy			Corner Numbers		
Team	Won	Draw	Lost	0-9	10-12	13+
A	0	0	5	1	2	2
B	2	1	0	1	1	1
C	3	2	0	2	1	2
D	3	1	2	3	2	1
Total	8	4	7	7	6	6
%	42.11	21.05	36.84	36.84	31.58	31.58
Odds	2.38	4.75	2.71	2.71	3.17	3.17

Summary

- Sunderland lost nine of 13 away games (69% / odds 1.45) against grade A, B and C sides with a half-time/full-time result of H/H.
- Ten of Sunderland's 14 away matches (71% / odds 1.40) against grade B, C and D sides finished in under 2.5 goals.
- Sunderland only won twice away from home – both times against grade D sides, and both times only by one goal.
- Only one of Sunderland's 11 away matches (9% / odds 11.10) against grade C and D sides featured two or less bookings.
- They won eight of 14 away matches (57% / odds 1.75) against grade B, C and D sides in corner superiority.

TOTTENHAM HOTSPUR (Grade B)

Season record

	Home					Away						
Pld	Won	Draw	Lost	F	A	Won	Draw	Lost	F	A	GD	Points
38	14	2	3	40	12	7	5	7	27	29	26	70

Top Scorers

Player	Started	Goals	First	Last	Each Way	Anytime
Jermain Defoe	31	18	7	2	12	12
Peter Crouch	21	8	6	3*	7	7
Robbie Keane	15	6	2	1	3	4
Niko Kranjar	19	6	1	4	4	5

*__Last scorer__ – Peter Crouch, 1-0 victory away to Man City.

Scoring

	Matches Scored In	Clean Sheets	Won to Nil	Both Teams Scored	A Goal 1st Half	A Goal 2nd Half
Home	15	9	7	8	15	14
Away	14	4	3	11	12	17
Total	29	13	10	19	27	31

Match Goal Times

	First Goal of Match			
	1st 10 mins	Before 27 mins	After 27 mins	No Goals
Home	4	9	6	4
Away	6	6	6	7
Total	10	15	12	11
%	26.32	39.47	31.58	28.95
Break-Even Odds	3.80	2.53	3.17	3.45

	Last Goal of Match			
	Before 75 mins	After 75 mins	90+ min Goal	No Goals
Home	4	10	4	5
Away	4	13	4	2
Total	8	23	8	7
%	21.05	60.53	21.05	18.42
Break-Even Odds	4.75	1.65	4.75	5.43

Half Time/Full time

	Half Time / Full Time Results								
	H/H	H/D	H/A	D/H	D/D	D/A	A/H	A/D	A/A
Home	13	0	0	1	2	1	0	0	2
%	68.42	0.00	0.00	5.26	10.53	5.26	0.00	0.00	10.53
Break-Even Odds	1.46	N/A	N/A	19.00	9.50	19.00	N/A	N/A	9.50
Away	5	1	0	1	4	3	1	0	4
%	26.32	5.26	0.00	5.26	21.05	15.79	5.26	0.00	21.05
Break-Even Odds	3.80	19.00	N/A	19.00	4.75	6.33	19.00	N/A	4.75

Goals

	Match goals				
	1 or More	Ov. 1.5	Ov. 2.5	Ov. 3.5	Ov. 4.5
Home	17	14	10	4	2
Away	18	16	12	6	2
Total	35	30	22	10	4
%	92.11	78.95	57.89	26.32	10.53
Break-Even Odds	1.09	1.27	1.73	3.80	9.50

Bookings

	Yellow Cards		Red Cards		Betfair Points		
	F	A	F	A	0-5	6-8	9+
Home	26	40	0	2	6	5	8
%	N/A	N/A	N/A	N/A	31.58	26.32	42.11
Break-Even Odds	N/A	N/A	N/A	N/A	3.17	3.80	2.38
Away	31	32	1	2	8	4	7
%	N/A	N/A	N/A	N/A	42.11	21.05	36.84
Break-Even Odds	N/A	N/A	N/A	N/A	2.38	4.75	2.71

Corner Superiority

	Corner Supremacy			Corner Numbers		
	Won	Draw	Lost	0-9	10-12	13+
Home	11	1	7	4	7	8
%	57.89	5.26	36.84	21.05	36.84	42.11
Break-Even Odds	1.73	19.00	2.71	4.75	2.71	2.38
Away	9	2	8	7	6	6
%	47.37	10.53	42.11	36.84	31.58	31.58
Break-Even Odds	2.11	9.50	2.38	2.71	3.17	3.17

Summary

- Ten of Tottenham's 38 matches (26.32%) contained a goal in the first ten minutes, the second highest number in the Premier League last season.
- 22 matches out of their full 38 (57.89%) finished with three or more goals; backing over 2.5 goals at above 1.60 would have yielded a level stake profit last season.
- 11 of all Tottenham's matches were 0-0 at H-T (28.95%).
- In the matches Tottenham were losing at half time, they didn't win any, losing seven (87.50%) and drawing one.
- In the 18 matches Tottenham *led* at half time, they went on win the match in 17 of them (94.44%).
- 14 of Tottenham's matches (36.84%) featured two or less bookings.
- 13+ corners occurred in only 14 of their matches (36.84%).

Home (Graded Analysis)

	Home Record					
Team	Won	Draw	Lost	F	A	Pts
A	4	0	1	10	6	12
B	1	1	0	2	1	4
C	5	0	1	11	3	15
D	4	1	1	17	2	13
Total	14	2	3	40	12	44
%	73.68	10.53	15.79			
Odds	1.36	9.50	6.33			

	Half Time / Full Time Results								
Team	H/H	H/D	H/A	D/H	D/D	D/A	A/H	A/D	A/A
A	4	0	0	0	0	0	0	0	1
B	1	0	0	0	1	0	0	0	0
C	4	0	0	1	0	1	0	0	0
D	4	0	0	0	1	0	0	0	1
Total	13	0	0	1	2	1	0	0	2
%	68.42	0.00	0.00	5.26	10.53	5.26	0.00	0.00	10.53
Odds	1.46	N/A	N/A	19.00	9.50	19.00	N/A	N/A	9.50

Goals

	Match goals				
Team	1 or More	Ov. 1.5	Ov. 2.5	Ov. 3.5	Ov. 4.5
A	5	5	5	1	0
B	2	1	1	0	0
C	6	5	2	1	0
D	5	3	4	3	3
Total	18	14	12	5	3
%	94.74	73.68	63.16	26.32	15.79
Odds	1.06	1.36	1.58	3.80	6.33

	Clean Sheet		Scored	
Team	Yes	No	Yes	No
A	1	4	5	0
B	1	1	1	1
C	3	3	5	1
D	4	2	4	2
Total	9	10	15	4
%	47.37	52.63	78.95	21.05
Odds	2.11	1.90	1.27	4.75

	Won By			Draw	Lost By		
Team	+3	2	1	0	1	2	+3
A	1	0	3	0	0	1	0
B	0	0	1	1	0	0	0
C	0	4	1	0	1	0	0
D	2	1	1	1	1	0	0
Total	3	5	6	2	2	1	0
%	15.79	26.32	31.58	10.53	10.53	5.26	0.00
Odds	6.35	3.80	3.16	9.50	9.50	19.00	N/A

Bookings

	Yellow Cards		Red Cards		Betfair Points		
Team	F	A	F	A	0-5	6-8	9+
A	13	13	0	2	0	1	4
B	1	4	0	0	1	0	1
C	6	11	0	0	2	3	1
D	6	12	0	0	3	1	2
Total	26	40	0	2	6	5	8
				%	31.58	26.32	42.11
				Odds	3.17	3.80	2.38

Corners

	Corner Supremacy			Corner Numbers		
Team	Won	Draw	Lost	0-9	10-12	13+
A	2	0	3	0	4	1
B	1	0	1	0	0	2
C	4	1	1	2	3	1
D	4	0	2	2	0	4
Total	11	1	7	4	7	8
%	57.89	5.26	36.84	21.05	36.84	42.11
Odds	1.73	19.00	2.71	4.75	2.71	2.38

Summary

- Tottenham won 13 of their 19 home games (68% / odds 1.46) with a half-time/full-time result of H/H.
- Nine of Tottenham's 11 home matches (82% / 1.22) against grade A and D sides featured over 2.5 goals.
- Tottenham won eight of their 19 home games (42% / 2.40) by two goals or more.
- Five of Tottenham's seven home games (71% / odds 1.40) against grade A and B sides featured five or more bookings.
- They won corner superiority in nine of 14 home games (64% / odds 1.56) against grade B, C and D opponents.

Away (Graded Analysis)

	Away Record					
Team	Won	Draw	Lost	F	A	Pts
A	1	0	4	2	11	3
B	0	2	0	3	3	2
C	3	2	1	8	6	11
D	3	1	2	14	9	10
Total	7	5	7	27	29	26
%	36.84	26.32	36.84			
Odds	2.71	3.80	2.71			

	Half Time / Full Time Results								
Team	H/H	H/D	H/A	D/H	D/D	D/A	A/H	A/D	A/A
A	3	0	0	1	0	1	0	0	0
B	0	1	0	0	1	0	0	0	0
C	1	0	0	0	2	2	0	0	1
D	1	0	0	0	1	0	1	0	3
Total	5	1	0	1	4	3	1	0	4
%	26.32	5.26	0.00	5.26	21.05	15.79	5.26	0.00	21.05
Odds	3.80	19.00	N/A	19.00	4.75	6.33	19.00	N/A	4.75

Goals

	Match goals				
Team	1 or More	Ov. 1.5	Ov. 2.5	Ov. 3.5	Ov. 4.5
A	5	4	3	1	0
B	1	2	1	1	0
C	5	5	3	1	0
D	6	5	5	3	2
Total	17	16	12	6	2
%	89.47	84.21	63.16	31.58	10.53
Odds	1.12	1.19	1.58	3.17	9.50

	Clean Sheet		Scored	
Team	Yes	No	Yes	No
A	1	4	2	3
B	0	2	2	0
C	2	3	4	1
D	1	6	7	0
Total	4	15	15	4
%	21.05	78.95	78.95	21.05
Odds	4.75	1.27	1.27	4.75

	Won By			Draw	Lost By		
Team	+3	2	1	0	1	2	+3
A	0	0	1	0	0	2	2
B	0	1	0	2	0	0	0
C	0	0	0	2	0	1	0
D	2	0	3	1	1	1	0
Total	2	1	4	5	1	4	2
%	10.53	5.26	21.05	26.32	5.26	21.05	10.53
Odds	9.50	19.00	4.75	3.80	19.00	4.75	9.50

Bookings

	Yellow Cards		Red Cards		Betfair Points		
Team	F	A	F	A	0-5	6-8	9+
A	9	4	0	0	3	1	1
B	5	4	0	0	1	0	1
C	6	11	0	1	3	1	2
D	11	13	1	1	1	2	3
Total	31	32	1	2	8	4	7
				%	42.11	21.05	36.84
				Odds	2.38	4.75	2.71

Corners

	Corner Supremacy			Corner Numbers		
Team	Won	Draw	Lost	0-9	10-12	13+
A	1	1	3	3	0	2
B	2	0	0	1	0	1
C	3	1	2	2	2	2
D	3	0	3	1	4	1
Total	9	2	8	7	6	6
%	47.37	10.53	42.11	36.84	31.58	31.58
Odds	2.11	9.50	2.38	2.71	3.17	3.17

Summary

- Tottenham lost three of their five away games against grade A and B sides with a half-time/full-time result of H/H.
- Eight of their 12 away matches (67% / odds 1.50) against grade C and D sides finished in over 2.5 goals.
- Seven of 19 Tottenham away matches (37% / odds 2.70) were lost by Spurs by two or more goals.
- Seven of their 13 away matches (54% / odds 1.86) against grade A, B and C sides featured two bookings or less.
- Four of their seven away matches (57% / odds 1.75) against grade A and B sides produced under 10 corners.

WEST HAM UNITED (Grade C)

Season record

	Home					Away						
Pld	Won	Draw	Lost	F	A	Won	Draw	Lost	F	A	GD	Points
38	7	5	7	30	29	1	6	12	17	37	-19	35

Top Scorers

Player	Started	Goals	First	Last	Each Way	Anytime
Carlton Cole	26	10	2	1	9	10
Alessandro Diamanti	18	7	3	2	6	7

Scoring

	Matches Scored In	Clean Sheets	Won to Nil	Both Teams Scored	A Goal 1st Half	A Goal 2nd Half
Home	16	5	4	12	15	17
Away	11	3	1	10	13	17
Total	27	8	5	22	28	34

Match Goal Times

	First Goal of Match			
	1st 10 mins	**Before 27 mins**	**After 27 mins**	**No Goals**
Home	3	9	6	4
Away	3	8	4	7
Total	6	17	10	11
%	15.79	44.74	26.32	28.95
Break-Even Odds	6.33	2.24	3.80	3.45

	Last Goal of Match			
	Before 75 mins	**After 75 mins**	**90+ min Goal**	**No Goals**
Home	5	12	5	2
Away	7	10	2	2
Total	12	22	7	4
%	31.58	57.89	18.42	10.53
Break-Even Odds	3.17	1.73	5.43	9.50

Half Time/Full time

	Half Time / Full Time Results								
	H/H	**H/D**	**H/A**	**D/H**	**D/D**	**D/A**	**A/H**	**A/D**	**A/A**
Home	6	2	0	1	2	3	0	1	4
%	31.58	10.53	0.00	5.26	10.53	15.79	0.00	5.26	21.05
Break-Even Odds	3.17	9.50	N/A	19.00	9.50	6.33	N/A	19.00	4.75
Away	7	2	0	5	3	0	0	1	1
%	36.84	10.53	0.00	26.32	15.79	0.00	0.00	5.26	5.26
Break-Even Odds	2.71	9.50	N/A	3.80	6.33	N/A	N/A	19.00	19.00

Goals

	Match goals				
	1 or More	Ov. 1.5	Ov. 2.5	Ov. 3.5	Ov. 4.5
Home	18	16	12	7	3
Away	17	15	11	7	3
Total	35	31	23	14	6
%	92.11	81.58	60.53	36.84	15.79
Break-Even Odds	1.09	1.23	1.65	2.71	6.33

Bookings

	Yellow Cards		Red Cards		Betfair Points		
	F	A	F	A	0-5	6-8	9+
Home	27	43	1	5	5	5	9
%	N/A	N/A	N/A	N/A	26.32	26.32	47.37
Break-Even Odds	N/A	N/A	N/A	N/A	3.80	3.80	2.11
Away	39	28	2	3	6	5	8
%	N/A	N/A	N/A	N/A	31.58	26.32	42.11
Break-Even Odds	N/A	N/A	N/A	N/A	3.17	3.80	2.38

Corner Superiority

	Corner Supremacy			Corner Numbers		
	Won	Draw	Lost	0-9	10-12	13+
Home	8	2	9	8	6	5
%	42.11	10.53	47.37	42.11	31.58	26.32
Break-Even Odds	2.38	9.50	2.11	2.38	3.17	3.80
Away	5	0	14	4	9	6
%	26.32	0.00	73.68	21.05	47.37	31.58
Break-Even Odds	3.80	N/A	1.36	4.75	2.11	3.17

Summary

- 23 of West Ham's matches (60.53%) contained three or more goals; backing over 2.5 goals, at odds over 1.70, would have yielded a level stake profit last season.
- Both teams scored in 22 of West Ham's matches (57.89%), the second highest number in the Premier League last season.
- In the 14 matches West Ham were drawing at half-time, they went on win the match just once (7.14%), going on to lose in eight of them (57.14%).
- In the 14 matches West Ham were losing at half-time, they went on lose in 11 of them (78.57%).
- 35 of their matches (92.10%) had at least one goal in the second half, the highest in the Premier League last season.

Home (Graded Analysis)

	Home Record					
Team	Won	Draw	Lost	F	A	Pts
A	0	3	2	6	11	3
B	1	0	2	4	5	3
C	2	2	1	5	3	8
D	4	0	2	15	10	12
Total	7	5	7	30	29	26
%	36.84	26.32	36.84			
Odds	2.71	3.80	2.71			

	Half Time / Full Time Results								
Team	H/H	H/D	H/A	D/H	D/D	D/A	A/H	A/D	A/A
A	0	1	0	0	1	1	0	1	1
B	1	0	0	0	0	1	0	0	1
C	1	1	0	1	1	1	0	0	0
D	4	0	0	0	0	0	0	0	2
Total	6	2	0	1	2	3	0	1	4
%	31.58	10.53	0.00	5.26	10.53	15.79	0.00	5.26	21.05
Odds	3.17	9.50	N/A	19.00	9.50	6.33	N/A	19.00	4.75

Goals

	Match goals				
Team	1 or More	Ov. 1.5	Ov. 2.5	Ov. 3.5	Ov. 4.5
A	5	5	3	3	1
B	3	3	3	0	0
C	4	3	1	1	0
D	6	6	5	3	2
Total	18	17	12	7	3
%	94.74	89.47	63.16	36.84	15.79
Odds	1.06	1.12	1.58	2.71	6.33

	Clean Sheet		Scored	
Team	Yes	No	Yes	No
A	0	5	4	1
B	0	3	3	0
C	3	2	3	2
D	2	4	6	0
Total	5	14	16	3
%	26.32	73.68	84.21	15.79
Odds	3.80	1.36	1.19	6.33

	Won By			Draw	Lost By		
Team	+3	2	1	0	1	2	+3
A	0	0	0	3	1	0	1
B	0	0	1	0	2	0	0
C	0	1	1	2	1	0	0
D	1	2	1	0	1	1	0
Total	1	3	3	5	5	1	1
%	5.26	15.79	15.79	26.32	26.32	5.26	5.26
Odds	19.00	6.33	6.33	3.80	3.80	19.00	19.00

Bookings

	Yellow Cards		Red Cards		Betfair Points		
Team	F	A	F	A	0-5	6-8	9+
A	12	9	1	0	2	0	3
B	4	10	0	1	0	1	2
C	5	10	0	1	2	2	1
D	6	14	0	3	1	2	3
Total	27	43	1	5	5	5	9
				%	26.32	26.32	47.37
				Odds	3.80	3.80	2.11

Corners

	Corner Supremacy			Corner Numbers		
Team	Won	Draw	Lost	0-9	10-12	13+
A	1	2	2	2	2	1
B	1	0	2	1	1	1
C	2	0	3	2	1	2
D	4	0	2	3	2	1
Total	8	2	9	8	6	5
%	42.11	10.53	47.37	42.11	31.58	26.32
Odds	2.38	9.50	2.11	2.38	3.17	3.80

Summary

- West Ham won four of six home matches (67% / odds 1.50) against grade D sides with a full-time/half-time result of H/H.
- 11 of 14 West Ham home matches (78% / odds 1.27) against grade A, B and D sides finished in over 2.5 goals.
- West Ham won three of six home matches (50% / odds 2.00) against grade D sides by two goals or more.
- Eight of 14 West Ham home matches (57% / odds 1.75) against A, B and D sides featured five or more bookings.
- They lost nine of 13 home games (69% / odds 1.44) in corner superiority.

Away (Graded Analysis)

	Away Record					
Team	Won	Draw	Lost	F	A	Pts
A	0	0	5	2	15	0
B	0	2	1	2	4	2
C	0	2	3	5	8	2
D	1	2	3	8	10	5
Total	1	6	12	17	37	9
%	5.26	31.58	63.16			
Odds	19.00	3.17	1.58			

	Half Time / Full Time Results								
Team	H/H	H/D	H/A	D/H	D/D	D/A	A/H	A/D	A/A
A	4	0	0	1	0	0	0	0	0
B	1	1	0	0	1	0	0	0	0
C	1	0	0	2	1	0	0	1	0
D	1	1	0	2	1	0	0	0	1
Total	7	2	0	5	3	0	0	1	1
%	36.84	10.53	0.00	26.32	15.79	0.00	0.00	5.26	5.26
Odds	2.71	9.50	N/A	3.80	6.33	N/A	N/A	19.00	19.00

Goals

	Match goals				
Team	1 or More	Ov. 1.5	Ov. 2.5	Ov. 3.5	Ov. 4.5
A	5	5	4	2	1
B	2	2	1	1	0
C	4	3	3	2	0
D	6	5	3	2	1
Total	17	15	11	7	2
%	89.47	78.95	57.89	36.84	10.53
Odds	1.12	1.27	1.73	2.71	9.50

	Clean Sheet		Scored	
Team	Yes	No	Yes	No
A	0	5	2	3
B	1	2	1	2
C	1	4	3	2
D	1	5	5	1
Total	3	16	11	8
%	15.79	84.21	57.89	42.11
Odds	6.33	1.19	1.73	2.38

	Won By			Draw	Lost By		
Team	+3	2	1	0	1	2	+3
A	0	0	0	0	0	2	3
B	0	0	0	2	0	1	0
C	0	0	0	2	3	0	0
D	0	1	0	2	2	1	0
Total	0	1	0	6	5	4	3
%	0.00	5.26	0.00	31.58	26.32	21.05	15.79
Odds	N/A	19.00	N/A	3.17	3.80	4.75	6.33

Bookings

	Yellow Cards		Red Cards		Betfair Points		
Team	F	A	F	A	0-5	6-8	9+
A	9	2	0	1	4	0	1
B	9	5	0	0	0	1	2
C	13	10	2	1	1	1	3
D	8	11	0	1	1	3	2
Total	39	28	2	3	6	5	8
				%	31.58	26.32	42.11
				Odds	3.17	3.80	2.38

Corners

	Corner Supremacy			Corner Numbers		
Team	Won	Draw	Lost	0-9	10-12	13+
A	1	0	4	1	2	2
B	1	0	2	0	2	1
C	1	0	4	1	3	1
D	2	0	4	2	2	2
Total	5	0	14	4	9	6
%	26.32	0.00	73.68	21.05	47.37	31.58
Odds	3.80	N/A	1.36	4.75	2.11	3.17

Summary

- West Ham lost four of five away games against grade A sides, with a half-time/full-time result of H/H.
- 11 of their 19 away matches (58% / odds 1.73) featured over 2.5 goals.
- Six of their 14 away matches (43% / odds 2.33) against grade B, C and D sides finished in a draw.
- Only four of West Ham's five away matches against grade A sides featured two bookings or less.
- West Ham lost 14 of 19 away matches (74% / odds 1.36) in corner superiority.

WIGAN ATHLETIC (Grade D)

Season record

	Home					Away						
Pld	Won	Draw	Lost	F	A	Won	Draw	Lost	F	A	GD	Points
38	6	7	6	19	24	3	2	14	18	55	-42	36

Top Scorers

Player	Started	Goals	First	Last	Each Way	Anytime
Hugo Rodallega	38	10	5	5*	8	9

*__Last Scorer__ – Hugo Rodallega (four times), 1-0 victories at home against West Ham, Liverpool, Sunderland and Burnley.

Scoring

	Matches Scored In	Clean Sheets	Won to Nil	Both Teams Scored	A Goal 1st Half	A Goal 2nd Half
Home	13	6	4	9	12	14
Away	12	2	2	10	15	18
Total	25	8	6	19	27	32

Match Goal Times

	First Goal of Match			
	1st 10 mins	Before 27 mins	After 27 mins	No Goals
Home	1	5	7	7
Away	6	10	5	4
Total	7	15	12	11
%	18.42	39.47	31.58	28.95
Break-Even Odds	5.43	2.53	3.17	3.45

	Last Goal of Match			
	Before 75 mins	After 75 mins	90+ min Goal	No Goals
Home	5	9	6	5
Away	6	12	6	1
Total	11	21	12	6
%	28.95	55.26	31.58	15.79
Break-Even Odds	3.45	1.81	3.17	6.33

Half Time/Full time

	Half Time / Full Time Results								
	H/H	H/D	H/A	D/H	D/D	D/A	A/H	A/D	A/A
Home	2	2	1	3	4	3	1	1	2
%	10.53	10.53	5.26	15.79	21.05	15.79	5.26	5.26	10.53
Break-Even Odds	9.50	9.50	19.00	6.33	4.75	6.33	19.00	19.00	9.50
Away	10	0	0	3	1	2	1	1	1
%	52.63	0.00	0.00	15.79	5.26	10.53	5.26	5.26	5.26
Break-Even Odds	1.90	N/A	N/A	6.33	19.00	9.50	19.00	19.00	19.00

Goals

	Match goals				
	1 or More	Ov. 1.5	Ov. 2.5	Ov. 3.5	Ov. 4.5
Home	17	11	7	5	3
Away	19	18	15	9	4
Total	36	29	22	14	7
%	94.74	76.32	57.89	36.84	18.42
Break-Even Odds	1.06	1.31	1.73	2.71	5.43

Bookings

	Yellow Cards		Red Cards		Betfair Points		
	F	A	F	A	0-5	6-8	9+
Home	27	38	0	2	4	9	6
%	N/A	N/A	N/A	N/A	21.05	47.37	31.58
Break-Even Odds	N/A	N/A	N/A	N/A	4.75	2.11	3.17
Away	37	34	3	1	6	7	6
%	N/A	N/A	N/A	N/A	31.58	36.84	31.58
Break-Even Odds	N/A	N/A	N/A	N/A	3.17	2.71	3.17

Corner Superiority

	Corner Supremacy			Corner Numbers		
	Won	Draw	Lost	0-9	10-12	13+
Home	8	3	8	7	5	7
%	42.11	15.79	42.11	36.84	26.32	36.84
Break-Even Odds	2.38	6.33	2.38	2.71	3.80	2.71
Away	8	0	11	10	6	3
%	42.11	0.00	57.89	52.63	31.58	15.79
Break-Even Odds	2.38	N/A	1.73	1.90	3.17	6.33

Summary

- There was at least one second-half goal in 32 of Wigan's 38 matches (84.21%), with the last goal of the match coming after the 75th minute in 21 matches (55.26%).
- A total of 12 Wigan matches (31.58%) had a goal in 90+ minutes, the second highest in the Premier League last season.
- 22 matches out of Wigan's 38 (57.9%) finished with three or more goals; backing over 2.5 goals at above 1.52 would have yielded a level stake profit last season.
- In the eight matches Wigan were winning at half time, they went on to win just two (25%).
- 17 of their matches (44.73%) produced nine or less corners.
- Just ten of their matches (26.31%) had two or less bookings.

Home (Graded Analysis)

Home Record						
Team	Won	Draw	Lost	F	A	Pts
A	3	1	1	8	9	10
B	0	0	3	1	6	0
C	2	3	1	7	6	9
D	1	3	1	3	3	6
Total	6	7	6	19	24	25
%	31.58	36.84	31.58			
Odds	3.17	2.71	3.17			

Half Time / Full Time Results									
Team	H/H	H/D	H/A	D/H	D/D	D/A	A/H	A/D	A/A
A	2	1	0	0	0	1	1	0	0
B	0	0	0	0	0	2	0	0	1
C	0	1	1	2	1	0	0	1	0
D	0	0	0	1	3	0	0	0	1
Total	2	2	1	3	4	3	1	1	2
%	10.53	10.53	5.26	15.79	21.05	15.79	5.26	5.26	10.53
Odds	9.50	9.50	19.00	6.33	4.75	6.33	19.00	19.00	9.50

Goals

	Match goals				
Team	1 or More	Ov. 1.5	Ov. 2.5	Ov. 3.5	Ov. 4.5
A	5	4	3	3	2
B	3	2	2	0	0
C	6	4	1	1	1
D	3	1	1	1	0
Total	17	11	7	5	3
%	89.47	57.89	36.84	26.32	15.79
Odds	1.12	1.73	2.71	3.80	6.33

	Clean Sheet		Scored	
Team	Yes	No	Yes	No
A	1	4	4	1
B	0	3	1	2
C	2	4	6	0
D	3	2	2	3
Total	6	13	13	6
%	31.58	68.42	68.42	31.58
Odds	3.17	1.46	1.46	3.17

	Won By			Draw	Lost By		
Team	+3	2	1	0	1	2	+3
A	0	1	2	1	0	0	1
B	0	0	0	0	2	0	1
C	0	0	1	3	2	0	0
D	0	0	1	3	1	0	0
Total	0	1	4	7	5	0	2
%	0.00	5.26	21.05	36.84	26.32	0.00	10.53
Odds	N/A	19.00	4.75	2.71	3.80	N/A	9.50

Bookings

	Yellow Cards		Red Cards		Betfair Points		
Team	F	A	F	A	0–5	6–8	9+
A	8	11	0	2	0	2	3
B	5	7	0	0	1	1	1
C	9	12	0	0	1	3	2
D	5	8	0	0	2	3	0
Total	27	38	0	2	4	9	6
				%	21.05	47.37	31.58
				Odds	4.75	2.11	3.17

Corners

	Corner Supremacy			Corner Numbers		
Team	Won	Draw	Lost	0–9	10–12	13+
A	1	1	3	1	4	0
B	1	0	2	1	1	1
C	3	1	2	2	0	4
D	3	1	1	3	0	2
Total	8	3	8	7	5	7
%	42.11	15.79	42.11	36.84	26.32	36.84
Odds	2.38	6.33	2.38	2.71	3.80	2.71

Summary

- Three of Wigan's five home matches (60% / odds 1.66) against grade D sides finished with a full-time/half-time result of D/D.
- Ten of Wigan's 11 home matches (91% / 1.09) against grade C and D sides finished in under 2.5 goals.
- Six of Wigan's 11 home matches (55% / odds 1.83) against grade C and D sides ended in a draw.
- Nine of their 19 home games (47% / odds 2.11) ended up with between 6 and 8 Betfair booking points.
- Seven of their eight home matches (87% / odds 1.14) against grade A and B sides finished with under 13 corners.

Away (Graded Analysis)

Team	Away Record					
	Won	Draw	Lost	F	A	Pts
A	0	0	5	1	22	0
B	1	0	2	4	11	3
C	0	2	4	7	11	2
D	2	0	3	6	11	6
Total	3	2	14	18	55	11
%	15.79	10.53	73.68			
Odds	6.33	9.50	1.36			

Team	Half Time / Full Time Results								
	H/H	H/D	H/A	D/H	D/D	D/A	A/H	A/D	A/A
A	4	0	0	1	0	0	0	0	0
B	1	0	0	1	0	0	0	0	1
C	3	0	0	0	1	0	1	1	0
D	2	0	0	1	0	2	0	0	0
Total	10	0	0	3	1	2	1	1	1
%	52.63	0.00	0.00	15.79	5.26	10.53	5.26	5.26	5.26
Odds	1.90	N/A	N/A	6.33	19.00	9.50	19.00	19.00	19.00

Goals

	Match goals				
Team	1 or More	Ov. 1.5	Ov. 2.5	Ov. 3.5	Ov. 4.5
A	5	3	5	3	2
B	3	3	2	1	1
C	6	5	4	2	1
D	5	5	4	3	0
Total	19	16	15	9	4
%	100.00	84.21	78.95	47.37	21.05
Odds	1.00	1.19	1.27	2.11	4.75

	Clean Sheet		Scored	
Team	Yes	No	Yes	No
A	0	5	1	4
B	1	2	3	0
C	0	6	5	1
D	1	4	4	1
Total	2	17	13	6
%	10.53	89.47	68.42	31.58
Odds	9.50	1.12	1.46	3.17

	Won By			Draw	Lost By		
Team	+3	2	1	0	1	2	+3
A	0	0	0	0	1	0	4
B	0	1	0	0	1	0	1
C	0	0	0	2	4	0	0
D	0	2	0	0	1	0	2
Total	0	3	0	2	7	0	7
%	0.00	15.79	0.00	10.53	36.84	0.00	36.84
Odds	N/A	6.33	N/A	9.50	2.71	N/A	2.71

Bookings

	Yellow Cards		Red Cards		Betfair Points		
Team	F	A	F	A	0–5	6–8	9+
A	8	8	2	0	2	1	2
B	7	4	0	0	1	1	1
C	14	15	0	0	0	4	2
D	8	7	1	1	3	1	1
Total	37	34	3	1	6	7	6
				%	31.58	36.84	31.58
				Odds	3.17	2.71	3.17

Corners

	Corner Supremacy			Corner Numbers		
Team	Won	Draw	Lost	0–9	10–12	13+
A	2	0	3	2	2	1
B	1	0	2	0	1	2
C	4	0	2	5	1	0
D	1	0	4	3	2	0
Total	8	0	11	10	6	3
%	42.11	0.00	57.89	52.63	31.58	15.79
Odds	2.38	N/A	1.73	1.90	3.17	6.33

Summary

- Wigan lost ten of their 19 away matches (53% / odds 1.90) with a half-time/full-time result of H/H.
- 15 of their 19 away matches (79% / odds 1.27) produced over 2.5 goals.
- They lost five of eight away matches (63% / odds 1.60) against grade A and B sides by three goals or more.
- Only three of their 11 away matches (27% / odds 3.67) against grade C and D sides featured two or less bookings.
- Eight of their 11 away matches (73% / odds 1.37) against grade C and D sides produced less than ten corners.

WOLVERHAMPTON WANDERERS (Grade D)

Season record

	Home					Away						
Pld	Won	Draw	Lost	F	A	Won	Draw	Lost	F	A	GD	Points
38	5	6	8	13	22	4	5	10	19	34	-24	38

Top Scorers

Player	Started	Goals	First	Last	Each Way	Anytime
Kevin Doyle	33	9	5	2	7	8

Scoring

	Matches Scored In	Clean Sheets	Won to Nil	Both Teams Scored	A Goal 1st Half	A Goal 2nd Half
Home	9	5	2	7	13	13
Away	12	3	2	10	15	14
Total	21	8	4	17	28	27

Match Goal Times

	First Goal of Match			
	1st 10 mins	Before 27 mins	After 27 mins	No Goals
Home	4	7	6	6
Away	4	10	5	4
Total	8	17	11	10
%	21.05	44.74	28.95	26.32
Break-Even Odds	4.75	2.24	3.45	3.80

	Last Goal of Match			
	Before 75 mins	After 75 mins	90+ min Goal	No Goals
Home	7	6	0	6
Away	7	7	3	5
Total	14	13	3	11
%	36.84	34.21	7.89	28.95
Break-Even Odds	2.71	2.92	12.67	3.45

Half Time/Full time

	Half Time / Full Time Results								
	H/H	H/D	H/A	D/H	D/D	D/A	A/H	A/D	A/A
Home	4	0	0	1	4	2	0	2	6
%	21.05	0.00	0.00	5.26	21.05	10.53	0.00	10.53	31.58
Break-Even Odds	4.75	N/A	N/A	19.00	4.75	9.50	N/A	9.50	3.17
Away	7	2	0	2	2	0	1	1	4
%	36.84	10.53	0.00	10.53	10.53	0.00	5.26	5.26	21.05
Break-Even Odds	2.71	9.50	N/A	9.50	9.50	N/A	19.00	19.00	4.75

Goals

	Match goals				
	1 or More	Ov. 1.5	Ov. 2.5	Ov. 3.5	Ov. 4.5
Home	16	12	5	1	1
Away	18	13	11	8	1
Total	34	25	16	9	2
%	89.47	65.79	42.11	23.68	5.26
Break-Even Odds	1.12	1.52	2.38	4.22	19.00

Bookings

	Yellow Cards		Red Cards		Betfair Points		
	F	A	F	A	0-5	6-8	9+
Home	24	26	1	3	8	7	4
%	N/A	N/A	N/A	N/A	42.11	36.84	21.05
Break-Even Odds	N/A	N/A	N/A	N/A	2.38	2.71	4.75
Away	40	14	3	0	8	6	5
%	N/A	N/A	N/A	N/A	42.11	31.58	26.32
Break-Even Odds	N/A	N/A	N/A	N/A	2.38	3.17	3.80

Corner Superiority

	Corner Supremacy			Corner Numbers		
	Won	Draw	Lost	0-9	10-12	13+
Home	10	4	5	8	7	4
%	52.63	21.05	26.32	42.11	36.84	21.05
Break-Even Odds	1.90	4.75	3.80	2.38	2.71	4.75
Away	8	1	10	4	6	9
%	42.11	5.26	52.63	21.05	31.58	47.37
Break-Even Odds	2.38	19.00	1.90	4.75	3.17	2.11

Summary

- Wolves scored in only 21 of their total 38 matches (55.26%), the lowest number of matches for any team in the Premier League last season.
- In only 13 of all their matches (34.21%) was the last goal of the game scored after the 75th minute.
- Just 16 matches out of their 38 (42.11%) finished with three or more goals; backing under 2.5 goals at above 1.75 would have yielded a level stake profit last season.
- In the ten matches Wolves were winning at half time, they went on to win eight times (80%).
- 16 Wolves matches (42.11%) had two or less bookings.
- Wolves achieved corner supremacy in 18 out of 38 games (47.37%).

Home (Graded Analysis)

	Home Record					
Team	Won	Draw	Lost	F	A	Pts
A	0	1	4	1	10	1
B	1	2	0	2	1	5
C	2	2	2	5	6	8
D	2	1	2	5	5	7
Total	5	6	8	13	22	21
%	26.32	31.58	42.11			
Odds	3.80	3.17	2.38			

	Half Time / Full Time Results								
Team	H/H	H/D	H/A	D/H	D/D	D/A	A/H	A/D	A/A
A	0	0	0	0	1	1	0	0	3
B	1	0	0	0	2	0	0	0	0
C	1	0	0	1	1	0	0	1	2
D	2	0	0	0	0	1	0	1	1
Total	4	0	0	1	4	2	0	2	6
%	21.05	0.00	0.00	5.26	21.05	10.53	0.00	10.53	31.58
Odds	4.75	N/A	N/A	19.00	4.75	9.50	N/A	9.50	3.17

Goals

	Match goals				
Team	1 or More	Ov. 1.5	Ov. 2.5	Ov. 3.5	Ov. 4.5
A	4	3	2	1	1
B	2	1	0	0	0
C	5	4	2	0	0
D	5	4	1	0	0
Total	16	12	5	1	1
%	84.21	63.16	26.32	5.26	5.26
Odds	1.19	1.58	3.80	19.00	19.00

	Clean Sheet		Scored	
Team	Yes	No	Yes	No
A	1	4	1	4
B	2	1	2	1
C	1	5	3	3
D	1	4	3	2
Total	5	14	9	10
%	26.32	73.68	47.37	52.63
Odds	3.80	1.36	2.11	1.90

	Won By			Draw	Lost By		
Team	+3	2	1	0	1	2	+3
A	0	0	0	1	1	1	2
B	0	0	1	2	0	0	0
C	0	0	2	2	1	1	0
D	0	1	1	1	1	1	0
Total	0	1	4	6	3	3	2
%	0.00	5.26	21.05	31.58	15.79	15.79	10.53
Odds	N/A	19.00	4.75	3.17	6.33	6.33	9.50

Bookings

	Yellow Cards		Red Cards		Betfair Points		
Team	F	A	F	A	0-5	6-8	9+
A	7	8	0	0	2	1	2
B	4	4	0	0	1	2	0
C	4	5	0	2	4	1	1
D	9	9	1	1	1	3	1
Total	24	26	1	3	8	7	4
				%	42.11	36.84	21.05
				Odds	2.38	2.71	4.75

Corners

	Corner Supremacy			Corner Numbers		
Team	Won	Draw	Lost	0-9	10-12	13+
A	1	1	3	4	1	0
B	1	0	2	0	3	0
C	4	2	0	3	1	2
D	4	1	0	1	2	2
Total	10	4	5	8	7	4
%	52.63	21.05	26.32	42.11	36.84	21.05
Odds	1.90	4.75	3.80	2.38	2.71	4.75

Summary

- 14 of Wolves' 19 home matches (74% / odds 1.35) finished with the same result at full time as at half time.
- 14 of Wolves' 19 home matches (74% / 1.35) finished with under 2.5 goals.
- Five of their eight losses at home came by two or more goals.
- 15 of their 19 home games (79% / odds 1.27) had less than five bookings.
- Wolves won eight of 11 home matches (73% / odds 1.37) against grade C and D sides in corner superiority.

Away (Graded Analysis)

	Away Record					
Team	Won	Draw	Lost	F	A	Pts
A	0	0	5	0	11	0
B	1	2	0	4	3	5
C	1	2	3	9	13	5
D	2	1	2	6	7	7
Total	4	5	10	19	34	17
%	21.05	26.32	52.63			
Odds	4.75	3.80	1.90			

	Half Time / Full Time Results								
Team	H/H	H/D	H/A	D/H	D/D	D/A	A/H	A/D	A/A
A	3	0	0	2	0	0	0	0	0
B	0	0	0	0	1	0	0	1	1
C	2	1	0	0	1	0	1	0	1
D	2	1	0	0	0	0	0	0	2
Total	7	2	0	2	2	0	1	1	4
%	36.84	10.53	0.00	10.53	10.53	0.00	5.26	5.26	21.05
Odds	2.71	9.50	N/A	9.50	9.50	N/A	19.00	19.00	4.75

Goals

	Match goals				
Team	1 or More	Ov. 1.5	Ov. 2.5	Ov. 3.5	Ov. 4.5
A	5	3	2	1	0
B	3	2	1	1	1
C	5	5	5	4	1
D	5	3	3	2	0
Total	18	13	11	8	2
%	94.74	68.42	57.89	42.11	10.53
Odds	1.06	1.46	1.73	2.38	9.50

	Clean Sheet		Scored	
Team	Yes	No	Yes	No
A	0	5	0	5
B	1	2	3	0
C	1	5	5	1
D	1	4	4	1
Total	3	16	12	7
%	15.79	84.21	63.16	36.84
Odds	6.33	1.19	1.58	2.71

	Won By			Draw	Lost By		
Team	+3	2	1	0	1	2	+3
A	0	0	0	0	2	1	2
B	0	0	1	2	0	0	0
C	0	1	0	2	1	1	1
D	0	0	2	1	1	1	0
Total	0	1	3	5	4	3	3
%	0.00	5.26	15.79	26.32	21.05	15.79	15.79
Odds	N/A	19.00	6.33	3.80	4.75	6.33	6.33

Bookings

	Yellow Cards		Red Cards		Betfair Points		
Team	F	A	F	A	0-5	6-8	9+
A	7	1	2	0	3	1	1
B	10	2	1	0	0	1	2
C	13	8	0	0	2	3	1
D	10	3	0	0	3	1	1
Total	40	14	3	0	8	6	5
				%	42.11	31.58	26.32
				Odds	2.38	3.17	3.80

Corners

	Corner Supremacy			Corner Numbers		
Team	Won	Draw	Lost	0-9	10-12	13+
A	2	0	3	1	3	1
B	1	0	2	1	2	0
C	2	0	4	1	0	5
D	3	1	1	1	1	3
Total	8	1	10	4	6	9
%	42.11	5.26	52.63	21.05	31.58	47.37
Odds	2.38	19.00	1.90	4.75	3.17	2.11

Summary

- Wolves lost four of 11 away matches (36% / odds 2.75) against grade C and D sides with a half-time/full-time result of H/H.
- Eight of Wolves' 11 away matches (73% / odds 1.37) against grade C and D sides produced over 2.5 goals.
- Six of Wolves' ten away defeats were by two goals or more.
- Five of their 11 away matches (45% / odds 2.20) against grade C and D sides featured two or less bookings
- Eight of Wolves' 11 away matches (73% / odds 1.37) against grade C and D sides featured 13 or more corners.

Premier Betting 2010/11 Top Betting Trend Tips

Below are listed, by team, the top trends from last season that we believe may continue to be profitable through the current season.

ARSENAL

Look to back Arsenal in the corner supremacy markets home and away.

Last season they won in corner supremacy in 32 out of 38 games (84.21%, odds 1.19).

Look to back Arsenal at home on the Asian Handicaps, giving away -1.5 goals against grade B, C and D sides.

In 15 away games against grade B, C and D sides, Arsenal won by at least two goals 13 times (86%). This equates to odds of 1.15.

ASTON VILLA

Look to back under 2.5 goals in Villa's home and away matches.

Last season only 15 of their matches out of 38 (39.47%) finished with three or more goals; backing under 2.5 goals at above 1.65 would have yielded a level stake profit for the year.

Look to oppose Villa in the corner superiority markets away from home.

Last season, in corner superiority against grade A, B and C opposition, Villa lost 11 of 13 away matches (85%, odds 1.18).

BIRMINGHAM CITY

Look to back under 2.5 goals in Birmingham's home games.

Last season, 13 of their 19 home games finished in under 2.5 goals (68% / odds 1.47).

BLACKBURN ROVERS

Look to back under 9 corners in Blackburn's home and away matches.

Last season, 20 out of their total 38 matches (52.63%) had nine or less corners in the match.

Look to back under 2.5 goals in Blackburn's away matches against grade D opposition.

Last season all six of their games away to grade D sides finished with under 2.5 goals.

BOLTON WANDERERS

Look to back over 3.5 goals in Bolton's home and away matches.

Last season, 14 matches out of their total 38 matches (36.84%) finished with four or more goals; backing over 3.5 goals at above 2.75 would have yielded a level stake profit.

CHELSEA

Look to back over 2.5 goals in Chelsea's home and away matches.

27 matches out of their 38 (71.05%) finished with three or more goals; backing over 2.5 goals at above 1.41 would have yielded a level stake profit last season.

Look to back Chelsea at home on the Asian Handicaps giving away -1.5 goals against grade B, C and D sides.

Last season Chelsea won by three goals or more in ten of 15 home matches (67%, odds 1.50) against grade B, C and D sides.

EVERTON

Back Everton at home against grade C and D sides in the corner superiority markets.

Last season Everton won 10 of 12 home matches (84%, odds 1.20) in corner superiority markets against grade C and D sides.

Look to back over 2.5 goals in Everton's away matches at sides graded A, B and C.

Last season, 11 of 13 away matches (85%, 1.18) at grade A, B and C sides featured over 2.5 goals.

FULHAM

Back 0-5 points on the Betfair booking markets in Fulham's home and away games.

Last season Fulham had two or less bookings in 23 matches (60.53%).

When away from home, back Fulham's grade A, B and C opponents to keep a clean sheet.

Last season Fulham only scored in five of 13 away matches (38%, odds 2.60) against sides graded A, B and C.

LIVERPOOL

Look to back Liverpool under 1.5 goals away from home.

Only 11 of Liverpool's matches away from home (57.90%, odds 1.73) had two or more goals last season. Backing under 1.5 goals at odds of over 2.40 would have yielded a profit and you would have received a bigger price than that in every single game.

Look to back Liverpool at home on the Asian Handicaps giving away -1.5 goals against grade C and D sides.

Last season, in eight of 12 home games (67%, odds 1.50) against grade C and D sides, Liverpool won by two goals or more.

MANCHESTER CITY

Back over 3.5 goals in matches both home and away.

Last season 13 matches (34.21%) contained four or more goals, and backing over 3.5 goals at odds over 3.0 would have yielded a level stake profit.

Back the draw in Man City's away matches.

Last season nine of Man City's 19 away matches (47%, odds 2.11) finished in a draw.

MANCHESTER UNITED

Look to back late goals in the last 15 minutes of Manchester United's home and away matches.

Last season the last goal of the match was scored after 75 minutes in 71.05% of all their matches, the highest rate in the Premier League last season.

Back over 2.5 goals in Manchester United's home and away matches.

Last season 25 matches out of their full 38 (65.79%) finished with three or more goals; backing over 2.5 goals at above 1.52 would have yielded a level stake profit.

STOKE CITY

Back under 2.5 goals in Stoke's home and away matches.

Last season only 14 matches out of 38 (36.84%) finished with three or more goals; backing under 2.5 goals at above 1.58 would have yielded a level stake profit.

Back the draw in Stoke's away matches to grade B, C and D sides.

Last season Stoke drew eight of 14 away matches (57%, odds 1.75) against grade B, C and D opposition.

SUNDERLAND

Look to back the first goal before the 27th minute in Sunderland's home and away matches.

Last season in 28 matches out of 38 (73.68%) the first goal of the match came before the 27th minute.

Back under 2.5 goals in Sunderland's away matches against B, C and D sides.

Ten of Sunderland's 14 away matches (71%, odds 1.40) against grade B, C and D sides finished under 2.5 goals.

TOTTENHAM HOTSPUR

Look to back over 2.5 goals in Spurs' home and away matches.

Last season 24 matches out of their 38 (63.16%) finished with three or more goals; backing over 2.5 goals at above 1.60 would have yielded a level stake profit.

Back over 9 booking points on the Betfair markets when Spurs are playing away at grade A and B sides.

Last season, five of seven away games (71%, odds 1.40) against grade A and B sides featured five or more bookings.

WEST HAM

Look to back over 2.5 goals in West Ham's home and away matches.

Last season 23 matches of their 38 (60.53%) contained three or more goals in the game and backing over 2.5 goals at over 1.70 would have yielded a level stake profit.

Look to back West Ham's opponents away from home in the corner superiority markets.

Last season, away from home, West Ham lost 14 of 19 matches (74%, odds 1.36) in corner superiority.

WIGAN

If Wigan are ahead at half time, look to oppose them in the second half.

In the eight matches Wigan were winning at half time, they went on to win just two (25%).

At home, look to back the draw when Wigan are playing grade C and D sides.

Six of 11 home matches (55%, dds 1.83) against grade C and D sides ended in a draw.

WOLVERHAMPTON WANDERERS

Look to back Wolves if leading at half time home and away.

In the ten matches Wolves were winning at half time, they went on to win eight (80%) of them.

Look to back under 2.5 goals in Wolves' away matches.

14 of Wolves' 19 away matches (74%, odds 1.35) finished in under 2.5 goals.

Promoted Sides

Looking at the promoted sides for 2010/11 – Newcastle, West Brom and Blackpool – you clearly cannot read too much into last season's stats, as they were playing at a lower level.

Normally all three of these sides would be regarded as grade D, but on this occasion we are going to raise Newcastle to grade C status. This is because in previous seasons they have performed reasonably well in the Premiership and they won the Championship with commensurate ease.

West Brom are the eternal one season up, one season down club, and we would be surprised if Blackpool managed to hold on to their Premiership status by the end of the 2010/11 season. We anticipate that they will be very much the Burnley of this term, though perhaps with more colourful press conferences (their manager, Ian Holloway, is something of a character, having recently lamented the prohibition on players removing shirts in celebrations, and the trend to longer, looser shorts, as both driving prospective female fans away from the game…).

So for these three teams, rather than give you nothing dependable, or leave you with nothing at all, we've provided a brief overview of their performances last year and a tailored summary for what might be of particular interest or use in the 2010/11 Premier League season.

NEWCASTLE UNITED (C)

Home

Played 23, Won 18, Drew 5, Lost 0

Newcastle were undefeated at home and only dropped ten points there all season. Of their 18 victories, 13 resulted in a half-time/full-time H/H result.

Goals

Over 2.5 goals occurred in 14 of their home matches. They scored at least two goals in 18 home matches and on only two occasions did they concede more than one goal (and that includes the final home game against Ipswich, where they drew 2-2).

Bookings

When it came to discipline, Newcastle kept their cool on most home occasions and their opponents invariably had more bookings than them – with a W13 D6 L4 record. Indeed, Newcastle only picked up two or more bookings in five matches.

Corners

With regards to the corner markets, Newcastle were not as strong as you would expect from a team that won the league so comfortably. In their 23 home matches their corner superiority record reads W13 D1 L9.

Summary

Considering Newcastle won this league at a canter, their corner superiority record is not that good. Something to bear in mind this year.

Away

Played 23, Won 12, Drew 7, Lost 4

Newcastle had the best away, as well as home, record in the league, and of their 12 victories, eight came about by the half-time/full-time result A/A.

Goals

No real goal scoring trends emerged, although they did only fail to score in three matches.

Bookings

When it came to discipline, they were almost the complete opposite and were shown more cards than their opponents in 15 matches away, with a W6 D2 L15 record.

Corners

As at home, when it came to the corners markets they did not perform as you would expect, with a W8 D1 L14 record.

Summary

As with their home form this season, we would certainly suggest that you look to oppose Newcastle on the corner superiority markets.

WEST BROMWICH ALBION (D)

Home

Played 23, Won 16, Drew 3, Lost 4

West Brom had the third best home record in the Championship, behind only Newcastle and Nottingham Forest. Ten of their 16 home victories resulted in a half-time/full-time H/H result. They were only behind at half time in two matches.

Goals

Over 3.5 goals appeared in 11 home matches.

Bookings

When it came to discipline, 11 of the matches played at the Hawthorns produced two or less bookings.

Corners

In terms of corner superiority, West Brom were W16 D2 L5, with only four matches featuring under nine corners.

Summary

Looking at these home stats from last season, it is hard to see any trends that may apply to West Brom at the Premiership level. That said, when it came to discipline the home matches tended not to be feisty affairs.

Away

Played 23, Won 10, Drew 10, Lost 3

West Brom had the second best away form in the league, only losing three matches.

Goals

Once again, some of the matches tended to be high scoring with 11 matches producing over 3.5 goals. Indeed West Brom only failed to score in two away matches.

Bookings

West Brom's disciplinary record away from home was completely the opposite of their home record. They received more cards than their opponents in ten matches, and the same number of cards in eight. West Brom received four cards or over in eight matches.

Corners

Away from home, West Brom had a good record in the corner superiority stakes, with a W16 D2 L5 record. Interestingly, though, 11 matches featured nine or under corners.

Summary

West Brom's disciplinary record away from home could be interesting in the 2010/11 Premier League contest – since away points will be at a premium, and they are almost certain to be in a relegation dog fight, these stats could come to the fore again.

BLACKPOOL (D)

Home

Played 23, Won 13, Drew 6, Lost 4

Blackpool had the fourth best home record in the Championship, behind Newcastle, Nottingham Forest and West Brom. Eight of their 13 home victories resulted in a half-time/full-time H/H result. They were behind at half time in four of their matches.

Goals

Only two of their matches featured under 1.5 goals.

Bookings

When it came to discipline, 12 of the matches played at home produced two or less bookings.

Corners

In the corner superiority stakes, Blackpool were W13 D0 L10, with 15 matches featuring over 10.5 corners.

Summary

Looking at the stats from last season, it would appear that games played at Blackpool tend to be fairly clean affairs (with only two red cards being shown all season).

Away

Played 23, Won 6, Drew 7, Lost 10

Blackpool had a very average away record, finishing tenth in the away table.

Goals

They have average stats in the away goals count, with a tendency towards low scoring. 12 of Blackpool's away games featured under 2.5 goals and they also kept seven clean sheets away.

Bookings

As at home, Blackpool's away matches were fairly disciplined affairs, with 12 matches featuring two or less bookings.

Corners

Away from home, Blackpool had a mediocre record in the corner superiority stakes with a W7 D4 L12 record.

Summary

Blackpool had a very mediocre record away last season and it would be a major surprise to see them do anything other than struggle away from home throughout 2010/11.

11

The Referees

Martin Atkinson

PREMIER LEAGUE						BETFAIR POINTS		
Year	Games	Yellow	Red	Y-Ave	R-Ave	5	6-8	9+
2005/06	18	49	1	2.72	0.06	10	4	4
2006/07	24	74	3	3.08	0.13	9	9	6
2007/08	26	81	3	3.12	0.12	6	13	7
2008/09	26	85	6	3.27	0.23	10	6	10
2009/10	32	126	5	3.94	0.16	4	13	15
Total	126	415	18	3.29	0.14	39	45	42

OTHER MATCHES						BETFAIR POINTS		
Year	Games	Yellow	Red	Y-Ave	R-Ave	5	6-8	9+
2005/06	20	29	1	1.45	0.05	14	5	1
2006/07	18	54	3	3.00	0.17	5	11	2
2007/08	18	28	2	1.55	0.11	10	4	4
2008/09	14	50	5	3.57	0.36	4	3	7
2009/10	17	64	1	3.76	0.06	6	5	6
Total	87	225	12	2.59	0.14	39	28	20

COMBINED TOTAL						BETFAIR POINTS		
Year	Games	Yellow	Red	Y-Ave	R-Ave	5	6-8	9+
Overall total	213	640	30	3.00	0.14	78	73	62

The trend with Martin Atkinson seems to be him giving out more yellow cards season on season. And with an average of just under four a game, you certainly wouldn't be looking to back 5 points in the Betfair market.

Over the past two Premier League seasons, 43% of all his matches yielded 9+ points compared with an average of just 25% over the previous three Premier League seasons.

Premier Betting 2010/11 value tip – look to back 9+ points if the odds on Betfair are 2.36 or above.

Stuart Attwell

PREMIER LEAGUE						BETFAIR POINTS		
Year	Games	Yellow	Red	Y-Ave	R-Ave	5	6-8	9+
2005/06	0	0	0	0	0	0	0	0
2006/07	0	0	0	0	0	0	0	0
2007/08	0	0	0	0	0	0	0	0
2008/09	5	17	2	3.40	0.40	2	2	1
2009/10	15	58	2	3.87	0.13	4	5	6
Total	20	75	4	3.75	0.20	6	7	7

OTHER MATCHES						BETFAIR POINTS		
Year	Games	Yellow	Red	Y-Ave	R-Ave	5	6-8	9+
2005/06	0	0	0	0	0	0	0	0
2006/07	0	0	0	0	0	0	0	0
2007/08	32	52	9	1.63	0.28	19	8	5
2008/09	25	77	6	3.08	0.24	9	6	10
2009/10	11	37	2	3.36	0.18	3	3	5
Total	68	166	17	2.44	0.25	31	17	20

COMBINED TOTAL						BETFAIR POINTS		
Year	Games	Yellow	Red	Y-Ave	R-Ave	5	6-8	9+
Overall total	88	241	21	2.74	0.24	37	24	27

Stuart Attwell is one of the referees new to the Premier League, having started officiating in 2008, and it's a little early in his career to spot any definitive trends. There is a fairly even spread of points/cards so far on the 20 games he has officiated at. However, in his last ten games, eight of them contained at least three or more bookings.

In his 17 matches since the beginning of December 2009 (all matches) only three (18%) have had two or less bookings.

Premier Betting 2010/11 value tip – look to lay 5 points if the odds on Betfair are less than 6.0.

Steve Bennett

PREMIER LEAGUE						BETFAIR POINTS		
Year	Games	Yellow	Red	Y-Ave	R-Ave	5	6-8	9+
2005/06	30	109	10	3.63	0.33	3	11	16
2006/07	28	93	5	3.32	0.18	9	12	7
2007/08	31	99	5	3.19	0.16	9	13	9
2008/09	22	78	0	3.55	0.00	4	14	4
2009/10	29	108	5	3.72	0.17	6	11	12
Total	140	487	25	3.48	0.18	31	61	48

OTHER MATCHES						BETFAIR POINTS		
Year	Games	Yellow	Red	Y-Ave	R-Ave	5	6-8	9+
2005/06	11	32	2	2.91	0.18	5	4	2
2006/07	18	66	9	3.67	0.5	4	5	9
2007/08	14	44	4	3.14	0.29	6	3	5
2008/09	12	41	1	3.42	0.08	5	3	4
2009/10	4	15	1	3.75	0.25	2	1	1
Total	59	198	17	3.36	0.29	22	16	21

COMBINED TOTAL						BETFAIR POINTS		
Year	Games	Yellow	Red	Y-Ave	R-Ave	5	6-8	9+
Overall total	199	695	42	3.49	0.21	53	77	69

Steve Bennett has been fairly consistent, with the majority of his games falling into the 6-8 point bracket. However, he has shown a tendency to give out more cards over the past two Premier League seasons, with matches involving two or less cards equating to less than 20% of those he officiated over, compared with his 24% average.

But it's the overall average of nearly 44% over the past five seasons on 6-8 points that interests us the most, as we would expect every match to be over the break-even price of 2.36 on Betfair.

Premier Betting 2010/11 value tip – look to back 6-8 points if the price on Betfair is 2.36 and above.

Mark Clattenburg

PREMIER LEAGUE						BETFAIR POINTS		
Year	Games	Yellow	Red	Y-Ave	R-Ave	5	6-8	9+
2005/06	16	56	0	3.5	0.00	6	7	3
2006/07	27	111	0	4.11	0.00	2	15	10
2007/08	26	95	8	3.65	0.31	5	11	10
2008/09	1	0	0	0.0	0.00	1	0	0
2009/10	31	84	5	2.71	0.16	12	11	8
Total	101	346	13	3.43	0.13	26	44	31

OTHER MATCHES						BETFAIR POINTS		
Year	Games	Yellow	Red	Y-Ave	R-Ave	5	6-8	9+
2005/06	8	25	4	3.13	0.5	2	1	5
2006/07	15	55	3	3.67	0.20	3	7	5
2007/08	13	29	2	2.23	0.15	8	2	3
2008/09	1	0	0	0.00	0.00	1	0	0
2009/10	11	21	0	1.91	0.00	8	2	1
Total	48	130	9	2.71	0.19	22	12	14

COMBINED TOTAL						BETFAIR POINTS		
Year	Games	Yellow	Red	Y-Ave	R-Ave	5	6-8	9+
Overall total	149	476	22	3.19	0.15	48	56	45

Mark Clattenburg is a hard one to work out, because if you look at his first three seasons in this five-year cycle, you would certainly expect him to dish out the cards. But it's the 39% of matches in the more recent 2009/10 season where only two or less cards were shown that clouds the water from a betting point of view.

As with Steve Bennett, it might be worth siding with the middle ground (6-8 points) with just under a 44% success rate on all Clattenburg's Premier League games over the past five seasons. We looked into his Premier League games from January 2010 and with seven out of 13 (54%) matches finishing within 6-8 points, you would have been successful backing within this range.

Premier Betting 2010/11 value tip – look to back 6-8 points if the price on Betfair is 2.36 and above.

Mike Dean

PREMIER LEAGUE						BETFAIR POINTS		
Year	Games	Yellow	Red	Y-Ave	R-Ave	5	6-8	9+
2005/06	23	77	6	3.35	0.26	7	4	12
2006/07	23	98	7	4.26	0.30	7	4	12
2007/08	25	104	9	4.16	0.36	5	5	15
2008/09	30	116	6	3.87	0.2	7	12	11
2009/10	30	114	6	3.8	0.2	7	10	13
Total	131	509	34	3.89	0.26	33	35	63

OTHER MATCHES						BETFAIR POINTS		
Year	Games	Yellow	Red	Y-Ave	R-Ave	5	6-8	9+
2005/06	18	57	4	3.17	0.22	8	2	8
2006/07	18	75	9	4.17	0.5	1	7	10
2007/08	17	50	1	2.94	0.06	6	9	2
2008/09	13	34	4	2.61	0.31	7	2	4
2009/10	13	30	1	2.31	0.08	8	3	2
Total	79	246	19	3.11	0.24	30	23	26

COMBINED TOTAL						BETFAIR POINTS		
Year	Games	Yellow	Red	Y-Ave	R-Ave	5	6-8	9+
Overall total	210	755	53	3.59	0.25	63	58	89

Looking at Mike Dean's stats, it is fairly obvious that he likes to dish the cards out – with 75% of his matches over the past five seasons containing three or more bookings. But it is the 48% of matches in the Premier League producing 9+ points that is the standout stat.

Because the trend is quite obvious, there could be value elsewhere – you may struggle to get odds against in the vast majority of Mr Dean's matches. But with a strike rate of 25% on two or less bookings in the Premier League, and 30% on all matches in total over the past five seasons, if you get over 3/1 (4.0) on Betfair for two or less cards, it would give you a bit of value.

Premier Betting 2010/11 value tip – back 5 points at 3/1 (4.0) or above on Betfair.

Phil Dowd

PREMIER LEAGUE						BETFAIR POINTS		
Year	Games	Yellow	Red	Y-Ave	R-Ave	5	6-8	9+
2005/06	23	100	7	4.35	0.30	4	6	13
2006/07	17	51	2	3	0.12	7	6	4
2007/08	22	66	7	3	0.32	5	10	7
2008/09	30	97	6	3.23	0.2	10	10	10
2009/10	29	87	5	3	0.17	14	8	7
Total	121	401	27	3.31	0.22	40	40	41

OTHER MATCHES						BETFAIR POINTS		
Year	Games	Yellow	Red	Y-Ave	R-Ave	5	6-8	9+
2005/06	23	83	1	3.61	0.04	6	9	8
2006/07	16	48	1	3.00	0.06	6	5	5
2007/08	23	58	4	2.52	0.17	10	6	7
2008/09	15	51	5	3.4	0.33	4	4	7
2009/10	9	45	0	5	0	1	2	6
Total	86	285	11	3.31	0.13	27	26	33

COMBINED TOTAL						BETFAIR POINTS		
Year	Games	Yellow	Red	Y-Ave	R-Ave	5	6-8	9+
Overall total	207	686	38	3.31	0.18	67	66	74

Phil Dowd seems fairly even with the split of cards he gives out, although there was a slight bias last season to not giving many cards out in the Premier League.

What interests us is the fact that less than 25% of all his matches over the past four Premier League seasons have resulted in 9+ points and this is where we could pinpoint some value, by either dutching 5 points with 6-8 points if we can get combined odds over 1.33, or laying 9+ if the price is under 3/1 (4.0) on Betfair.

Premier Betting 2010/11 value tip – dutch 5 points with 6-8 points; you should be able to receive above 1.50 on most matches (break-even price 1.33).

Chris Foy

PREMIER LEAGUE						BETFAIR POINTS		
Year	Games	Yellow	Red	Y-Ave	R-Ave	5	6-8	9+
2005/06	22	58	6	2.64	0.27	10	5	7
2006/07	22	44	4	2	0.18	14	5	3
2007/08	23	74	5	3.22	0.22	7	8	8
2008/09	24	82	3	3.42	0.13	6	11	7
2009/10	26	69	2	2.65	0.08	12	7	7
Total	117	327	20	2.79	0.17	49	36	32

OTHER MATCHES						BETFAIR POINTS		
Year	Games	Yellow	Red	Y-Ave	R-Ave	5	6-8	9+
2005/06	21	45	4	2.14	0.19	12	4	5
2006/07	19	67	3	3.53	0.16	5	8	6
2007/08	14	42	1	3	0.07	7	3	4
2008/09	11	35	0	3.18	0	4	4	3
2009/10	11	38	3	3.45	0.27	3	4	4
Total	76	227	11	2.99	0.14	31	23	22

COMBINED TOTAL						BETFAIR POINTS		
Year	Games	Yellow	Red	Y-Ave	R-Ave	5	6-8	9+
Overall total	193	554	31	2.87	0.16	80	59	54

With Chris Foy there is an obvious trend for two or less bookings per match over the past five seasons, with 42% of all his matches finishing 5 points or under. This is backed up by his Premiership stats, which produce an overall 41% on all 193 matches.

You should obtain level stakes profits if you back Mr Foy (5 points) if the price on Betfair is bigger than 6/4 (on average). Also, if you are laying at less than 5/2 (3.50) on 9+ points, then you are also squeezing some value out of the market.

Premier Betting 2010/11 value tip – back 5 points at 6/4 (2.5) or above on Betfair.

Kevin Friend

PREMIER LEAGUE						BETFAIR POINTS		
Year	Games	Yellow	Red	Y-Ave	R-Ave	5	6-8	9+
2005/06	0	0	0	0	0	0	0	0
2006/07	0	0	0	0	0	0	0	0
2007/08	0	0	0	0	0	0	0	0
2008/09	0	0	0	0	0	0	0	0
2009/10	12	40	4	3.33	0.33	3	6	3
Total	12	40	4	3.33	0.33	3	6	3

OTHER MATCHES						BETFAIR POINTS		
Year	Games	Yellow	Red	Y-Ave	R-Ave	5	6-8	9+
2005/06	21	45	2	2.14	0.1	10	7	4
2006/07	34	87	6	2.56	0.18	19	9	6
2007/08	41	100	11	2.43	0.27	22	9	10
2008/09	46	124	6	2.69	0.13	19	18	9
2009/10	22	93	3	4.22	0.14	3	8	11
Total	164	449	28	2.74	0.17	73	51	40

COMBINED TOTAL						BETFAIR POINTS		
Year	Games	Yellow	Red	Y-Ave	R-Ave	5	6-8	9+
Overall total	176	489	32	2.78	0.18	76	57	43

2009/10 was a Premier League debut for Kevin Friend, with him taking charge of just 12 matches. His overall average didn't match his previous four seasons as a referee outside the Premier League.

His overall profile suggests he doesn't like to give out too many cards, but with his newbie status it's best to keep a watching brief during the next season.

Mark Halsey

PREMIER LEAGUE						BETFAIR POINTS		
Year	Games	Yellow	Red	Y-Ave	R-Ave	5	6-8	9+
2005/06	21	37	5	1.76	0.24	13	5	3
2006/07	25	53	5	2.12	0.2	14	7	4
2007/08	24	58	3	2.42	0.13	13	5	6
2008/09	27	36	1	1.33	0.04	22	4	1
2009/10	1	0	0	0	0.0	1	0	0
Total	**98**	**184**	**14**	**1.88**	**0.14**	**63**	**21**	**14**

OTHER MATCHES						BETFAIR POINTS		
Year	Games	Yellow	Red	Y-Ave	R-Ave	5	6-8	9+
2005/06	17	17	1	1	0.06	15	1	1
2006/07	17	51	4	3	0.24	6	6	5
2007/08	20	33	2	1.65	0.1	14	4	2
2008/09	17	37	1	2.17	0.06	11	3	3
2009/10	5	8	0	1.6	0	3	2	0
Total	**76**	**146**	**8**	**1.92**	**0.11**	**49**	**16**	**11**

COMBINED TOTAL						BETFAIR POINTS		
Year	Games	Yellow	Red	Y-Ave	R-Ave	5	6-8	9+
Overall total	174	330	22	1.9	0.13	112	37	25

We are not sure if Mark Halsey will make it back as a Premier League referee after recovering from cancer. As you can see from his past stats, he certainly doesn't give out too many cautions. However much he takes charge next season, any price odds against on 5 points is worth considering.

Michael Jones

PREMIER LEAGUE						BETFAIR POINTS		
Year	Games	Yellow	Red	Y-Ave	R-Ave	5	6-8	9+
2005/06	0	0	0	0	0	0	0	0
2006/07	0	0	0	0	0	0	0	0
2007/08	0	0	0	0	0	0	0	0
2008/09	12	40	3	3.33	0.25	3	6	3
2009/10	20	64	1	3.2	0.05	7	10	3
Total	32	104	4	3.25	0.13	16	16	6

OTHER MATCHES						BETFAIR POINTS		
Year	Games	Yellow	Red	Y-Ave	R-Ave	5	6-8	9+
2005/06	39	109	5	2.79	0.13	17	12	10
2006/07	41	160	12	3.90	0.29	6	12	23
2007/08	45	134	7	2.98	0.16	19	12	14
2008/09	26	70	3	2.69	0.12	10	10	6
2009/10	13	46	5	3.54	0.38	4	3	6
Total	164	519	32	3.16	0.2	56	49	59

COMBINED TOTAL						BETFAIR POINTS		
Year	Games	Yellow	Red	Y-Ave	R-Ave	5	6-8	9+
Overall total	196	623	36	3.18	0.18	72	65	65

Jones is another fairly new referee in the Premier League ranks, and it looks like his stats on the Premier League don't really match those of when he was a football league official.

His overall percentage is 19% on 9+ points in two seasons of the top flight and 25% on all games, comparing with an overall average of 38% on 9+ points in the previous three seasons.

Again, until we can ascertain a more structured trend, we suggest keeping a watching brief on Mr Jones.

André Marriner

PREMIER LEAGUE						BETFAIR POINTS		
Year	Games	Yellow	Red	Y-Ave	R-Ave	5	6-8	9+
2005/06	7	17	1	2.43	0.14	4	2	1
2006/07	6	22	1	3.67	0.17	1	3	2
2007/08	20	53	4	2.65	0.20	9	6	5
2008/09	21	74	4	3.52	0.19	7	8	6
2009/10	28	97	9	3.46	0.32	9	6	13
Total	82	263	19	3.21	0.23	30	25	27

OTHER MATCHES						BETFAIR POINTS		
Year	Games	Yellow	Red	Y-Ave	R-Ave	5	6-8	9+
2005/06	21	59	6	2.81	0.29	8	6	7
2006/07	26	74	3	2.85	0.12	12	8	6
2007/08	19	65	2	3.42	0.11	7	5	7
2008/09	12	34	3	2.83	0.25	3	5	4
2009/10	9	18	1	2	0.11	5	2	2
Total	87	250	15	2.87	0.17	35	26	26

COMBINED TOTAL						BETFAIR POINTS		
Year	Games	Yellow	Red	Y-Ave	R-Ave	5	6-8	9+
Overall total	169	513	34	3.03	0.2	65	51	53

The first thing we noticed with André Marriner's stats was the number of red cards he issued last season; it has somewhat distorted his figures on 9+ points, with nearly half his overall total over five Premier League seasons coming in the one season of 2009/10.

We feel the overall trends suggest siding against 9+ points. If you can obtain less than 2/1 (3.0) on Betfair, we recommend that you lay that market. Alternatively you could consider backing 5 points if the price on Betfair is bigger than 2/1 (3.0).

Premier Betting 2010/11 value tip – back 5 points at 2/1 (3.0) or above on Betfair.

Lee Mason

PREMIER LEAGUE						BETFAIR POINTS		
Year	Games	Yellow	Red	Y-Ave	R-Ave	5	6-8	9+
2005/06	3	8	0	2.67	0	1	2	0
2006/07	12	27	1	2.25	0.08	7	3	2
2007/08	8	32	1	4	0.13	2	4	2
2008/09	16	54	3	3.38	0.19	4	6	6
2009/10	22	62	6	2.82	0.27	11	5	6
Total	61	183	11	3.00	0.18	25	20	16

OTHER MATCHES						BETFAIR POINTS		
Year	Games	Yellow	Red	Y-Ave	R-Ave	5	6-8	9+
2005/06	34	82	3	2.41	0.09	18	12	4
2006/07	21	60	2	2.86	0.1	8	9	4
2007/08	23	82	3	3.57	0.13	8	5	10
2008/09	18	78	5	4.33	0.27	3	3	12
2009/10	13	43	1	3.31	0.08	3	6	4
Total	109	345	14	3.17	0.13	40	35	34

COMBINED TOTAL						BETFAIR POINTS		
Year	Games	Yellow	Red	Y-Ave	R-Ave	5	6-8	9+
Overall total	170	528	25	3.11	0.15	65	55	50

One thing that you can conclude from Lee Mason's Premier League stats is that, on the reasonably rare occasion that he issues a red card, he isn't going to hold back in that match, and it is likely to result in 9+ points. A red card has been produced in around 18% of his Premiership games, and if you look at the overall stats for the league they suggest that he isn't too frequent on dishing out the cards, with 74% of matches sitting in the 5 points and 6-8 points region.

Once again, we feel the angle here would be backing 5 points if you can obtain over 7/4 (2.75) on Betfair – it's highly likely you could obtain that in almost every game he officiates.

Premier Betting 2010/11 value tip – back 5 points at 7/4 (2.75) or above on Betfair.

Lee Probert

PREMIER LEAGUE						BETFAIR POINTS		
Year	Games	Yellow	Red	Y-Ave	R-Ave	5	6-8	9+
2005/06	0	0	0	0	0	0	0	0
2006/07	2	3	0	1.5	0	2	0	0
2007/08	10	19	0	1.9	0	5	5	0
2008/09	11	26	0	2.36	0.0	6	4	1
2009/10	22	74	6	3.36	0.27	8	5	9
Total	**45**	**122**	**6**	**2.71**	**0.13**	**21**	**14**	**10**

OTHER MATCHES						BETFAIR POINTS		
Year	Games	Yellow	Red	Y-Ave	R-Ave	5	6-8	9+
2005/06	40	127	8	3.18	0.2	13	12	15
2006/07	36	104	5	2.89	0.14	17	8	11
2007/08	27	63	3	2.33	0.11	15	7	5
2008/09	24	68	4	2.83	0.17	8	11	5
2009/10	11	45	1	4.09	0.09	3	4	4
Total	**138**	**407**	**21**	**2.95**	**0.15**	**56**	**42**	**40**

COMBINED TOTAL						BETFAIR POINTS		
Year	Games	Yellow	Red	Y-Ave	R-Ave	5	6-8	9+
Overall total	**183**	**529**	**27**	**2.89**	**0.15**	**77**	**56**	**50**

Lee Probert is taking charge of more Premier League games each season and can now be classed as one of the established referees on the list.

Again he would be another referee we would be happy siding with in the 5 points market, as you would only need prices above 6/4 (2.50) to secure level stake profits.

Premier Betting 2010/11 value tip – back 5 points at 6/4 (2.5) or above on Betfair.

Anthony Taylor

PREMIER LEAGUE						BETFAIR POINTS		
Year	Games	Yellow	Red	Y-Ave	R-Ave	5	6-8	9+
2005/06	0	0	0	0	0	0	0	0
2006/07	0	0	0	0	0	0	0	0
2007/08	0	0	0	0	0	0	0	0
2008/09	0	0	0	0	0	0	0	0
2009/10	2	5	0	2.50	0	1	1	0
Total	2	5	0	2.50	0	1	1	0

OTHER MATCHES						BETFAIR POINTS		
Year	Games	Yellow	Red	Y-Ave	R-Ave	5	6-8	9+
2005/06	0	0	0	0	0	0	0	0
2006/07	26	78	5	3	0.19	11	9	6
2007/08	36	105	10	2.92	0.28	14	7	15
2008/09	38	91	4	2.39	0.11	21	11	6
2009/10	34	87	8	2.56	0.24	14	12	8
Total	134	361	27	2.69	0.20	60	39	35

COMBINED TOTAL						BETFAIR POINTS		
Year	Games	Yellow	Red	Y-Ave	R-Ave	5	6-8	9+
Overall total	136	366	27	2.69	0.2	61	40	35

With only two games officiated so far in the Premier League, we should keep a watching brief for now; but if you look at his stats from the football league it certainly appears that he is a referee who likes to keep his cards in his pocket, and footballers are no more saintly there than in the Premier League.

Peter Walton

PREMIER LEAGUE						BETFAIR POINTS		
Year	Games	Yellow	Red	Y-Ave	R-Ave	5	6-8	9+
2005/06	13	40	1	3.08	0.08	5	6	2
2006/07	16	48	0	3	0	7	7	2
2007/08	24	74	3	3.08	0.13	8	9	7
2008/09	27	66	3	2.44	0.11	13	8	6
2009/10	27	66	4	2.44	0.15	12	9	6
Total	107	294	11	2.75	0.1	45	39	23

OTHER MATCHES						BETFAIR POINTS		
Year	Games	Yellow	Red	Y-Ave	R-Ave	5	6-8	9+
2005/06	29	86	5	2.97	0.17	9	14	6
2006/07	24	80	4	3.33	0.17	8	7	9
2007/08	20	56	2	2.8	0.1	8	8	4
2008/09	17	33	1	1.94	0.06	10	6	1
2009/10	8	22	2	2.75	0.25	3	3	2
Total	98	277	14	2.83	0.14	38	38	22

COMBINED TOTAL						BETFAIR POINTS		
Year	Games	Yellow	Red	Y-Ave	R-Ave	5	6-8	9+
Overall total	205	571	25	2.78	0.12	83	77	45

With 9 points and above appearing in only 22% of the Premier League matches that Peter Walton has officiated at over the past five seasons, the stats certainly suggest you should avoid backing that option. Looking at his overall stats, he is just over a 1/4 (1.25) shot to keep his bookings count down to four or less.

Continuing with the trend of this book, you shouldn't look beyond backing 5 points if you can obtain minimum odds of 6/4 (2.50).

Premier Betting 2010/11 value tip – back 5 points at 6/4 (2.50) or above on Betfair.

Howard Webb

PREMIER LEAGUE						BETFAIR POINTS		
Year	Games	Yellow	Red	Y-Ave	R-Ave	5	6-8	9+
2005/06	30	87	5	2.9	0.17	12	9	9
2006/07	28	110	4	3.93	0.14	10	6	11
2007/08	27	101	1	3.74	0.04	12	4	11
2008/09	34	119	6	3.5	0.18	14	8	12
2009/10	28	101	3	3.61	0.11	9	7	12
Total	147	518	19	3.52	0.13	57	34	55

OTHER MATCHES						BETFAIR POINTS		
Year	Games	Yellow	Red	Y-Ave	R-Ave	5	6-8	9+
2005/06	17	30	2	1.76	0.12	8	5	3
2006/07	17	46	5	2.71	0.29	7	6	4
2007/08	18	65	3	3.61	0.17	4	6	8
2008/09	13	41	0	3.15	0	5	5	3
2009/10	14	49	1	3.5	0.07	2	9	3
Total	79	231	11	2.92	0.14	26	31	21

COMBINED TOTAL						BETFAIR POINTS		
Year	Games	Yellow	Red	Y-Ave	R-Ave	5	6-8	9+
Overall total	226	749	30	3.31	0.13	83	65	76

Mr Webb is currently rated the top English referee (though these stats exclude any matches refereed at this year's World Cup finals), and the vast majority of his other matches involve him taking charge of the big European matches (he officiated the 2009/10 Champions League final).

He is pretty consistent in the number of cards he issues, with a five season average of 3.5 yellow cards a game. Also, because of the high percentage of his matches resulting in 9+ (37%), the chances are that you will see quite a few of his matches next season being odds-on in this market, especially if the match on paper looks a little feisty.

Premier Betting 2010/11 value tip – lay 9+ points, lower than 6/4 (2.50) on Betfair.

Alan Wiley

PREMIER LEAGUE						BETFAIR POINTS		
Year	Games	Yellow	Red	Y-Ave	R-Ave	5	6-8	9+
2005/06	31	97	5	3.13	0.16	10	12	9
2006/07	30	96	4	3.2	0.13	12	9	9
2007/08	30	96	1	3.2	0.03	14	10	6
2008/09	28	81	2	2.89	0.07	8	9	11
2009/10	26	81	5	3.12	0.19	7	10	9
Total	145	451	17	3.11	0.12	51	50	44

OTHER MATCHES						BETFAIR POINTS		
Year	Games	Yellow	Red	Y-Ave	R-Ave	5	6-8	9+
2005/06	13	45	2	3.46	0.15	2	8	3
2006/07	12	39	0	3.25	0	6	3	3
2007/08	14	39	2	2.79	0.14	5	7	2
2008/09	14	48	2	3.43	0.14	6	3	5
2009/10	12	46	0	3.83	0	4	3	5
Total	65	217	6	3.34	0.09	23	24	18

COMBINED TOTAL						BETFAIR POINTS		
Year	Games	Yellow	Red	Y-Ave	R-Ave	5	6-8	9+
Overall total	210	668	23	3.18	0.11	74	74	62

You can see by Mr Wiley's five years of stats that he is pretty consistent in the number of cards that he gives out on a season-by-season basis. As with many referees we have looked at in this report, the 6-8 points range seems pretty stable each season.

If we look at the last two Premier League seasons, in 39 of his matches (72%) there have been at least three bookings and in our view, if you can get over 2/1 (3.0) on Betfair for 6-8 points, you would be getting fair value.

Premier Betting 2010/11 value tip – back 6-8 points at 2/1 (3.0) or above on Betfair.

Conclusion

And that's the final whistle: book over! (With only the injury time of the Glossary there if you need it.)

Well, of course, that's not quite true. As you'll have seen, this book should be really helpful to have on hand – or tucked up with your match programme – from week to week throughout the 2010/11 Premier League season.

We hope and trust that it's a great source of help and insight in all your betting over the term – and, of course, wish you the best of luck in all your trips to the bookies or betting exchanges.

If you would like to continue the journey with us throughout the season, then do please check out premier-betting.com. Subscriptions start at £8 and as a buyer of this book you can get 2 weeks free by going to premier-betting.com. In the 2010/11 season we will be providing our unique ratings, analysis and top tips for all 380 Premiership matches. It'd be great to see you there!

Pete and Matt

Glossary

Accumulators – A multiple bet which involves several selections in different events. All the selections made must win for you to win the accumulator.

Alternative handicaps – Each team is given a goals handicap and you bet on the match result after that handicap. Unlike Asian Handicaps the draw is taken into account.

Anytime goal scorer – A bet placed on a player to score a goal at anytime during the match.

Asian handicap – Asian handicaps are, as the name suggests, a special type of handicap betting popular in the Far East. Each team is given a certain number of goals handicap and you bet on the match result after that handicap.

Book – Running a 'book' is the act of quoting odds and accepting bets on an event.

Bookings market – A betting market that takes into account the amount of red and yellow cards shown by the referee to either side during the match.

Commission – On Betfair a commission of 5% is payable on all winning bets.

Corners market – A betting market that deals with the number of corners forced by both sides during a match.

Corner supremacy – A team that forces more corners than their opponents has corner supremacy.

Correct score – This is predicting the score at the end of normal time.

Double chance – The betting market where you are selecting 2 out of 3 outcomes and if either one wins your bet wins i.e. Home/Draw, Home/Away Draw/Away.

Draw, the – A game outcome where competitors in an event finish evenly.

Draw no bet – This is like a full time result bet other than there is no option for the draw. You can bet on either team to win and if it's a draw you get your stake back.

Dutching – Backing two or more selections in an event to achieve the same profit whichever selection wins.

Drifters – A selection whose odds get longer during a period of time.

Each way – A bet on a selection to be placed as well as to win.

Exchanges – A site where punters exchange bets anonymously. The betting exchange's only involvement is to charge a commission of around 2% to 5% on the punters' winnings.

First/last goal scorer – A bet placed on a player to score the first goal or last goal in the event.

Fixed-odds – Your dividend is fixed at the odds when you placed your bet.

Half-time/full-time – Also known as "double result" this is a bet on predicting the result at half time and full time in the same bet.

- **H/A** = Home side leading at half time; away side win at full time.
- **H/D** = Home side leading at half time; a draw at full time.
- **H/H** = Home side leading at both half time and full time.
- **A/A** = Away side leading at half time; away win at full time.
- **A/D** = Away side leading at half time; a draw at full time.
- **A/H** = Away side leading at half time; home side win at full time
- **D/A** = A draw at half time; an away win at full time.
- **D/D** = A draw at half time; a draw at full time.
- **D/H** = A draw at half time; a home win at full time.

Half-goal – Used in Asian Handicaps where one team is given a half goal start.

In-running – A bet placed whilst the match is in play.

Juice – see: 'over round'.

Lay – When a bookmaker accepts bets it is often said that they lay a bet.

Long odds – A team or selection unlikely to win.

Over round – The margin the bookmaker builds into their odds to ensure they make a profit on an event.

Over/Under [x] goals – This is a two option bet on whether there will be more or less than the number of goals quoted. Normally the bet is more or less than 2.5 goals but you will often see many variations such as 0.5, 1.5, 3.5 and 4.5.

Payout – How much money you will receive after your selection has won.

Real odds – Odds based purely on what has happened in the past and not based on opinion.

Stake – This is how much money you are placing on a bet

Steamers – An outcome that has been very well backed all day

Quarter-goal – This is quoted on Asian Handicap bets where a team receives a ¼ of a goal start.

Win Market – The most common football bet is on the match result or 90 minutes result. This can be called 'Full time Result', 'WLD' (for win lose draw) and "1x2" (being the notation for home win, draw and away win).